£1

SPIDER WOMAN

SPIDER WOMAN

A LIFE

BRENDA HALE

The Rt Hon the Baroness Hale of Richmond

THE BODLEY HEAD
LONDON

1 3 5 7 9 10 8 6 4 2

The Bodley Head, an imprint of Vintage, is part of the
Penguin Random House group of companies whose addresses
can be found at global.penguinrandomhouse.com

First published by The Bodley Head in 2021

www.penguin.co.uk/vintage

A CIP catalogue record for this book is available from the British Library

Hardback ISBN 9781847926593

Typeset in 11.5/14 pt Dante MT Std
by Integra Software Services Pvt. Ltd, Pondicherry

Printed and bound in Great Britain by Clays Ltd, Elcograf S.p.A.

The authorised representative in the EEA is Penguin Random House Ireland,
Morrison Chambers, 32 Nassau Street, Dublin D02 YH6.

Penguin Random House is committed to a sustainable future for
our business, our readers and our planet. This book is made from
Forest Stewardship Council® certified paper.

For
Julia, Patrick and Amelia
The Future

Omnia feminae aequisssimae

Contents

Forethoughts

We all have our imposter moments. I defy any woman to say that she doesn't. Here are four of mine.

Imposter moment no. 1

It is September 1955. I am ten years old. I am standing all alone in the playing field at Richmond High School for Girls, in North Yorkshire. I am wearing a navy-blue gymslip with a square neck and a pale blue blouse also with a square neck. It looks absurd – why on earth are we not allowed to wear shirts with a collar and tie until the sixth form? But I am glad to be wearing it because it means that I am at the High School and not at the dreaded Secondary Modern School on Catterick Camp where rumour has it that everyone gets the cane in their first term, even goody-goodies like me. I look like a goody-goody. Long hair in pigtails. Round National Health Service spectacles. A speccy swot. Short. Rather overweight. The youngest girl in the school because they entered me for the 11-plus a year early and unbelievably I passed. My older sister Jill is the oldest girl in the school and head girl. Impossibly godlike and no company for her baby sister. Alone because I am the only girl from Bolton-on-Swale Church of England primary school to have passed the 11-plus that year. All the other girls in the class seem to have at least one friend from the same primary school as them. Am I an imposter? Should I be here yet? Can I cope?

Imposter moment no. 2

It is October 1963. I am eighteen years old. Still a speccy swot. Rather more attractive spectacles. Pigtails gone and a short bob. Not thin but not noticeably overweight. Still short. I am walking along King's Parade in Cambridge. On my left is King's College. Intricately carved stone tracery separates its grounds from the street. The east end of its magnificent chapel faces the street: one of the most glorious church buildings in the country. Ahead of me is the Senate House, an elegant eighteenth-century stone building, where one day I may kneel before the vice chancellor to receive my degree. To my right is Great St Mary's, the university church. Tucked away between King's College Chapel and the Senate House are the Old Schools, more eighteenth-century elegance, where the Law Faculty is based, and the Squire Law Library. That is where I am headed. Unbelievably, Girton College, the first women's college in either Oxford or Cambridge, has awarded me an exhibition to read law. The first girl from Richmond High School to go to Cambridge and the first to read law. I pinch myself. Am I really here? Am I an imposter? Can I cope?

Imposter moment no. 3

It is May 1984. I am thirty-nine years old. Rather more stylish spectacles. Still with a short bob. Still not fat but not thin. Still short. I am sitting at my desk in my office in Conquest House, at the corner of Theobalds Road and John Street, just north of Gray's Inn. A long way from home. Unbelievably, I am the first woman and the youngest ever Law Commissioner. I am ploughing through an immensely detailed and learned discussion of what should be done with the law of blasphemy: abolish, modernise or replace it? That is the sort of thing the Law Commission does. The other commissioners are some of the cleverest men I have ever known. Am I an imposter? Can I cope?

Imposter moment no. 4

It is 13 January 2020. I am seventy-four years old. Smart spectacles by Elle. Still with a short bob, rather smarter than the earlier cut (though Anne Robinson had said I ought to get a proper haircut when I announced the Supreme Court's decision in the great prorogation case), and more grey than dark brown. Not thin but not noticeably overweight. I am walking through St James's Park in London. To my left is the lake with its pelicans and wildfowl and a distant view of Buckingham Palace (last visited for the banquet for President Trump), also the pretty little fake cottage with its traditional cottage garden.

To my right are the Treasury, with the Churchill War Rooms beneath, the Foreign and Commonwealth Office, the other end of Downing Street, the back of Dover House (where the Scottish Office lives), and Horse Guards Parade. Where am I coming from? Earlier in the morning I had been in Courtroom No. 1 in the Supreme Court of the United Kingdom applauding as my successor was sworn in as president of the Supreme Court. After that I was in the House of Lords, being welcomed back by the Clerk of the Parliaments after ten years' absence as a Justice of the Supreme Court, presenting my writ of summons in the Chamber and taking the oath, necessary if I want to take part in parliamentary business. Swearing the oath of allegiance to Her Majesty, her heirs and successors according to law, I slightly emphasised the word 'law' and was surprised when many of Their Lordships said 'Hear, hear.' Where am I going to? Up the Duke of York steps, along Waterloo Place, and into the Athenaeum club to have lunch at the club table, before checking the arrangements for a dinner I am giving for my fellow justices that evening. Unbelievably, I was one of the first group of women to become members eighteen years ago. If I was an imposter, I must have learned to love her.

This is the story of how that little girl from a little school in a little village in North Yorkshire became the most senior judge in the United Kingdom. How she found that she could cope. And how all those other people who feel they are imposters can learn to cope too. Some of them may even be men.

1 Village Life

My Lords, town and village greens are not just picturesque reminders of a bygone age. They are a very present amenity to the communities they serve. The village green in Scorton, in the North Riding of Yorkshire, is a perfect example. Most of it is contained within a three-foot-high stone wall and raised to the level of the top of that wall, thus giving it a character all of its own. It is surrounded by the old village houses, including the former vicarage, the two remaining pubs, the shop, the village institute, and the eighteenth-century building which was until recently the old grammar school. It was and is the centre of the community. Both villagers and grammar school boys played cricket there in the summer; archery contests were held there; a bonfire was built for Guy Fawkes day; the fair and other events of Scorton feast were held there every August; and all the villagers could walk and play games upon it.[1]

This idyllic place was the village where I grew up, five miles down the road from the medieval town of Richmond in Yorkshire, the first Richmond, from which all the other Richmonds in the world are named. Scorton is the largest village in the parish of Bolton-on-Swale. Apart from its village green, its main claim to fame is the archery competition for 'The Antient Silver Arrow' or 'Scorton Arrow'. Founded in 1673, this is said to be the oldest recorded sporting event and is still going strong, though hardly ever in Scorton, for whoever wins the competition hosts the next one. Even so, the village is proud of the archery tradition. But it is neither the sort of place where you would expect a top judge to grow up nor the sort of place for people like us. My family are not country people. What were we doing there?

In 1721, a local gentleman called Leonard Robinson left all his land and buildings in Scorton to establish 'a free school for all persons after being qualified to enter upon learning the Latin tongue'. That meant it was to be a grammar school. The schoolmaster had not only to be 'qualified in learning the Latin and Greek tongues but also [lead an] exemplary life'. He had to take the boys to church in Bolton-on-Swale every Sunday. He was to have Mr Robinson's house to live and teach in, but the trustees might also build a schoolhouse if they thought it more proper. They soon built a fine red-brick Georgian schoolhouse, standing next to Mr Robinson's much older home. The village green was built on top of a rubbish dump, for use as a school playing field. This was no brutal Dotheboys Hall, although Dickens' models were not many miles away. Its fortunes fluctuated over the eighteenth and nineteenth centuries, but it flourished between the two world wars. Then came the Second World War. Airfields were built in North Yorkshire, to defend the industrial towns in Teesside and later to fly bombing missions to Germany, one of them in Scorton. In 1941, the school was closed and its buildings taken over by the RAF. After the war, the trustees, led by the vicar, decided to reopen the school as an independent grammar school catering for boarding and day boys. They appointed my father, Cecil Hale, the headmaster. My mother was to run the boarding house.

So it was that we arrived in Leonard Robinson's old home in autumn 1948 to prepare for the school's reopening in January 1949. I was three years old and my little sister Frances was two. We looked quite alike and our mother dressed us alike, so the schoolboys thought that we were twins. We found it a scary house. The headmaster's quarters were at the front, overlooking the green. Behind them on the ground floor were the boys' dining hall and a long stone-flagged corridor leading down to the school kitchen. Meals were cooked on a huge coke-fired Aga which took up almost the whole of one wall. Going down there at night was not advised: turning the light on provoked a scuttling of cockroaches for cover. Beyond that was the scullery, housing among other vital pieces of school equipment, a large potato-peeling machine. On the other side of the corridor were the larders where the food was kept, the rationed goods under lock and key, and great earthenware jars full of eggs pickled in isinglass.

Upstairs were four dormitories for the boys, named after Elizabethan explorers, Drake, Raleigh, Grenville and Frobisher. There were also bedrooms for two or three unmarried schoolmasters and the sick bay, presided over by matron. There were odd spaces between the internal walls which could not be accounted for – what mysteries lurked there? The ancient radiators gurgled and clanked. The ill-fitting windows whistled in the wind. The old floorboards creaked. The ghost of Leonard Robinson was said to haunt the top floor. No wonder we found it scary.

When the school reopened in January 1949, there were just seventeen boarders and thirty-two day boys and two schoolmasters as well as our father. From these small beginnings, it grew to around 150 boys, roughly a third of them boarders. Despite its frightening features, the school was a lovely place for young children to live. Frances and I could play anywhere in the grounds. There was a kitchen garden where we could have our own little plot, two tennis courts where we were allowed to learn to play tennis, and a large playing field surrounded by hedgerows where we could make dens. But there was more to village life than that.

So much was coloured by the fervent desire of everyone who had lived through the Second World War that nothing like it should ever happen again. The relics of war were all around us. The airfield had closed but the runway was still there. There was still a working RAF base three miles away at Catterick village. There was a whole estate of Nissen huts and other temporary dwellings. Some of the people living there had been bombed out of their homes in the industrial towns of Teesside. There was another large site on the edge of the village where the air-force personnel had also been housed in huts, but only the large gymnasium (used by the grammar school) remained. There was a smaller site down the road on the edge of Bolton-on-Swale which Mr Pigg the farmer later took over for his pig farm (yes, really). And there was an army engineers' site a mile or two out of the village which was still in use.

Just a few miles away, over the river Swale, lay Catterick Camp. This was and remains a large army garrison, then housing both regular soldiers and national servicemen, for compulsory military service did not finally end until 1963. Catterick Camp was a bleak place on the edge of the moors between Swaledale and Wensleydale, surrounded by military training grounds and roads built for tanks. There were some permanent houses for the officers and barracks for the men, but there were also acres of Nissen huts surrounded by barbed wire. There were very few shops and places of entertainment – the soldiers went into Richmond for their rest and recreation. The place was a constant reminder, not only of the Second World War, but also of the UK's extensive military commitments all over the world.

The struggle to feed the nation a balanced diet was still going on. We children were urged to collect the rose hips which were plentiful in the hedgerows so that they could be sold (for a song) to make rose-hip syrup, rich in vitamin C. Food rationing lasted into the early 1950s. We went to the village shop with our coupons each week to buy our small allowance of sweets or chocolate (I always chose Fry's Chocolate Cream). Somehow our mother managed to feed the growing numbers of hungry teenage schoolboys on what was available but it cannot have been easy. We ate the same food that they did. Some of it was pretty hard to take – sausages with impenetrably thick skins and more gristle than meat, a mincemeat loaf in pastry known as rissole, Yorkshire pudding with a burnt base and uncooked batter. There were also puddings, steamed in little basins in a great vat on the top of the Aga, rich in carbohydrate – jam sponge, spotted dick, roly-poly. With custard of course. No wonder I got plump. There was much excitement when the last vestiges of rationing were gone and the food began to improve. But English food was never very exciting in the 1950s and boarding-school food even less so. The end of rationing, the phasing out of national service, the demolition of the Nissen huts, and a gradually increasing sense of prosperity – in 1957, Prime Minister Harold Macmillan told us that 'most of our people have never had it so good' – all these brought home, even to a child, the benefits of peace and an international rule-based community, not only in Europe, but also in the rest of the world.

Then there was the persistence and strength of the great British class system. One day in the late 1950s, our headmistress accused us of holding the mistaken belief that Britain was now a classless society. I indignantly denied it. It was difficult to hold that belief living in a village like Scorton. The hierarchy of rural society was plain for all to see.

At the top there was – and still is – something called 'the county': minor aristocrats and major landowners who socialised and inter-married with one another and with their like in neighbouring counties. The Lord Lieutenant and the High Sheriffs came from 'the county' and by and large they still do. (The Lord Lieutenant is the Queen's representative in the county; the High Sheriff used to be the Crown's enforcer but now spends a year doing good works in support of the justice system in the county.) So too did the Members of Parliament then. Sir Thomas Dugdale, of Crathorne Hall, near Yarm, was MP for Richmond from 1929 until 1959. In 1954 he became famous for the 'Crichel Down affair'. Crichel Down in Dorset had been bought for military use during the war. The previous owners thought that they had been promised the right to buy it back when it was no longer needed by the military, but the Ministry of Agriculture refused them. There was a tremendous fuss. Sir Thomas resigned as Minister of Agriculture. I knew nothing of this at the time, but in the late 1960s, when I was teaching constitutional law in the University of Manchester, Sir Thomas was widely regarded as the best – nay the only – example of a minister responsible to Parliament doing the honourable thing and resigning when his civil servants had got things wrong. His successor as MP for Richmond was Sir Timothy Kitson, another local landowner and farmer, who served until 1983. But they were the last 'county' MPs. Their successors were even more prominent in national politics but very different: Leon Brittan from 1983 to 1988, William Hague from 1989 to 2015, and Rishi Sunak since then. The Richmondshire constituency can attract star candidates because it is one of the safest Conservative seats in the country: it taught me that the rural working classes still vote Conservative.

Top of the social tree in Scorton, grander even than the 'county', was undoubtedly Miss Bridget Talbot. Miss Talbot was the owner of Kiplin Hall, built in the 1620s. It is a pleasingly symmetrical square red-brick building with a square, domed tower jutting out from the middle of each of the walls. A library wing was added early in the nineteenth century and a service wing later on, but these do not spoil the elegant shape of the main house. Miss Talbot was a truly remarkable woman. Among her many achievements was the invention of a waterproof torch for merchant seamen, provided to the navy and RAF during the Second World War and saving many lives. She was a well-known figure driving around the village in a battered old car. My sister Jill, eight years older than I, remembers going for tea at the hall. But even Miss Talbot could not find a way to save the hall from apparently terminal decay.

In the eighteenth and nineteenth centuries the Kiplin estate had grown to cover most of the land in the parish. However, this was sold off in the early twentieth century, leaving only the hall and its grounds. There was scarcely any money to spend on maintaining the building, which steadily became more and more dilapidated. This was not helped by its being requisitioned by the army in the Second World War (two rooms have been left in the state in which the army left them, to make the point). Miss Talbot battled for forty years to save Kiplin but nothing worked. In 1958, the National Trust having refused to take it on, the hall was to be demolished. But Miss Talbot was knocked down on a pedestrian crossing and broke her leg, so she did not telephone the demolition firm. In 1968, she set up a private charitable trust to take over the hall and left the contents to the trustees when she died in 1971. The trust has found ways to raise the money to restore the building, not least by quarrying the sand and gravel on what remains of the estate. The house and gardens are now a charming and slightly quirky visitor attraction – definitely not the National Trust. I do hope that Miss Talbot would be pleased rather than horrified by what they have done.

Also in the upper ranks of Scorton society were Miss Hillyard, who lived at Bolton Old Hall, an attractive eighteenth-century house next to the church, attached to an ancient pele tower, and Colonel Hall and his wife. Doesn't every village have a retired colonel, who is also a churchwarden and an independent member of the county council? The colonel both looked and sounded the part – tall, thin, moustached and ram-rod straight. He was also the heir to a baronetcy but he kept very quiet about that.

Next came the large local farmers. Several substantial farmhouses surround the village, their similar design indicating that they were built by the Kiplin estate. There was Tancred, where much of the land near to the river Swale was given over to extracting sand and gravel. There was Bolton Grange, whose owner became our landlord when we moved out of the grammar school. And there was Cross Hills, where lived Miss Wilson and Miss Matty Wilson, one of the three pairs of genteel unmarried sisters who were such a feature of village life. Miss Jones and Miss Annie Jones lived in the Manor House in the village. Despite its name, this is not a very large house, but it too had a Kiplin connection, as their father had been the agent for the Kiplin estate. Miss Rogers and Miss Lucy Rogers lived in a much smaller cottage on the village green. Miss Lucy had been a senior civil servant but returned to live with her older sister when she retired. They were all stalwarts of the church and great friends of my mother. I don't remember any of them cycling to church (as so fondly pictured by John Major in his vision of how England would still be fifty years on from his speech to the Conservative Group for Europe in 1993) but they might well have done had not one of each pair been rather lame.

After the farmers were the various tradesmen who served the village. When I was a child, there were three pubs in Scorton – the Royal, the Farmers Arms and the White Heifer – and another – St Cuthbert's Inn – half a mile down the road next to the railway station. There was a garage which had once been a blacksmith's. There were two general stores, one of which sold the local Wensleydale cheese in slices cut from a massive whole cheese. There was also a post office. There was a butcher, who traded from a van which he took around the village and its surroundings, before getting a shop. There was a milkman, who supplied milk from his own cows. The stores sold some rudimentary vegetables – potatoes, onions, carrots and perhaps tomatoes. But many people grew their own and others would make a weekly trip into Richmond to buy vegetables and fruit at the Saturday market there. There was also a police station, with a resident sergeant, and a magistrates' court above the police station.

Then there were the majority of the village people, who worked on the land or in the building trade or in Catterick Camp, the rural working classes. There was even, for a time, one incoming 'problem' family.

So where did our family fit into all of this? We were undeniably middle class (we called the sitting room the 'drawing room' and had staff), and teachers then had a respected status, but we were not well off or propertied. We were not – and never would be – 'county', not local farmers, not local business or tradesmen, not local workers. We were incomers and outsiders: one of a small group of professional families whose work had brought us to the village. Another was the doctor, who had his surgery and a dispensary in his substantial house on the village green. And another was the vicar, the Revd F. F. le Brun Crankshaw, chairman of the governors of Scorton Grammar School and also of Bolton-on-Swale Church of England primary school, and my father's closest friend. There were a few others, who worked outside the village, but it was not then a commuter village. Later, of course, there would be many more such incomers – people who worked in Richmond, Darlington, and further afield but liked the idea of village life.

Village life was very different then. It was very cold: heating was mostly by coal fires and immersion water heaters. Life was lived where the fire was and baths were once a week. Most people did not have cars. The primary school children walked from the large village of Scorton to school in the much smaller village of Bolton-on-Swale, half a mile away. Most of them had school dinners but not, I'm sorry to say, Frances and I. Our mother sent the handyman, Joe, to collect us from school in our modest Morris car and bring us back to the grammar school for lunch. I have no idea why. It cannot have been the quality of the food – the school dinners in Bolton were a good deal tastier than the school dinners in the grammar school. It could have been economy – we were provided with our meals free of charge by the grammar school while school dinners had to be paid for. It could have been snobbery – but why object to our eating with the village children if there was no objection to our learning with them? It was another thing that set us apart from the other children in the school, another sign (along with our academic prowess) that we were outsiders.

The secondary school children took the bus, either to Richmond, where the boys' grammar school and the girls' high school were, or to Catterick Camp, where the dreaded secondary modern school was. They took the train home if they had to stay late. Even those parents with cars did not ferry their children about. School friends visiting us from other villages stayed overnight rather than be driven back home. Joining the Girl Guides in Richmond (as I really wanted to do because my father was a keen Scout) was out of the question. Despite these little frustrations, we were very happy with our village life. But all three of us were anxious to leave it for the greater educational and career opportunities offered by the big wide world when the time came. In the 1970s, the church's marriage register showed that only the Hale sisters had married someone coming from more than thirty miles away.

Dinner was at lunchtime. After school, we had high tea. My elder sister Jill had hers with the grammar school boys in the school dining hall. Our father was adamant that his children would not be treated differently from the boys (but Frances and I were too young to join them). It was awkward for them all at first, but gradually they got used to one another, grew up together and became firm friends. How many people eat high tea these days? There was a savoury course, such as bacon and egg, followed by bread and butter, with jam, malt loaf and cake. In that order. Washed down with tea for the grown-ups and water or squash for the children. After tea, and some play time with his children, our father would retire to his study for a rest. He had a traffic light system outside his study door: red meant 'your headmaster is enjoying a well-earned rest and cannot see you now'. There was no need: his snores reverberated around the house. But when he woke up, he would work until the early hours – a habit which still runs in the family.

What did the adults do for recreation? There was the radio and eventually a television set. Grandma Hale, our father's mother, bought one for the Queen's coronation in 1953, as so many people did. It was housed in a handsome mahogany cabinet but had a tiny screen. We all travelled down to her home in Sheffield to watch it with her, curtains drawn, as in a cinema. The set came with her when she came to live with us during her final illness. Of course, we children were only allowed to watch *Children's Hour*. I have no idea whether or what the adults watched after we had gone to bed.

Outside the home, there were the village pubs, but I don't think that my father, let alone my mother, spent much if any time there.

Each of them had its own distinct clientele, mostly men. Our parents did a little socialising at home, but not much: they would invite a few people in for sherry after church on Sundays and there was the occasional 'at home'. I remember once asking why Mrs X was not invited: our mother said that she would not feel comfortable, but the real explanation was the great British class system. It showed itself in so many ways, not just in social life but also in schooling and in life chances. The village children were not expected to pass the 11-plus and go to the high school or grammar school. I well remember my mother's delight when, as head teacher of Bolton-on-Swale school, she saw one of her village boys pass the 11-plus and go to the grammar school.

Church played quite a prominent part in village life. There was the Anglican church in Bolton-on-Swale. There was a Methodist chapel in Scorton, which was the main rival to the Church of England. Unusually, there was also a Roman Catholic church. This was next door to the other Scorton institution, the St John of God hospital, established in the late nineteenth century to cater for 'unwanted people', 'cripples and incurables'. It developed into a more general hospital in the 1950s, but some of the original residents remained and were often seen around the village, being taken for walks and down the road to church at Bolton-on-Swale in a variety of wheelchairs. The St John of God Brothers also began to develop links with Africa. Extraordinary as it may seem today, the very first black people I remember seeing were two African doctors who were visiting the hospital. We were delighted: rural Yorkshire was not the most diverse of places. It still is not.

Frances and I went to Sunday school until we were deemed old enough to go to church. Morning service was at 10.45 a.m., mattins except on the third Sunday of the month when it was Holy Communion. We learned to love the Book of Common Prayer. The grammar school boarders went every Sunday, as Leonard Robinson had commanded, which made the congregation look a respectable size. The vicar's sermons were commendably short. Our father was a lay reader. He used to take the services in other parishes when their vicar was away or on holiday – he had a bank of a hundred sermons and a card index which told him when and where he had preached each one, so that he would not repeat himself. One of the churches he used to visit was in Arkengarthdale, more than twenty miles away. In those days, it was unthinkable that he would drive there and back for the morning service and then there and back again for evensong. The local pub, the CB Inn (still going strong), gave him a private room. Jill used to go with him sometimes to keep him company (she had a lot more fun than we did, but that's only natural given the age difference).

Our mother ran the local branch of the Mothers' Union, founded in 1876 by Mary Sumner, who wanted to create 'an organisation for women that brought together rich and poor to build a network that would support mothers of all kinds as they brought up their children in Christian faith'. These days, the Mothers' Union is 'an international Christian membership movement that aims to demonstrate Christian faith by action'. But to us it was always the women's movement of the Church of England, at a time when women were not allowed to become priests. For one week each year, envelopes were delivered round the parish in an attempt to raise money for something called 'moral welfare': an Anglican charity which ran homes for unmarried mothers and their babies. Not everyone approved. Morality was more censorious and less tolerant, even illogical, then. One of the Mothers' Union stalwarts was not allowed to take Communion in church because she was the innocent party to a divorce. Village life did teach us something about hypocrisy and injustice. But I have reason to be grateful to the Mothers' Union. When I was sitting my Bar Final examinations in September 1967, I stayed in a little room at the top of Mary Sumner House, its headquarters in Westminster. It was perfect for a country girl who knew nothing of London: quiet and conveniently situated with no distractions. Perhaps that's why I did so well.

The other activity for women in the village was the Women's Institute, famous for jam and 'Jerusalem'. Our mother was a member but not, I think, a very keen one. Even so, the members gave a stirring rendition of 'Jerusalem' at her funeral in August 1981. They met in the Village Institute, where all sorts of other events took place. There was an amateur dramatic society, run by the vicar, which produced a play every year. Overacting was encouraged. There was barn dancing. In my teens, the wife of the head teacher of Bolton-on-Swale school put on country dancing lessons. These were great fun – and gave me my first and only schoolgirl romance with a carpenter's apprentice from a nearby village. We used to go off to barn dances in the local villages to put what we had learned into practice.

There were other highlights of the village year: the vicarage garden party, with the usual flower and produce competitions; the three-day Scorton Feast, with a fair on the village green, sporting events including a gymkhana, and evening entertainments; the harvest festival, when the church was full for the only time in the year; and bonfire night, with a huge bonfire on the village green, built over several weeks, and do-it-yourself fireworks which would now be banned.

Scorton still looks much the same as it did then, but a good deal has changed. There is still the garage, but only two pubs and one shop. The police station and the magistrates' court have gone. The hospital, the Roman Catholic church, and the grammar school are no more. There are small housing estates where the Nissen huts used to be and many other new houses. The primary school has moved from Bolton to Scorton and thrives. There are many, many more cars. Its society has changed too. There are many more people who live in the village and work elsewhere. It is a 'popular' commuter village. We would not be seen as outsiders now.

The grammar school closed in 1991, as did many similar small independent schools. Pupil numbers had declined and it was no longer financially viable. The advent of comprehensive education meant that failing the 11-plus did not condemn a child to a second-class education, so middle-class parents saw less need to 'go private'. The school had had to borrow to build a new sports hall after the Ministry of Defence had sold the gymnasium. It was a sad day for the Hale sisters. Our parents had poured so much effort and their own money into building it up. As late as 1985, we had seen the opening of the Hale building. This, along with all the other school buildings, has now been converted into houses and flats. Leonard Robinson's old home has become three houses. My elder sister Jill and her family own one of them. This just goes to show what a lovely and loveable old place it is.

Looking back, I learned three big lessons from growing up in Scorton. First was a love of place – of the beauty of the North

Yorkshire countryside and buildings, and especially of the ancient town of Richmond. As a child, I thought that everywhere had a ruined but still magnificent medieval castle, a ruined abbey down the road, a cobbled marketplace with eighteenth-century shopfronts covering even older buildings, in a splendid setting above the fast-running river Swale. Second was a love of peace – or a fear of war – which led eventually to an interest in international organisations, international treaties and the international legal order. And third was a love of social justice – that so-called morality should not be cruel; that people should not be pigeonholed into social classes, their futures determined by who their parents were and where they went to school; that education was the way out and up for all of us, not just a favoured few.

2 A Family Life

Hanging in the dining room of my house in Yorkshire is a large portrait which probably should not be there. We knew it first in our maternal grandmother's house in Leeds. After our mother's death, it moved to me – not because my sisters agreed that it should be mine, but because I had a suitably large wall upon which to hang it. It shows a handsome, dark-haired man in middle age, sitting down, looking serious but friendly. As children we were fascinated by the fact that his eyes followed us round the room. Sister Jill used to be so scared that she would hide behind the furniture in the hope that he would not see her. He is wearing the academic robes of a Cambridge MA and holding his mortar board on his knee. In the background is a coat of arms with the motto '*Semper Eadem*' – always the same. This was the motto of Queen Elizabeth I of England and of the grammar school built with her authority in 1567 in Mansfield, Nottinghamshire.

It is the portrait of John Bates Dashwood Godfrey, my maternal grandfather, no doubt commissioned by Queen Elizabeth's Grammar School while he was headmaster there from 1918 to 1926, when he left because of ill health. The family story is that our maternal grandmother insisted on taking the portrait with her: 'that is my husband and my portrait'. The family moved to Leeds and he was appointed to teach history at Leeds Grammar School, but never did so. He died in 1934 at the age of fifty-six. A letter to our grandmother said this: 'When I knew Mr Godfrey he was a little boy attending a ladies' school where I went also: he was a dear, lovable little boy with a pale face and big dark eyes and I feel sure he would grow up to still have that lovable disposition ... ' If the portrait is anything to go by, he did.

He was also a great inspiration to the granddaughters he never knew. We wanted his academic success. We wanted to go to Oxford like our father, or to Cambridge like him. He came from a long line of clergymen and teachers. His father was vicar of Goole, but died when our grandfather was seven years old. John and his brother Richard were sent to the Clergy Orphan School in Canterbury,[1] which must have been a good school because John went up to Peterhouse College, Cambridge, in 1898, and gained first-class honours in both parts of the history tripos. It gave me quite a thrill when I looked him up in the *Gazette* while I was there. After Cambridge, he taught at various schools, including Sir William Turner's School in Coatham, Redcar, the King's School Grantham, where my mother, Marjorie, was born in 1908, and King Edward VII's School in Sheffield.

By a curious coincidence, our father (who was born in 1909) was educated at King Edward VII's School in Sheffield and they might just have overlapped there. He also spent more than ten years of his teaching career at Sir William Turner's School in Coatham. Our father did not come from a family of teachers. His father and grandfather were engravers in the silver industry in Sheffield. But education was taken seriously and after King Edward VII's school, he went up to Wadham College, Oxford, to read Spanish – a curious choice in those days but apparently there was a scholarship available. After Oxford, he taught at Blackburn Grammar School, then at Birkenhead School, before moving to Coatham. It was in Birkenhead that he met our mother, who was teaching in the prep school of Birkenhead High School for Girls.

We owe that too to Grandpa Godfrey. Our mother told us that he used to take her out for walks and drum into her how important it was that she should pass her school certificate and go on to train as a teacher. She would much rather have been playing tennis (or so she said). He must also have had quite advanced ideas about education, because she qualified to teach under the Froebel system, which emphasised the needs of the individual child and the importance of play (rather than the opposite, which was then the more orthodox educational philosophy).

Our parents were married on 1 January 1936, just over a year after our grandfather's death in December 1934. It was a small affair. The photos were taken several months later. Our mother wore an elegant midnight blue velvet gown and a matching cap. Her strong-minded mother was firmly opposed to her marrying so soon after her father's death. She compromised by not wearing a white gown and veil. Yet marriage meant that she had to give up teaching: in the 1930s there was a marriage bar for women in most public sector jobs, in the Civil Service, in local government and in teaching. She would have had to give up soon afterwards anyway, as my elder sister Jill was born in April 1937, and it was a difficult birth. But teaching was obviously in her blood. When Jill was old enough to go to school, our mother set up a little private school in the family home in Coatham. There were seven pupils including Jill. Recently one of her pupils sent me a photo of the seven and of the inscription our mother wrote in the little book she gave to each child: 'Timothy Marley – With love from Mrs Hale, hoping he will always remember his first little school happily'. He must have done to have kept it all these years. His mother, Minnie Marley, was one of my godparents.

The school cannot have lasted long, because my mother was advised that it would be safe for her to have another child, and in 1944 she became pregnant with me. For the next few years our mother was fully occupied with two young children – my younger sister Frances was born in 1946 while our father was on sabbatical working for the British Council in Spain – and then with helping to run the grammar school in Scorton. As the school expanded, she also began to do some teaching there. Then our whole world fell apart.

It was August 1958. Sister Jill was twenty-one, between her second and third years reading Spanish at Nottingham University, on holiday in Austria with her boyfriend Mike (later to become her husband). Sister Frances was twelve and I was thirteen. Our father had just got back from taking the school cricket team on a tour. He appeared in his normal robust health – despite smoking a pipe, being seriously overweight, leading a largely sedentary lifestyle (he would get into the car to go and see the vicar across the village green), and working long into the night. Frances and I were playing in the school grounds as usual. There was a tall stone wall running down from one corner of the main school building towards the drive, with a line of trees beside it. We liked to climb up it and walk along the top. We saw an ambulance beside the door into the school office. We saw a person being taken into the ambulance on a stretcher. We wondered who it was. When we eventually came down from the wall and went indoors, we found that our father had been suddenly taken ill and driven the short distance to Scorton hospital. He died there two days later at the age of forty-nine. The certified cause of death was a heart attack.

Six months later, our mother wrote this touching story in a 'commonplace book' which we found after her death:

> It was very quiet in the house; and outside too. The dull light of a heavy February sky hung low over the village, and the few sounds – a car driving slowly through, a solitary child running – were deadened by it. The low room, soon shadowy, was shadowy now, though it was not long after luncheon, and she sat back in her chair. It was not comfortable to read any more; why put on the lamp when she was tired of reading, anyhow? Tired of reading, tired of thinking, tired of making an effort, tired of being bright, being normal, 'for the children's sake'. The children were all out, now; she was alone. She was always alone. Oh! People came to see her: quite often: they were wonderfully kind: it was extraordinary how kind people were: and she was very fond of them and very grateful and humbled in receiving their kindness: but still she was alone, carrying on endless conversations in her mind with the one who was not there, who never would be there any more, and who was the only one she ever really wanted ...
>
> How did one pick oneself up when one's life suddenly changed? When one's husband's life was suddenly ended? When half one's personality was cut off and one was left shattered and torn and desolate? One tried to behave as if it hadn't happened; one pretended to oneself that life must go on, that one must do things as usual, that this must be done and that must be done; and one did them; and often enjoyed doing them, too. One was playing a part ...

I now know exactly how she felt, but then, in the selfishness of youth, we saw very little of her anguish. But we always knew that theirs was the greatest love affair of all time. And we were included in that love: even though our mother had firm ideas of what it was suitable for young children to do, there was never any doubt that she and our father loved us all dearly. To her, at twelve and thirteen Frances and I were still young children when our father died, so for the days surrounding the funeral we were sent to stay with my school friend Claire. I don't recall that we objected at the time. Jill and Mike were only told about our father's death when they got back from their holiday, because she didn't want to spoil it for them. They were very cross. But at least they got to the funeral.

We too were devastated by our loss, not only of the fun and laughter which our father always brought with him, but more fundamentally of the sense of security. What was to become of us? Where would we live? What would we live on? And where would we go to school?

Our mother was under pressure from her mother and her younger sister, our Aunt Mary, to go and live with them in the Godfrey family home in Leeds. I doubt that she relished the prospect. Our grandmother was a demanding woman and by then an invalid. Our Aunt Mary, three years younger than our mother, had not been persuaded (or allowed?) to acquire academic qualifications. She was extremely beautiful – so much so that our mother was worried that our father might fall for her sister when she took him home (he didn't). None of Aunt Mary's friendships ripened into marriage. Her destiny was to look after her mother. But she too went into teaching, at Miss Rider's Froebelian Kindergarten and Preparatory School in Moortown, a suburb of Leeds. Our sister Jill spent two periods living with Grandma Godfrey and Auntie Mary and going to the school. Living away from home does not seem to have been so unusual or so traumatic in those days. Jill found it much more traumatic when she was brought back from Moortown to the much larger and rougher Church of England primary school in Coatham for her 11-plus year. But she stuck it out. I come from a family of strong-minded women.

Teachers could get away with quite outrageous behaviour in those days. Lord Dyson, a very fine judge who later became a justice of the Supreme Court and then Master of the Rolls (head of civil justice in England and Wales), lived in the same road as Moortown Preparatory School. He tells how, aged around seven, he was playing with snowballs in his front garden and hit some of Miss Rider's pupils who were walking by. Miss Rider promptly arrested him and marched him off to the school where he was detained for a while as a punishment. Perhaps it was the memory of his false imprisonment that eventually impelled Lord Dyson into the law.

Our mother put the idea of moving to Leeds to Frances and me. We did not fancy it at all – we were thriving in the small pond which was Richmond High School for Girls and were afraid of getting lost in the much larger pond which would be Leeds Girls' High School. Then Mr Davey, head teacher of Bolton-on-Swale primary school, decided to retire. Our mother picked herself up in earnest, dusted off her Froebel certificate and was appointed to succeed him. For some reason we did not move into the head teacher's house which was next door to the school. Instead we moved into a pair of Edwardian farmworkers' cottages, which had been knocked into one house, overlooking the church. For Frances and me, this was the perfect solution. We could stay living in the same parish, with the same friends, and the same school. We had security. Our mother had a job.

Looking back, I feel sure that the sudden loss of security, and regaining it through our mother's resourcefulness, is what made me so determined to qualify for a career, to carry on working whether or not I married or had a family, and never to become wholly dependent upon anyone else, this at a time when marriage and a family were the height of most girls' ambitions. Frances was the same as me. But what career? Many occupations run in families, whether it is farming, the church, the forces, shopkeeping or whatever. Many farms and businesses in Scorton were in the same family for generations. My family's occupation was teaching. None of the three Hale sisters escaped it.

In order to teach, of course, you have first to learn. No doubt our family was much like countless other teachers' families in those days: not especially scholarly or intellectual but with a love of books and an atmosphere which was very conducive to learning. There were always lively conversations at mealtimes and we were encouraged to take part. 1956 was a momentous year, with a great deal to talk about – the Egyptian takeover of 'Colonel Nasser's bloody canal' as our father called Suez and its humiliating aftermath; the height of the civil war in Cyprus; and the Russian suppression of the Hungarian uprising. But I have no real sense of our parents' political beliefs. They took the *Daily Telegraph*, the *Yorkshire Post* and the weekly *Darlington and Stockton Times*. (In those days, *The Times* was seen as a paper for the upper classes: the colonel was the only person in the village who took it.) They also subscribed to the *Reader's Digest* and *Punch*. Churchill was still revered by those who had lived through the war. Aunt Mary wondered whether she should really be shopping at the Co-op next door, 'because we are not socialists'. But our parents did believe in the welfare state; if they were conservatives, they were very open-minded and forward-looking ones. Our father preferred the well-educated and determined sister over the more beautiful one; when they married, he insisted that she should have some money of her own to spend, not just the housekeeping; he clearly saw them as a partnership of equals, which they were. He believed in independent education, because the state should not dictate what everybody learned, but not in the socially divisive public school system. He held the belief that single-sex education should be compulsory for girls but forbidden for boys – obviously unattainable but supported by the evidence. Our mother was among the first to buy the unexpurgated Penguin edition of *Lady Chatterley's Lover* when it was published in 1960 and before its triumphant acquittal of the charge of obscenity (probably the first notorious court case I knew about). In these small but important ways, they were different from the people around them in the village.

Our father was also a dedicated Scout. He ran a Scout troop in the grammar school and he became an assistant county commissioner. In that capacity he was sent by the powers that be to spend a month inspecting how scouting was getting on in Ceylon, as Sri Lanka was then called. He toured the country and saw its wonderful sights. When he came home, he passed on his enthusiasm to the family.

All my adult life, I have wanted to go to Sri Lanka to see it for myself, but alas, since it descended into internal conflict, terror and repression, opportunities have been few and far between. I have seen more of its problems, through the lens of cases about Tamil Tiger asylum-seekers, than of its beauties and its charm.

Our parents were well aware of the educational value of foreign travel. They took a party of Scorton Grammar School boys to Spain every other year and sister Jill went with them. Frances and I were deemed too young. We did not have a family holiday abroad until, surprisingly, our mother hired a villa for a month on Ibiza while I was at university (before it became the party capital of the Balearics). Family holidays were by caravan to the Lake District or to Northumberland, where we just asked the farmers for permission to park in their fields. Frances and I did our best to have adventures like Arthur Ransome's Swallows and Amazons, though never quite as exciting. Our father's scouting skills were well in evidence and scouting songs were sung in the car: I can still sing many of them if called upon to do a turn.

There were also card and board games, although nothing as serious as bridge or chess. Most of the books in the house were out of bounds to the children until we went to the high school. Our mother had strict ideas about age-appropriate reading. As little ones, we were enchanted by Elleston Trevor's books about a bear called Wumpus who wrote silly little poems which we found hilarious: for example, when called upon to be a living dam:

> Poor old Wumpus sitting in the water
> Stopping up the river with what he shouldn't oughta.
> Freezing cold sit-upon stopping up the river
> Hope I needn't sit here for iver and iver.

We liked Wumpus much better than Winnie the Pooh. And *Alice's Adventures in Wonderland* scared me stiff – I had nightmares about suddenly shrinking in size while out in the car and ending up in the gutter.

Later on, we read the usual children's books: including Enid Blyton (I liked the Secret Seven much better than the Famous Five but I cannot now remember why) and Angela Brazil (impossibly alluring accounts of life in a girls' boarding school). We took the *Girl*, the girls' equivalent of the *Eagle* comic for boys (the *Dandy* and the *Beano* were unthinkably vulgar). We scarcely noticed the gender bias in our reading, but I do remember feeling outraged that I was not allowed Meccano because it was a boys' toy: early stirrings of the feminism to come? There were also more serious books: *Once Upon a Time: Children's Stories from the Classics*, retold by Blanche Winder, with memorable pictures of Prometheus chained to a rock, Narcissus falling in love with his reflection in the pool, Perseus with the gorgon's head, which taught us all we needed to know about the myths and sagas of ancient Greece and Rome; *Lamb's Tales from Shakespeare*, which taught us the plots of all the Shakespeare plays, including those which are rarely performed; and later on, Van Loon's *Lives,* imaginary dinner parties with some improbable guests, such as Plato and Confucius, or Dante and Leonardo da Vinci, an entertaining way to introduce us to some important historical figures. These were all wonderful stories. They made me feel well educated. They also awakened and then deepened my love of history.

When we got older, we moved on from the *Girl* to the *New Elizabethan*, a magazine for younger secondary school children. It held a short story competition when I was thirteen. My story was called 'A Case of Gules', a detective tale owing not a little to Agatha Christie and even more to my interest in heraldry. The denouement depended on knowing that a colour (Gules, Vert, etc.) or a metal (Or and Argent) could not be superimposed on each other in a heraldic device. Much to my surprise, I won the competition. But the magazine did not publish my story, so they cannot have thought it very good. Perhaps I was the only competitor? Perhaps the subject matter was a little abstruse? But it stood me in good stead when I came to devise my own coat of arms.

When we were no longer deemed too young, we were allowed to read the grown-up classics, but I don't remember enjoying them as much then as I did later in life. I was far more taken with the detective stories of Agatha Christie, Ngaio Marsh, and Dorothy L. Sayers. Dorothy L. Sayers, in particular, provoked an early interest in feminism: why was the well-educated Harriet Vane, a successful author, so reluctant to marry the rich and well-educated aristocrat, Lord Peter Wimsey? Georgette Heyer also wrote detective stories but we were especially fond of her historical romances, set mostly in the Regency period in a rather higher social stratum than Jane Austen's novels, entertaining and very well written. One, *The Spanish Bride*, was so full of rich historical detail about Wellington's campaigns in the peninsular war it proved remarkably useful in my A level history exam. We also devoured the historical novels of the Irish writer Maurice Walsh, who was very popular in the 1920s and 1930s but is little read today. His books were set in either Ireland or Scotland and dealt with the Irish struggle for independence and the bloody civil war which followed; they gave me a lasting fascination with the Irish people and the romantic Irish nationalism which he championed. Later on, I took to Graham Greene and Joseph Conrad with enthusiasm. This may have had something to do with a late teenage burst of religiosity: Frances and I were confirmed by the bishop of Ripon on 10 March 1961, when I was sixteen. We took our confirmation classes and our new duties as full members of the Church of England quite seriously: these included going to church every Sunday (which we did) and following 'the example of Christ in home and daily life, and [bearing] personal witness to Him' (which was harder).

There must have been non-fiction in the house, but I only remember the Bible, the complete works of Shakespeare and the annual edition of *Whitaker's Almanac*, which was a mine of useful information. In the sixth form, our headmistress, Miss Thornton, told me that I should be reading more non-fiction. She gave us a list: she must have been a more radical person than might be guessed from her stern and conventional appearance. The books which made a lasting impression were *Naught for your Comfort*, Trevor Huddleston's powerful attack on apartheid, and another by an author whom I cannot now trace, which I think was called *The Myth of National Character*, also a powerful attack on stereotyping people according to where they come from. That all people, wherever they came from and whatever the colour of their skin, were entitled to equal dignity and respect was instilled in me long before I had heard of the Universal Declaration of Human Rights.

So there were conversation, games and books. There was a lot of laughter. Our father liked making up limericks, but the only one I can remember was aimed at sister Jill:

> There is a young lady I know
> Whose dress sense is very so-so
> She wears red and green,
> With amber between,
> So they called her stop, caution and go!

There was also more tangible help with our education. Bolton-on-Swale school did not have high aspirations for most of its pupils. It had two classrooms which housed around sixty children aged from five to eleven. There was the infant school for the first two years, presided over by a teacher without formal qualifications but with a very assured touch. I was good at the three Rs but hopeless at needlework: to my shame, I dropped a stitch in the dishcloth I was knitting, so she looped down to pick it up, leaving a very sorry-looking object. But later on, I got good enough at it to make my own clothes – including a May Ball dress in Cambridge – then the cheapest way to acquire a larger wardrobe.

Linked to the infant school by a covered passageway was a late Victorian building which housed what were then called 'standards': one, two three and four. The room was divided by a curtain and one teacher took standards one and two, while the head teacher took standards three and four. It cannot have been easy handling all abilities in those conditions. But it must have been even worse when our mother was head teacher – for the school numbers hovered between those which qualified it for three teachers and those which only entitled it to two. She had sometimes to cope with four years of very mixed-ability pupils in the one room. And she was very deaf. But like many good teachers, she seemed to have a fifth sense of what was going on around her even if she could neither see nor hear it.

In those days, it felt as if one's whole future depended upon the 11-plus. Those who passed, and whose parents could afford and were prepared to pay for the uniform, went to the boys' grammar school or the girls' high school in Richmond. Those who failed went to the secondary modern school on Catterick Camp. This was not supposed to be an inferior education, just more suitable for children with practical rather than academic talents. The reality for many was quite different. And there was a very real postcode lottery. There was no national pass mark for the 11-plus. It depended upon how many grammar school places there were in your local authority area. There were far fewer grammar school places in the North Riding of Yorkshire than there were in counties such as Surrey and Cheshire. Not only that: there were fewer than half the high school places available for girls than there were grammar school places for boys. North Riding children had to do better than Cheshire children and North Riding girls had to do better than North Riding boys.

This was not illegal until the Sex Discrimination Act 1975. One of the landmark cases under the Act involved Birmingham City Council, which had fewer grammar school places for girls than for boys. This was not because of a conscious decision by the councillors to treat the girls less favourably than the boys. It was for historical reasons. Nevertheless, the House of Lords held that it was unlawful: if the effect of what the council did was to treat the girls less favourably than the boys the councillors' motive was irrelevant.[2]

None of this did I know in 1955 when I took the 11-plus a year early, at the age of ten. I must have been getting on well with English and arithmetic but as well as these, there was an IQ test. This was said to be a test of innate intelligence, so there was no need to prepare for it, but my parents must have thought otherwise, because I have a distinct recollection of taking several practice IQ tests produced by our father for all three of us: just one more unfair advantage of growing up in a family of teachers.

So I passed the 11-plus at the age of ten and went up to the high school in September 1955. The school was founded in the 1920s and moved into a spanking new building in 1939. Our father used to call it the 'jam factory' but in fact it was – and still is – a fine building, all glass, stone and concrete, a pioneer in modern school design and now Grade II listed. The classrooms are all on the ground floor off a long corridor with huge windows looking east towards the Cleveland Hills. Indeed they look over the fields to the collection of stone buildings which are now three houses in which I and my two stepdaughters live – a family compound. There are little gardens between the class-rooms. It was and is a building to be proud of. It now houses the sixth-form college of Richmond School but the honours board listing the high school head girls is still there, showing J. Hale in 1955, B. Hale in 1962, and F. Hale in 1963.

But when I arrived in 1955, I was scared and lonely: scared because I was so young, and no doubt less mature than my classmates, and lonely because I was the only one from my little primary school. My big sister Jill might have been head girl, but she was an impossibly remote figure. But I was soon befriended by a kind and thoughtful girl, my dear friend Claire, who took pity on my solitude and we became and still are the best of friends. So I got over my fright and began to enjoy myself. The school suited me down to the ground.

It was small: twenty-six girls in my first-year class. I was clever, a swot and a goody-goody: still a bit of an outsider. When I got hauled over the coals by the headmistress for once skipping choir practice, the class applauded – 'now, you're one of us' – and elected me form captain. I was always top of the class in the academic subjects, but the school did not want me to become complacent or big-headed: more 'good' than 'very good' in my school reports. On 7 December 1956 our father sent sister Jill, then in her first year at Nottingham University, a telegram reading 'Brenda averages full alpha stop fellow worm comma crawl'. I am amazed that she is still talking to me. Typically, the least enthusiastic reports were in art ('Brenda must try to be more imaginative'), needlework ('Brenda must try to pay more careful attention to detail') and physical education ('Brenda is a willing worker'). All of those comments are true to this day, and apply to far more than art, needlework and sport (cross-check the personality test on page 121). But my father was reassuring: you mustn't be good at everything.

I was entered for nine subjects at O level but might never have got to sit them because I caught chickenpox and had to stay at home. Luckily, I could sit the exams there, invigilated by Miss Lucy Rogers, but had to miss the French oral and aural exams. Whether despite or because of these arrangements, my results were respectable: 80% in six subjects, but only 70% in biology, Latin and French. So what to do in the sixth form? The school's expectations of its students were not adventurous. About three or four of the fifteen or sixteen in the upper sixth would go to university. Another three or four would go to conventional teacher training colleges. Others would go into nursing or become bank or insurance clerks or secretaries. My best friend Claire wanted to be an occupational therapist, which was unheard of. She eventually went to train as a child care officer, which was equally unheard of. Another girl wanted to do Froebel teacher training, as my mother had done, but this was not encouraged, although she did in fact go and do it. Even then, I must have been thinking of law, because I chose to do history, Latin and French, an excellent preparation. It meant that I had to go down to the boys' grammar school to study Latin: my first (and entirely enjoyable) experience of co-education.

The high school was a strange mixture of rather restricted career expectations, petty rules typical of the girls' schools of the day, and some really quite forward-looking ideas. One of these was to enter those of us who wanted to for the European Schools Day competition in 1962, when I was in the upper sixth. Looking back, this was one of the most formative experiences of my school days. It certainly helped me to grow up and learn to look after myself.

European Schools Day was an essay competition to attract 'the attention of youth ... to the deep-laid unity of the cultural heritage of Europe and to the benefits of a real understanding between our diverse national communities'. There were roughly a dozen winners from each of the twelve countries then belonging to the Council of Europe. I cannot now remember what the exact subject of the essay was or what I wrote, but it was good enough to win me the second-best prize: my first trip abroad, at the age of seventeen.

I was excited but nervous about the trip – my first visit to London had only been the year before, at the age of sixteen when I went to stay with sister Jill for a week. So I kept a narrative diary. The British prizewinners met at Victoria station and travelled by train to Dover where we took the ferry to Ostend, then travelled by train through Bruges, Ghent, Brussels ('Belgium is very dull', I wrote, but I seem to remember tasting my first beer over dinner in Brussels), then Aachen, Cologne, after which I went to bed in my couchette, sharing the compartment with one of the boys, an Austrian couple, two Austrian women who had married Englishmen, and a toddler. 'Germany – what little I saw – did not impress me; Austria was better – more hills, more woods, and quaint little churches with onions on top (query: is this Turkish influence?). The Danube is wide, but a nasty grey-green ... '

The Austrian ladies gave us funny looks when we told them we would be staying in a *Bundeserziehungsanstalt für Mädchen*: we didn't realise then that it was a sort of borstal for delinquent girls, although that was certainly how it felt when we got there: 'the something or other *für Mädchen* is rather grim: absolutely huge, barrack-like archi-tecture, hospital beds, <u>no</u> baths (plenty of washbasins), all dully institutional'. One of the girls was engaged: 'don't like her ring and also think it's a bit queer – she's only eighteen, and going to university next year'.

The next day we were taken on a tour of Vienna, 'a very lovely city', though to my English eyes, the interior of St Stephen's Cathedral had 'neither beauty nor style' and the numerous altars and tombs were 'absolutely hideous'; then up through the Vienna woods to the Kahlenburg restaurant, where we had a 'spiffing blowout', high on a hill overlooking Vienna (food was quite a preoccupation). That evening there was a formal welcome reception given by the lord mayor of Vienna in the *Rathaus* (town hall), which 'turned out to be one short speech, a huge and wonderful buffet, and dancing'. We also learned that day that the gold medal for the best essay of all had been won for the first time by an English boy 'of King Edward VII's Grammar School, Sheffield (!!!)'. He was 'very brainy, very pleasant, just a little discouraging'.

The following day was the prize-giving and discussion held in the Hofburg Palace. There was music and 'rather ineffectual' speeches with 'brilliant but not always effective' simultaneous translation. The bright spot was the English boy getting the gold medal, although the Italian who won the prize offered by Vienna did better materially – a cine camera and projector. During the afternoon's discussion 'There were several times when I almost plucked up courage to speak, but they all sounded so erudite, and I was so nervous, I thought I'd better not.'

After four days in Vienna, we all set off in groups with members from each of the participating countries on our different prize holidays. Scary, but my French and even my German were a great deal better then than they are now. The second-best prize was a week as guests of the Council of Europe in Strasbourg. We stayed in a guest house in the old city. I shared a room with a Swiss girl who became a good friend. Once again, I was the youngest there and the Europeans thought I was young for my age. Being used to this, I just carried on regardless. It turned out to be a magical time, once we had got over the formal proceedings in the Maison de l'Europe. Even these were much better than in Vienna, 'more informal, and more argumentative'. Once again, 'I almost made a contribution, but not quite!'

Strasbourg is a beautiful city with more restaurants and churches than anywhere I had ever seen. In Vieux-Thann, on the Alsace wine route, we visited the church and 'I made the boob of saying to Marie, one of the English girls who works in the directorate of information (I think!), that I didn't like the interior of Catholic churches. She is, of course, a Catholic.' The next day, there was an organ concert in a beautiful old Protestant church, 'just for us. It was really wonderful: organ music is perhaps the one thing that can make me feel I ought to be religious – sitting in a dark, old church, listening to Bach superbly played is an unforgettable experience.' Odd, as I had been very religious the year before and was to become so again in the next. We also went over the Rhine, first to Baden-Baden, 'the original snob town', with a 'swish Harrogatish café' and a casino which I didn't like, then to the International Forum at Burg Liebenzell, where we found the discussion on European unity 'even more superficial than our own had been'.

After the week in Strasbourg I travelled back by train to Vienna. This was quite a challenge for such an inexperienced girl on her own in central Europe. Luckily, Heinz, the Austrian prizewinner, came with me to the station and as far as Stuttgart on the train (to my shame, the bus conductor could not understand my '*À la gare, s'il vous plait*' but instantly responded to Heinz's '*Zum Bahnhof*'). I was to spend the next four weeks in Klosterneuburg, near Vienna, with the family of Christl, an Austrian schoolgirl who had been staying with my family for the previous three weeks.

I had a very happy time in Klosterneuburg, lazing around, reading, going for walks and swimming in a backwater of the Danube. There were also some trips out – to Melk and the Wachau, to the Raxalpe, to Schönbrunn Palace – where I was fascinated by the huge and elaborately decorated stoves in the corner of each room – to Burgenland and the Neusiedlersee, and several times to Vienna, where I found St Stephen's 'slightly better than I thought, but still pretty awful'. I didn't like the monastery church in Klosterneuburg either or the Karlskirche, Vienna's example of late baroque, 'with a classical portico which is quite bearable, two columns with a spiral of relief work, which aren't, and an extremely ugly interior. By that I mean no disrespect to the God for whom it was created, or to the creators who thought it beautiful: I merely register my own dislike of it.'

On the middle Sunday,

I've decided that going to church would be pointless, as their Protestantism is very different from mine, and I wouldn't understand a word of it: it might be better if someone could go with me, but Catholics aren't allowed in Protestant services. But I am beginning to wish that I could take Communion – I wonder why, because as a rule I don't feel at all religious – perhaps it's a sort of vanity, or home-sickness. Anyway, I don't seem to want one enough to write to the consul about it.

A few days later I discovered that there was an Anglican church 'quite near our old borstal – I wonder?' The following Sunday, Christl and I went into Vienna for the Communion service there: 'somehow I'd been wanting to go to Communion quite a lot. There were not many people there ... Two pewsful knew each other – probably from the embassy and consulate: they gathered to talk outside in a most English country church manner!'

That trip meant such a lot. I was on my own. I had to get on with new people, some of them from foreign countries, speaking languages I didn't know or only knew in books. I had to find my way about. I had to learn about countries, architecture, religions I had not met before. It proved how much good it does to bring the young people from different parts of Europe together; to learn that they have more in common than they think; to learn about our common European heritage (though not necessarily our common European institutions); to respect our common European values, despite the ghastly history of the twentieth century, which had featured so strongly in my early childhood. I came back a different person, much better prepared to move on from school to university.

The results of my advanced- and scholarship-level examinations arrived while I was there – distinctions in A level history and French and high marks in the scholarship papers in both subjects. My diary doesn't mention Latin, where I didn't do so well. But the whole was good enough to get me a state scholarship to go to university. It was taken for granted that all three girls would go to university if we could and we wanted to (but we were also told that we could stay at home if we wanted). So on my return from Vienna (bearing gifts for all the family) I embarked on the first term of my third year in the sixth form with a view to sitting the entrance examinations to read law at either Oxford or Cambridge. But why law?

3 Why Law?

Miss Thornton's study was a small room with large windows looking over to the Cleveland Hills. The A level history class had their lessons there while her red setter dog sat quietly under her desk. She was a slight woman with pepper and salt hair and a stern appearance. The younger girls were scared stiff of her. She had soon seen me as potential Oxbridge material. But she had read history at Oxford and did not see me as a natural historian. So what was I going to study? History was my favourite subject but I had also developed an interest in the British constitution and suggested studying that for A level. She turned that down – they wouldn't be able to teach me and knew no one who could. So we settled for history, Latin and French, a good combination of storytelling, analysis and linguistic skills, well suited to a budding lawyer. But where had the idea of law come from?

I am convinced that it came from studying the political history of seventeenth-century England. That was the century of 'Rebellion, Restoration, Revolution'.[1] It should be taught in every school today, because it is the foundation of our modern constitution. The House of Commons, with some encouragement from the lawyers, rebelled against the king; there was a civil war which culminated in the king being tried and executed for treason in 1649 and the establishment of Cromwell's government; then there was the restoration of the monarchy in 1660; and the 'Glorious Revolution' of 1688, in which one king was deposed (or abdicated, depending on your point of view) and another monarch was installed by the authority of Parliament. Alongside the exciting stories of the battles between the Cavaliers ('wrong but wromantic') and the Roundheads ('right but repulsive') were the constitutional battles between the king, the judges and Parliament, brought to life by real legal cases involving real people who had the courage to stand up for what they believed in, despite the very real risks to their lives and their livelihoods, risks which are unimaginable in Great Britain today. How much of this I knew at the time, and how much I learned later at university, I cannot now remember. But the story is worth telling, because it says so much about what we now call the rule of law.

In 1603, after the death of Queen Elizabeth, King James VI of Scotland became James I of England. He believed that he ruled by divine right, answerable only to God. He also believed that he could judge lawsuits and change laws. He very soon came up against the formidable legal brain and scholarship of Sir Edward Coke. As Attorney General, Coke had led the prosecution of the conspirators in the Gunpowder Plot of 1605. But as a judge he was a staunch upholder of the ancient laws and liberties of England. In the *Case of Prohibitions del Roy*,[2] Coke relates how the king claimed to take what causes he wanted to determine from the judges and decide them for himself. But Coke responded, in the presence and with the consent of all the judges, that the king could not do this.

> Then the king said that he thought the law was founded upon reason and that he and others had reason, as well as the judges: to which it was answered by me, that true it was, that God had endowed His Majesty with excellent science, and great endowments of nature; but His Majesty was not learned in the laws of his realm of England, and causes which concern the life, or inheritance, or goods, or fortunes of his subjects, are not to be decided by natural reason but by the artificial reason and judgment of law, which law is an act which requires long study and experience, before that a man can attain to the cognisance of it: that the law was the golden met-wand and measure to try the causes of the subjects; and which protected His Majesty in safety and in peace.

Coke's law report does relate that the king was 'greatly offended' at the idea that he was subject to the law as well as to God, but not that he flew into a rage and made as if to strike the judge, who fell flat on his knees.

Only three years later, in the *Case of Proclamations*,[3] the question was whether the king could, by proclamation, prohibit new buildings in and around London or the making of starch from wheat, on pain of prosecution. Predictably, Coke's answer was that the king could not create any offence by his prohibition or proclamation which was not an offence before. In the same term, by the chief justices of all the common law courts – Common Pleas, King's Bench and Exchequer – 'it was resolved, that the king hath no prerogative, but that which the law of the land allows him'. Somehow Coke kept his place, although he was moved from chief justice of the Court of Common Pleas to chief justice of the Court of King's Bench, where it was thought that his higher status would make him less of a troublemaker. It didn't.

The end for Coke came in 1616. King James had used the writ of commendams to allow Richard Neile to hold a bishopric and associated revenues without actually performing its duties. The judges wrote to the king to tell him that this was illegal. The king summoned them to him and tore up the letter. The other judges fell to their knees and begged for pardon but Coke is reported to have said that 'when the case happens I shall do that which shall be fit for a judge to do'. He was dismissed from his post. In those days, judges held office 'during His Majesty's pleasure' and could be sacked at will. Coke went on to be just as troublesome as a Member of Parliament. He was, for example, a prime mover behind the Statute of Monopolies 1624, passed in an attempt to control the king's habit of raising money by granting monopolies to engage in a wide variety of profitable activities, such as draining the fens, or making and selling commodities like salt and starch.

Another of Coke's achievements was to resurrect the Magna Carta and give it almost mythical power. The original charter was sealed by King John at Runnymede in 1215, but swiftly repudiated. Much of it was resurrected by his successor, King Henry III, and reissued several times in the thirteenth century. The 1297 charter of Edward was passed into statute by Parliament. We can derive at least three powerful constitutional principles from the Magna Carta. They motivated many of the struggles of the seventeenth century and are with us to this day. The first is still on the statute book:

No free man shall be taken or imprisoned, or be disseised of his freehold or liberties or free customs, or be outlawed or exiled or in any other wise destroyed; nor will we pass upon him, nor condemn him, but by the lawful judgment of his peers or by the law of the land. We will sell to no man, we will not deny or defer to any man right or justice.

Those words still 'have the power to make the blood race', as
Lord Bingham, senior Law Lord and the greatest judge of the twenty-
first century, has said. They embody the individual's right to life,
liberty and property, not to be arbitrarily infringed by the rulers,
but only in accordance with the law. The closing words also embody
the individual's right to access to justice, before an incorruptible
decision-maker who will judge according to law and not by the size
of the bribe.

The second great principle found in the original charter can be
summed up in the later slogan, 'no taxation without representation': 'No scutage or aid is to be imposed in Our Kingdom except
by the Common Counsel of Our Kingdom unless for the ransoming
of Our person and knighting of Our firstborn son and for marrying
once Our firstborn daughter and for these only a reasonable aid is
to be taken.'

The king was generally expected to fund his regime from the royal
estates, apart from those traditional taxes. It also became customary
for Parliament to vote a new king 'tonnage and poundage' – excise
duties – for the duration of his reign. For anything else he needed,
the king had to go to Parliament, as the great council of the realm
became known in the thirteenth century, unless he could dream up
some other way to raise money.

The third great principle is that the king and his officials are as
much subject to the laws of the land as are his subjects. The rule of
law is not one-way traffic: not only do the governed have to obey the
law, but so do the governors. This was reinforced by the king's promise
that: 'We will not appoint justices constables sheriffs or bailiffs except
from such as know the law of the kingdom and are willing to keep
it well.'

This does, of course, beg the question of who makes the laws,
a question which was only resolved at the end of the seventeenth
century. The battles between the king and Parliament escalated
after 1625, when King Charles I succeeded King James. Parliament
refused to grant Charles the money he needed unless he would
address their grievances. His response was to devise new ways of
raising money. One was to demand loans and imprison without

trial those who refused to pay. Another was to declare martial law and force people to house, feed and clothe the soldiers and sailors. This led to the Petition of Right of 1628, drafted by Coke and accepted first by the House of Commons and then by the House of Lords and then reluctantly by King Charles, because he needed the money. This repeated the cardinal principles of Magna Carta, no taxation without parliamentary consent and no imprisonment without cause, as well as banning commissions to declare martial law in peacetime.

Soon afterwards, King Charles dissolved Parliament and tried to govern without it for eleven years. Again, he had to resort to novel ways of raising money, one of which was 'ship money'. It was accepted that in times of war or national emergency, coastal towns might be required to supply ships for the defence of the realm. But Charles expanded this by raising money rather than ships, not only from coastal towns but also from inland, and not only in wartime but also in peacetime. This led to another great legal case – the prosecution for failure to pay the tax of John Hampden, a Buckinghamshire landowner and cousin of Oliver Cromwell. His case[4] was heard by all twelve judges in the Court of Exchequer Chamber: seven of them held that the tax was legal but five held that it was not. The narrowness of the king's victory encouraged many more to refuse to pay and, when Parliament was eventually recalled in 1640, the tax was abolished by the Ship Money Act 1640. The civil wars followed.

There were fewer landmark legal cases after the monarchy was restored in 1660. Nor were the judges always so courageous. But juries could be. In *Bushel's Case*,[5] after a jury had acquitted two Quakers of an unlawful assembly, the chief justice ruled that jurors could not be punished for the verdicts they returned, even if these were obviously perverse: a principle which remains to this day. Another jury provoked a constitutional crisis in 1688 when they acquitted seven bishops of seditious libel. The bishops had objected to reading out the king's Declaration of Indulgence, granting exemption to Roman Catholics and Nonconformists from the Test Act 1678, which required the holders of public office to be members of the Church of England.

The 'Glorious Revolution', in which James II was replaced by King William and Queen Mary, followed soon afterwards.

This was the true revolution. William and Mary were the first to acknowledge, from the outset, that they were a constitutional, limited, monarchy. They were offered and accepted the throne on the terms laid down by Parliament in the Bill of Rights which received royal assent in December 1689. This was very clear. It was illegal for the Crown to suspend or dispense with laws, or to levy money for and to the use of the Crown, or to keep a standing army in peacetime, without the consent of Parliament. The election of Members of Parliament must be free, 'freedom of speech and proceedings in Parliament ought not to be impeached or questioned in any court or place out of Parliament', parliaments ought to be held frequently, and excessive bail or cruel and unusual punishments should not be imposed. The scene was set for a modern constitution governed by the sovereignty of the king-in-Parliament and the rule of law.

Who could not be excited by such a story – which laid the foundations for our democracy – but also by the courage of those who stood up for their principles, often at great personal cost? I knew only some of this when I suggested to Miss Thornton that I read law, but I knew that I wanted to know more. Even then I knew that there was more to law than the courtroom dramas shown on TV. At the back of my mind there may also have been a desire to escape from the family profession of schoolteaching – law was not taught in schools in those days. To her eternal credit, given her rather tramlined views of what her girls should do, Miss Thornton's reaction was not 'nonsense, girls do not read law, no one in this school has ever done so before, and we know nothing about it'. She embraced it as a good idea, while accepting that there was little the school could do to help. And a good idea it turned out to be, although I was not entirely successful in escaping the teaching profession. But I am fond of saying that I chose to study law because my headmistress did not think that I was clever enough to study history.

I had no idea then of the richness and complexity of the law, or of how one went about studying it. That is what I learned at university.

There I learned that the law touches every corner of our personal and business lives; that it is not always a straightforward system of easy-to-follow and uncontentious rules; that it can raise some hard-to-solve problems in the search for a just solution; and that it can be great fun to study.

4 University Life

It is December 1962. The school Christmas party. As head girl, I have to be there. But this is the day that the telegrams are due to arrive telling me whether I have been offered a place at Somerville College, Oxford, or Girton College, Cambridge. (In those days you could apply for both.) The teachers at the party know this. They also know that my mother is expected to telephone the school with the news. She does not do so. Nor does she say anything when she collects me from school at the end of the party. The teachers' disappointment is plain to see. We drive home. She still does not say anything. But there on the hall table is a telegram saying 'Girton offers Exhibition to read law'. This was wonderful news – not just a place but a minor scholarship to go with it. Why had my mother said nothing? Because she thought that I wanted to go to Oxford (which had only put me on the waiting list)! But I am elated – a dream come true.

Of course, I would have been delighted with either. But my censorious teenage self had been much more impressed with Girton than with Somerville. In those days, the colleges set their own entrance exams and the Girton papers had been fun to take. The interview process was more thorough. The Girton grounds and buildings were more attractive. Above all, the law tutor in Somerville had stressed that theirs was a course in jurisprudence, concentrating on the theory rather than the practicalities of the law, and even then I knew which I would prefer. In retrospect, of course, both Somerville and Girton were right. I might have managed the Oxford course, but I was much better-suited to the more concrete and down-to-earth approach in Cambridge.

So I rang the school to tell them the good news that I would be going to Cambridge and, better still, leaving school at Christmas.

The next three months were spent mainly in bed, while I arranged my second trip abroad: perhaps not as exciting as the adventures undertaken by today's students in their 'gap' years, but exciting enough for me.

It began in April with another long train trip to Vienna, where I was to spend three months as an au pair girl with the Lhotka family who lived in Kierling, a little village near Klosterneuburg, where I had stayed with Christl and her family the year before. Frau Dr Lhotka taught languages, and Herr Professor Lhotka taught sport, at the *gymnasium* in Klosterneuburg. They had five children, ranging from an eighteen-year-old son, Rudolf, who was doing his *abitur*, their school-leaving exam, down to a seven-year-old daughter, Burgi, who had just started school and came home earlier than the rest. I shared a room with their fourteen-year-old daughter, Roswitha, and we became good friends. They had two other sons, Johannes and Bernhard. In many ways they were quite like my own family, education-focused, child-centred and churchgoing, but there were differences. They were Roman Catholics, so for a taste of home I made my way into Vienna every other Sunday for the service at the Anglican church. But they encouraged me to join them in their local church which, unlike the Roman Catholic churches at home, welcomed Protestants. There they sang Mozart Masses.

The family were seriously musical. Herr Lhotka and the three sons played all the stringed instruments between them, apart from the double bass; Grossvati, Frau Lhotka's father, who lived with them, was an excellent violin player and teacher; Frau Lhotka and Roswitha played the piano and sang. The family could put on its own chamber music concerts. They encouraged me to join in the singing (*'wie hoch eine Stimme die Brenda hat'*). Grossvati developed quite a crush on me, and improved my piano playing enough for us to play duets (*Für Elise*, transcribed for piano and violin, among them). They sent me to see *La Bohème* at the Vienna Staatsoper, only the second opera I had ever seen, apart from Gilbert and Sullivan. They deepened my understanding of classical music and set me off on a lifelong enthusiasm for opera.

But to my untutored mind the family were also rather odd. They lived in an old house on a large plot of land on the side of a steep wooded valley. They had been extending it for years. There were two impressive reception rooms and a large music room but these were sparsely furnished and barely used. There was a television which was never watched. The family lived in a much smaller music room and the kitchen in the basement. There was running water in the two lavatories in the house but not in any of the taps. Water had to be fetched from the pump by the stream at the bottom of the valley.

I was very homesick at first but grew accustomed. I learned a lot. Not only music and conversational German, but also the history and culture of the Austro-Hungarian Empire. Budapest was only 134 miles away, and Bratislava even closer, yet behind the Iron Curtain they could have been in another world. I learned how Austria and Vienna had been divided into American, British, French and Russian zones after the war, as had Germany and Berlin. But they had been able to make a treaty with the Allies in 1956 and were now an independent nation once more. The romance of central Europe stayed with me: it was a thrill, in 1992, soon after the Iron Curtain came down, to travel by train from an ombudsman conference in Vienna to a family-law conference in Budapest. The Lhotkas and the Hales stayed friends. In the summer of 1966, my mother, Frances and I drove down to Kierling and listened to the World Cup on the Lhotkas' sunny terrace: England and Germany were 2–2 at full-time, then England scored a controversial (*unpopulär*) third, so we were all relieved when they scored a fourth.

After three months with the Lhotkas, I took another train from Vienna, through the Alpine glories of Salzburg, Innsbruck and Liechtenstein, to Zurich, where I changed for the train to Solothurn, a small town in the German-speaking part of Switzerland. There I spent a very happy holiday with my friend from Strasbourg the year before, and her family. In Strasbourg, we had spoken French, but after speaking German for three months, I found it well-nigh impossible to switch back to French. I learned that I am not a natural linguist. So we stuck to German: though the switch from *Wienerisch* to *Schwitzertüch* was almost as hard. Switzerland has, of course, some spectacular scenery. It was also quite the cleanest and tidiest place I had ever been. But remarkably, even in 1963, women still did not have the right to vote in federal elections (they did in a few of the cantons).

This would have required not only a majority of the popular (male) vote, but also the support of a majority of the cantons. So it was not surprising that change was slow (think of some of the London clubs). But it was surprising that my friend, due to pass her *abitur* and go to university the next year, did not think that women should have the vote – women were so much more emotional than men, she said. I was shocked. That was not the way I had been brought up to think or indeed what I had observed.

From Switzerland I travelled on to Rome, again by train through the Alps. There I was to spend four weeks with a party of English students, at a work camp organised by the Student Christian Movement, at Ecumene, a Methodist retreat centre in the hills near Velletri, south of Rome. It was a relief to be speaking English once more, although the others thought I was a foreigner when I first met them: after speaking German all the time I spoke English with a funny accent. There were Italian young people at the camp as well. Latin helped us to understand them but we got on better in French. The boys spent their time helping to build huts and the girls spent their time doing the washing and cooking. But we also had trips into Rome, where we saw the pope from a distance, and *Aida* rather closer, and down to Naples, where there was the worst poverty I had ever seen, but also the wonders of Herculaneum. Then back by train to England in time for the university term.

I was not nervous about going up to Cambridge. It was the culmination of everything I had been working towards for the past seven years. I knew how to study and how to work hard. My family knew what university – even Oxbridge – was all about. I was excited by the prospect of new friends and new experiences. My trip had been a good preparation for university life: I had learned to conquer homesickness, to live and get on with other people, including young people from very different backgrounds, to find my way around Europe by public transport without a guide, to understand a little of other cultures and how other people lived. So I boarded the train at Scorton station with much more confidence than I would have done a year earlier. There was no suggestion that my mother would drive me down to Cambridge – it wasn't generally done in those days. My trunk was sent on by 'passenger luggage in advance' but did not arrive in Cambridge until days after I did, which was the most nerve-wracking thing about the whole experience. My mother pressed an envelope into my hand as I left, 'Lord Chesterfield's advice to his son,' she said, but actually it was a healthy sum in cash. The advice I had was a copy of the letter our father had sent to Jill when she went up to Nottingham University:

I am now going to do a Polonius, so you have no need to read any further unless you want to. I have only three bits of advice for you:

1. We have brought you up to appreciate drink for what it is worth, neither more nor less. I am not in the least afraid that you will not treat it with discretion; but I would suggest that you be a thought careful with whom you drink; there are several well-known ways of making a drink much more potent than it ought to be and there are men about who would consider it a desirable thing to use such methods to get a girl drunk, either for the fun of it or for even more definite reasons ...

2. It generally takes more courage to refuse a dare than to take it.

3. Try and keep a clear idea of what you have gone up for. The obvious answer – a degree – is neither the whole truth nor anything less than the truth. Of course you want a degree and the best one you are capable of. If you get married the day you come down, or decide to go into dress-designing or running a tea shop or conducting a tram, you still want a degree, possibly as a qualification, certainly as an insurance policy but most certainly for the mental training and discipline that it involves. But you could get that by a correspondence course and a London external. Then you want some fun; and there is nothing essentially incompatible between scholarship and the one-step; but you can get that at the local palais and cinema. There remain the things which you can get at a University and nowhere else; contact with other minds, probably better than your own, the capacity to formulate a viewpoint and argue it, without diffidence on the one hand or arrogance on the other, above all the chance to explore and find out things, chief among which is yourself. Languages, dancing, dress-making: three things you do tolerably well and even more than tolerably: is there anything that you might do superlatively? This is your chance to find out. Failing that acquire as many interests as time and work allow; the

more avenues of expression you can discover, the less chance you have of finding later in life that circumstances have blocked all your outlets. And do try and avoid falling in love: I have nothing against falling in love, in fact I believe in it: but not please at the University: there are so many places and so many years in which it can be done, but a University is neither the time nor the place: passionate or platonic a love affair makes too many demands and knows a dozen ways of ruining a career without going to the melodramatic lengths of the popular novelette.

I shall now get behind the arras.

This is all still excellent advice for today's students. I don't know how much of it Jill followed – she didn't avoid falling in love. I did my best to follow it and managed to avoid falling in love.

The advice may be the same now but university life is not. There were then only twenty universities in England, one in Wales and five in Scotland. There were 118,000 university students in 1962/3. This was 4% of the eighteen- to twenty-one-year-old age group, but 5.6% of the men and only 2.5% of the women. These small numbers meant that the state could afford to support everyone who needed it. Tuition fees were paid for us all, regardless of means, and there were means-tested maintenance grants, paid for either by the county councils or by central government. I qualified for a full state scholarship, which was enough to pay my college bills and lead a happy student life in Cambridge, while spending my vacations at home.

All the Cambridge colleges were single-sex. There were twenty-one colleges for men and only three for women. The ratio of male-to-female undergraduates was roughly nine to one. This was, of course, grossly unfair to the women, but I'm not sure how conscious the class of 1963 was of it at the time. We just got on with enjoying it. The men came from a wide variety of schools, ranging from Eton, Winchester, Harrow and other major public schools, through what were then seen as minor public schools, the leading long-established grammar schools, the more recently established grammar schools, and I even knew one young man from a comprehensive school, then a very new idea. This was my first exposure to the innate sense of entitlement that so many of the public schoolboys had, and also to the noticeable and often resented hierarchy amongst them (one friend threatened that, come the revolution, he was going to dismantle Eton 'brick by brick'). By contrast, most of the women came from girls' grammar schools, many from those established at the end of the nineteenth century by the Girls' Public Day School Trust, and from the less august county council institutions such as my own. The leading academic girls' boarding schools did not feature as strongly in the women's colleges as the leading academic boys' boarding schools did in the men's. One reason could be that upper- and upper-middle-class parents were prepared to pay for their sons to go to university but not for their daughters.[1]

That sense of entitlement, exuded by some of the men, was another difference between the men and the women. Their fathers had been there. Or their schools had a long-standing relationship with their colleges. They thought it was their right to be there. They expected to walk into a good job in the City or the professions when they left. This was extremely irritating. But once I realised that I was at least as good at law as they were, it raised my sights: I too might aspire to being something other than a country solicitor. I do not recall a similar sense of entitlement amongst the women. Most of us were just thrilled to be there and very conscious of how privileged we were to be having this excellent education in this wonderful place. An incomer and outsider I may often have felt, but I am also conscious of how very privileged I am, compared with so many.

Girton itself was not quite so wonderful. It too was very different then. It had a proud history, founded in 1869 by Emily Davies and Barbara Bodichon as the first residential educational establishment offering degree-level education for women. The college began life with five students in a house in Hitchin, twenty miles away, but 'a great campaign' raised the money to buy a large tract of land near Girton village, two miles from the centre of Cambridge. The first buildings, designed by Alfred Waterhouse, opened in 1873. These are in the Victorian red-brick Gothic style which was not as well thought of in the 1960s as it is now. Unlike the ancient men's colleges, the rooms are not arranged on staircases, but along corridors – unusually, there are rooms on only one side of the corridor, with windows on the other, so the corridors are light and bright. Even so, the architecture, perhaps especially in the dining hall, has a noticeably masculine 'feel'. Unlike its sister college, Newnham, it is not pretty.

This reflects the educational philosophy of its founder. Emily Davies firmly believed that her students should attend the same lectures and classes and take the same examinations as the men. By 1881, the university had formally agreed that the women students at Girton and Newnham could take the standard tripos examinations and have their results published separately but alongside those of the men. Thus it was that, in 1890, Philippa Fawcett was known to have been placed above the 'senior wrangler' (that is, gained the top marks) in the mathematical tripos: Philippa was the daughter of Millicent Fawcett, leader of the suffragist movement which campaigned by lawful means for women's right to vote. The women's colleges played an enthusiastic part in that campaign.

But even Philippa could not get a degree. The campaign for women's degrees was resoundingly defeated in May 1897, amid scenes of astonishing violence and abuse, most of it from the male undergraduates. This is what one of the students at Newnham wrote to her mother:

> Friday was such an intense exciting day here. On Thursday night Miss Clough [principal of Newnham] and Miss Jex-Blake [Girtonian secretary of the Committee for Women's Degrees] were burnt in effigy by the undergraduates in the marketplace ... All the MAs had to go into the court in front of the university library and there they got cards either with '*placet*' or '*non placet*' on them and then they went into the Senate House to vote – the street in front of this court was packed with undergrads and so were the windows of the houses opposite; presently the men began pelting the MAs with oranges, bags of flour, eggs and especially squibs and crackers, each of which went off with a huge report so that it sounded like heavy firing.[2]

After the vote was lost, they had an 'excitement' at Newnham College:

> Between two and three hundred undergraduates rushed up to Newnham dragging an effigy of a woman on a bicycle ... They began to hurl themselves against our precious gates ... some of the men

began to climb in at the windows but the gardeners threw them out
... then they tore the effigy to pieces in front of the gates and threw
the pieces through ... The gardeners were so indignant about it – they
said that they had never seen men mob women before, and a craftsman
was heard to say 'Well, I thought the toffs was fonder of the females
than that.'

The Newnham Student found it all awfully funny – one of the men
had gone up a ladder which was placed against a tree and pasted a
'No Women' placard up there – but a garden boy took the ladder
away while he was up the tree, so he had to scramble down and then
the boy went up the ladder and tore the placard down. But the
excitement was not over: 'At 10 o'clock they came and fired on us
with squibs and broke three windows – what they would have done
if we had won I cannot think!' After that, there was a bonfire and
fireworks in Selwyn College across the road, where every now and
then they shrieked out 'down with women'. She thought it most kind
of them to provide them with so much amusement – and she was
sorry for Girton – two miles down the road – having all the disappointment and none of the fun and excitement. But she also felt 'sad
that they hate us so'.

Sad indeed: the men saw the women's quite reasonable requests
for equal treatment as an insult to them. Even after the Sex
Disqualification (Removal) Act 1919 had opened up the professions,
the universities and public life to women, Cambridge refused to give
them degrees, or to recognise Girton and Newnham as regular university colleges. This had to wait until 1948, when the first women
were able to call themselves BA (Cantab) rather than the humiliating
BA (tit) (for 'titular'). Fifty years later, the university made amends by
awarding degrees to the surviving women who had been so shabbily
treated. But it seems that most of these women had not been much
troubled by their exclusion from full membership of the university:
they took pride in being there at all. That Girton was not accepted
as a full college was felt more keenly by the fellows, who were excluded
from university administration and ceremonies.

I am not sure how much of this we all knew when we arrived in
1963. Did we know that it was only fifteen years ago that Girton had

become a full college and women were allowed to take degrees? Or, like those older Girtonians, did we just get on with enjoying it? We certainly knew that women could not become members of the Cambridge Union Society, the prestigious debating club where budding politicians such as Kenneth Clarke, Norman Fowler, Michael Howard, Leon Brittan and Norman Lamont had recently been honing their political skills. The only time that I ever remember the mistress, Dame Lucy Cartwright, addressing us in hall was on the day in 1965 when the union voted (by the necessary two-thirds majority) to admit women. I didn't join. I had no political ambitions and no experience of debating. But it was not long before Ann Mallalieu, now a Labour peer, became its first woman president.

Girton in those days was out on a limb in more ways than one. As women students, not only were we in a small minority, we also had very few senior women role models. Even the brilliant Cherry Hopkins, who had come top in the law tripos, in the postgraduate LLB and in the Bar Final examination, did not have a university teaching post. It was not until 1985 that the Law Faculty had a woman university teaching officer. As Girtonians, we had to cycle the two miles home up the only hill in Cambridge. Not surprisingly, many of us spent most of our time in town, attending lectures and supervisions, having picnic lunches or afternoon tea (a Cambridge habit) in other students' rooms, lounging around on the 'backs' (the lawns behind the college buildings) beside the river Cam, taking part in the many and various student societies, and going to a lot of parties. There was not much of a 'life' in college, the Junior Common Room was scarcely used, and there was no bar! On the whole, Girtonians went to visit their boyfriends in town rather than the other way about.

The age of majority was still twenty-one, so we were not seen as grown-ups. Everyone '*in statu pupillari*' had to spend almost the whole term within three miles of Great St Mary's Church; we were not allowed to have cars; we had to be back in college by midnight (in Girton we had to sign out if we wanted to come in between 10.30 p.m. and 12); we had to wear gowns for lectures, supervisions and examinations, and also when out on the streets of Cambridge after dinner. The university proctor and his two 'bulldogs' used to prowl the streets of central Cambridge policing this. It was a badge of honour to get 'progged' at least once and fined the traditional six shillings and eightpence. I still have the receipt. But it was better not to make a habit of it.

We had two lectures a week in each subject and a supervision once a fortnight. Supervisions were in small groups of between three and six students, for which essays were set and marked in advance. They were compulsory. Lectures were not. But generally I went to them, because I was still a speccy swot. Partly this was the ingrained habit of my school days. But partly it was because I found it all so fascinating. I enjoyed most of the lectures, even though our lecturer in criminal law refused to talk about sexual offences because there were women in the room. But I did skip land law: 9 a.m. is not a convenient time for a Girtonian. I loved going to the Squire Law Library, reading the cases in the law reports, and making a precis of each on an index card: no photocopying or downloading from the internet then. But there was no need to go into the main university library, a Stalinist 1930s building in stark contrast to the beauties of the ancient colleges, and (to my shame) I never did. I loved writing essays, especially when they were working out the solution to a legal problem. And I mostly enjoyed the supervisions. We had some of the best supervisors. Most inspirational of all was a brilliant young Scotsman called Tony Weir. He had only just joined the faculty then but went on to become a reader and an influential author, especially on the law of tort (civil wrongs for which the wrongdoer pays compensation to the person harmed). He was brimming with enthusiasm and ideas, a stickler for intellectual rigour, conservative in many ways, but a kind, conscientious and encouraging teacher. As Lord Hoffmann once remarked, 'If you want to know how a particular judge thinks about the law, find out how their university teachers thought.' If you want to know how I think about the law, read Tony Weir. I even enjoyed our family-law supervisions with John Hall, another kind and conscientious supervisor, but with some rather old-fashioned ideas about women: he advised his all-female group to forget what they had learned after the exams, as it was not good for wives and mothers to know their rights (such as they were in those days).

Our supervisor in constitutional law, Geoffrey Wilson, an inspirational lecturer who went on to found the law school at Warwick

University, gave us more sensible advice: decide how much time you want to spend working each day, including lectures and supervisions, and make sure you do it – whether it's two hours or eight hours. I decided that five hours a day during full term struck the right balance between work and play, so that's what I did. I also developed the habit of coming up to Cambridge a week before the start of full term and staying up a week after the end. This gave me plenty of quiet time to study. I tried to use my time efficiently – not just sitting in the library twiddling my thumbs. I made up my own set of notes in each subject, a distillation of what I had learned from lectures, textbooks and supervisions, together with the index cards of the decided cases. In the days running up to the examinations I would learn all these by heart, in my final year marching round my college room to the strains of either *Ein Heldenleben* by Richard Strauss or the *Grosse Fuge* by Ludwig van Beethoven. Try it: it works.

In those days there was a great deal of memory work needed for law exams – we were not allowed to take any materials into the room with us and the idea of an 'open book' exam or a dissertation instead of an exam had not yet been dreamt of. This suited me down to the ground. I had a very good memory. The exams were crammed into a stressful three or four days, but my observation of continuous assessment by essay while I was teaching at Manchester University was that it could be even more stressful. Each essay had to be as good as it could be. There was no time to learn from one's mistakes: it was very good for me, as well as hurtful, to be told by a contemptuous land-law supervisor (who shall remain nameless) that I obviously didn't understand the subject. He may have been right. But I made sure that I did the next time.

Most law exams contain a mixture of essay questions ('write all you know about … ') and problem questions, which are much more fun to do and a much better test of who is, and is not, good at legal reasoning. Whether from vanity or nostalgia, I have kept all my university and Bar Final exam papers (apart from the three I took in Roman law, for which I got the prestigious George Long Prize in my second year). It is striking how many of the questions in them are coming before the courts to this day. I hope that I can communicate something of the excitement I felt then and still feel by picking an example from our 1966 Family Law exam. Family law has changed out of almost all recognition since then, but the human dilemmas are still the same:

> (a) Eighteen months ago Edwina asked Mr and Mrs Smith to look after her illegitimate daughter, Frances, then aged two months, as she was unable to take care of her herself. The Smiths have looked after Frances ever since. Edwina is now demanding her return. The Smiths say that Frances regards them as her parents and insist that she should remain with them. Advise Edwina.
>
> (b) Dr Finlay calls in a consultant to his patient, Roger, aged eight. The consultant's view is that probably the only way of saving Roger's life is for him to go into hospital immediately for a blood transfusion. Roger's parents object to blood transfusion on religious grounds and refuse to let Roger go. Dr Finlay is anxious to do all he can to save Roger's life. What steps can be taken?

We abolished the label 'illegitimate' in 1987: there are no illegitimate children, only unmarried parents. But question (a) raises a fundamental issue for family law the world over: should the future of a child be governed solely by what is in that child's best interests, or do the parents who created the child have their own independent right to bring him or her up unless this would be actively harmful to the child? An early case[3] in the newly created Supreme Court of the United Kingdom was about a little boy, born in December 2005, who had lived all his life with his maternal grandmother because neither of his parents could look after him. In 2009, his father was out of prison, married and with another child. He wanted the little boy to live with him. The magistrates' court, having heard all the evidence, found that it was in the child's best interests to continue living with his grandmother where he was settled and doing well. But a judge allowed the father's appeal. The Supreme Court restored the magistrates' order. The child's best interests were the paramount consideration. Parenthood was only significant because it could play a part in the child's welfare. I had said the same in an earlier case about lesbian parents,[4] but perhaps it needed a male judge to say it for the message to get home?

A variant of question (b) will be familiar to anyone who has read Ian McEwan's book, *The Children Act*, or seen the film starring Emma Thompson as a very convincing High Court judge. In the book, the child is aged seventeen and firmly opposed on religious grounds to having a life-saving blood transfusion. It is one thing to override the wishes of the parents in the best interests of the child. It is another thing to override the wishes of a child who is old enough to make up his own mind. But the courts almost always decide in favour of preserving life if they can and that is what happened in the book and in the real case upon which it is based. Yet in the cases of Charlie Gard and Alfie Evans, the Supreme Court upheld the conclusion of the trial judges that it was not in the best interests of these terminally ill babies artificially to be kept alive, desperately though their parents longed for this.[5]

In those days, there were no internet, no email or social media, and no mobile phones. Communication with staff and students was face to face or by telephone or the occasional note. There was only one telephone for students to use in Girton. I wrote a letter home to my mother every week. She kept them all and labelled them meticulously with their dates. They tell the story of a busy student life but I don't suppose that they told her everything.

Five hours' work a day left plenty of time for fun. I joined the Gilbert and Sullivan Society, which put on an opera each year. I was only ever in the chorus, except in *Yeomen of the Guard*, where I also sang the small part of Kate (rather sharp, which I expect I still am). At the end of my first year, the society also supplied the chorus for three concert performances, in Cambridge, Oxford and London, of *Perelandra*, an opera by Donald Swann (more famous for his 'Drop of a Hat' comedy shows with Michael Flanders). In London, one of the chorus members who was also reading law said 'Oh, by the way, Brenda, did you know that you got a first?' I hadn't until then – our results were communicated by putting up a notice outside the Senate House in Cambridge. It was a big surprise and not at all what I had been expecting when I went up – having been a big fish in a very small pond I expected to be a very small fish in the much larger pond.

Some of the men's college choirs also wanted women singers for their concerts, so I did that. I joined the Mummers, an acting society which was not quite as grand as the Amateur Dramatic Society, but still far too precious to be much fun. The college drama societies were much more welcoming. I particularly enjoyed playing the wicked governor's wife in *The Caucasian Chalk Circle* by Bertolt Brecht with the Fitzwilliam College Society. I joined the Yorkshire Society, a very jolly social club, though the women were not allowed to be there when the society entertained the Yorkshire cricket team. I was at a Yorkshire Society dinner on 22 November 1963 when we all learned of the assassination of President Kennedy. I learned something else that evening. A senior member asked me how I pronounced 'one': was it 'wonne' or 'wun'? If the former, it was a dead giveaway that we came from the north.

And I joined the Liberal Club. This was the only time that I have ever engaged in anything approaching party political activity (although I don't think that I actually joined the party). Being a Liberal in those days meant that one had little or no interest in a political career. There were only six Liberal MPs in 1963, nine after the general election in October 1964, and twelve after the election in March 1966. Girtonians did not seem very interested in politics. Only a few of us gathered in the Junior Common Room to watch the exciting election in 1964, when the Labour Party squeezed into power with a majority of only four seats, and still fewer stayed up as long as I did.

There were plenty of parties of the other kind – some of them formal black-tie affairs but most of them not. One Lent term I made it my business to sign out – i.e. return to college between 10.30 p.m. and midnight – every night. There was also the gaiety of 'May Week' – in fact a fortnight in June after the exams had finished but before the term ended. All sorts of impromptu plays and performances were put on. There were the May bumping races on the Cam – the river is so narrow that boats cannot race side by side, so they set off in single file and the boat behind tries to catch and 'bump' the one in front. They swap places for the next round. I did a lot of cheering from the towpath. And there were the May Balls – extravagant affairs with several bands, cabaret acts, and lots to eat and drink, though not, as I recall, any fairground rides.

This was the swinging sixties. Labour had come to power in 1964, after 'thirteen years of Tory misrule'. The Beatles and the Rolling

Stones were playing everywhere. Our skirts were getting shorter and shorter. But we (or at least my friends and I) were still curiously innocent. We mainly stuck to the rules. We did not, as far as I know, do drugs. 'If you can remember the sixties, you weren't there' did not apply to us. The student rebellions of 1968 were yet to come and came late to Cambridge anyway. But there was a definite feeling that things were on the move, that change was in the air, that the old social order was breaking down and a more equal society was on the way. Life in the village felt twenty years behind the times but I knew little of life outside the charmed world of Cambridge.

The most momentous change in Girton since the Cambridge of my student days has been the arrival of men. In 1968, Churchill, one of the newer colleges for men, announced that it would admit women students in 1972. The ancient King's and Clare colleges soon followed suit. It was clear that the others would eventually do so too. This was not, says Professor Malveena McKendrick, 'because they believe in equal opportunities, not because they want a healthy, normal collegiate society, not even because they want their share of the good women around, but in order to continue to attract good men'.[6] Senior Cambridge might still not be taking women seriously, but the young men increasingly were. But what was Girton to do? It was caught between pride in its pioneering role in women's higher education and the fear that many of its best women candidates would be lured away by the ancient charms and central location of the men's colleges. It was conscious, too, that the students, rather than the academics, would benefit from the men's colleges going mixed: it would take those deeply sexist, even misogynistic institutions much longer to admit women as fellows. Should the college stay single-sex so that there would still be a place for the women academics? In the end, the momentous decision to go mixed was taken in 1976 and the first male undergraduates arrived in 1979.

This was undoubtedly the right thing to do. It transformed the place. There was now a bar! The facilities for students were greatly improved. There was a life in college which had not been there before. Music, sports and other college activities thrived. Why make the trek into town when you have everything you need on the spot? It may not have been the first choice for many male Girtonians, but they are proud to belong to a place with such a truly egalitarian spirit and pioneering history. It did not take long for undergraduate numbers to reach the rough parity which they still enjoy. The fellowship is also mixed. There has been a male vice mistress but so far not a male mistress. I used to think that those colleges which were led by a master should either adopt a neutral title, such as principal or warden, or allow women leaders to call themselves mistress. But I am quite looking forward to the first male leader of Girton being proud to call himself mistress.

All the men's colleges have now gone mixed. Magdalene was the last, in 1988. There are still three all-women colleges. But while the men's colleges were happy to attract some of the brightest and best of the women undergraduates, the Girton fellows were right to fear that it would take them longer to appoint women as college fellows or to give them university teaching posts. That too is one of the most striking changes. There were no women university teaching officers in law when I was there but by the summer of 2019, nearly half in the Law Faculty were women and women held two of the four long-established professorships. The staff are much more ethnically diverse as well, although the university still has some way to go before it is a truly inclusive institution.

Admitting men is not the only way in which the Girton student body has changed. The number of students admitted each year has gone up, but a much greater proportion are postgraduate or research students. Research has become a more and more important feature of university life in all disciplines, not just the sciences. But Cambridge is still admitting undergraduates and long may that continue: the whole idea is that students learn most from being taught by the people who are the leaders in their field, as I did, and perhaps those leaders can learn something from their students in return. The number of students from abroad has also increased. There are many advantages to having students – and fellows – from all over the world. We all have to learn to live and work with people from other countries, cultures and backgrounds, but this is especially so in universities, where so much research is the product of international collaboration.

Like many others, I had very little to do with Girton after I graduated in 1966. But I made some lifelong friends there and it had certainly changed my life. When I became a High Court judge, the college was kind enough to make me an honorary fellow. It cannot be a coincidence that so many of the 'first' women lawyers are Girtonians. Carrie Morrison was the first woman to qualify as a solicitor; Maud Crofts was the first to set up in practice as a solicitor; Sybil Campbell was the first professional woman judge, appointed a Metropolitan Stipendiary Magistrate in 1945; Mary Arden was the first to be appointed a High Court judge in the Chancery Division, which specialises in property, tax, company and other commercial business; she was also the first woman chair of the Law Commission; Rosalyn Higgins was the first to be appointed to the International Court of Justice in The Hague and its first woman president. I was the first woman Law Commissioner and the first woman Lord of Appeal in Ordinary. So Girton has been good for its lawyers.

After leaving Cambridge, I spent eighteen years teaching in the University of Manchester. But I left Manchester in 1984 for the Law Commission and then for the bench, so I had little contact with university life until 2004, when I became chancellor of the University of Bristol. Being chancellor is very like being queen. You are the titular head of the institution but you have no power: that is held by the vice chancellor in academic matters and the chair of the council or board of trustees in business matters. As chancellor I got to wear a magnificent and capacious robe (I believe that the Bristol robe was made for the first chancellor, W. O. Wills of the famous tobacco family, who was enormous). I presided over degree ceremonies, handed out prizes and medals, thanked the benefactors, and generally did all the jolly things. I also presided over the University Court and the Convocation, which is now the Alumni Association. I met many students and visited many departments. I could be a sounding board for the vice chancellor and chair of council – a concerned and hopefully knowledgeable person with whom they could share their concerns and generally let their hair down: very like the monarch's constitutional role to 'advise, encourage, warn'.

Also in 2004, Girton's 'Visitor', Queen Elizabeth the Queen Mother, died and the college appointed me to take her place. Historically, the role of the Visitor was to determine disputes between the college and its members. But this has now gone and a new role, not unlike that of chancellor of a university, has evolved. It gives me such a thrill to be back in the college hall, but sitting at high table next to the mistress, for formal dinners, listening to the college choir sing grace, cutting the odd commemorative cake and making the odd inspirational speech. It is still the same, rather masculine, red-brick Gothic room, with portraits of mistresses past and present on the walls, some of them rather good. But the chairs are much more comfortable and the food and drink are a great deal better.

The greatest proof of how Girton has changed was the weekend in June 2019 in which we celebrated our 150th anniversary. This was a joyous festival: a combination of serious lectures from the likes of the Astronomer Royal and our ambassador to the United Nations; panel discussions, including one on women in the law and another on men in the college; light-hearted events such as the Girton version of *University Challenge*; comedy acts; a brass band concert, with the mistress, Professor Susan Smith, playing the euphonium; a pop festival, at which the chaplain played a blinder, as did several old Girtonians; and theatrical performances, including *Bluestockings*, the play based on Jane Harrison's book about the shocking events of 1897. And almost all of this was done by Girtonians – truly a very different place from the one I left in 1966.

It has been a great privilege to have had so much contact with students over the years. Today's students have a much harder life than we did. The university sector has grown dramatically. At one point in the twenty-first century, the aim was that 50% of young people would go to university. Obviously this could not be funded in the way that our studies had been funded (and recouped from very high taxes when we joined the labour market). Most students now have to take out loans and many of them also have to take on part-time jobs to make ends meet. Strangely, this does not seem to put many of them off. I admire their courage and their optimism hugely.

5 Manchester – A Double Life

There I was at the beginning of 1966: what was I going to do when my degree course came to an end? I could have stayed on in Cambridge for a year as a postgraduate. But could that possibly be as much fun as my undergraduate days had been, with so many friends going out into the big wide world? And (perhaps contradictorily) I was worried that, if I stayed another year in Cambridge, I would be sucked in and never leave. That was not an attractive prospect when I could see the way that brilliant women academics struggled for recognition: Gillian White, for example, was only a college fellow, yet so distinguished in her field that she was appointed a professor at Manchester University in 1968.

So should I aspire to become a barrister, as many of the most able, but also not so able, young men planned to do? In those days, intending barristers usually joined an Inn of Court in their first year at university. This was because they had to 'keep term' for three years before being called to the Bar, a relic of the days when aspiring barristers learned their trade from keeping company with the practising members of their Inn of Court. It continued after the four Inns of Court set up their own School of Law to prepare students for the Bar Final examination. But most people just did the minimum: eating at least three dinners in each of four terms a year for the three years: a total of at least thirty-six dinners. The Bar Final exams were held in September and so students who started eating dinners in their first year could be called to the Bar within months of their graduation. Knowing this, and with friends who were set on going to the Bar, I applied to one of the Inns of Court for a scholarship in my first year. It was not a happy experience. The large interviewing panel seemed to be composed solely of ancient men who were clearly perplexed that someone like me might want to go to the Bar. I don't blame them. I had not yet begun to get first-class marks, I had absolutely no connections with the Bar, and I probably made a poor showing in the interview. But I lost heart when a scholarship was awarded to one of the young men, whose father was a High Court judge and who did not distinguish himself academically. It appeared that the criteria were neither merit nor need but something else, which I didn't have. Also, in the early 1960s, we were still being told how hard it was to make a living at the Bar, especially for women.

So what about becoming a solicitor? I knew a little bit more about that. I spent my first long vacation working – as what would now be called an 'intern' – in the small firm of solicitors which acted for my mother in Richmond. There were two partners, an assistant solicitor and an articled clerk. They were all very kind to me. I sat with the senior partner, Jack Garget, in his beautiful Georgian room with a fine view of the river Swale. He was also the part-time clerk to the local magistrates, so we spent one or two days a week sitting in court, watching the magistrates deal with petty crime and matrimonial disputes, and the occasional committal for trial by jury on some more serious charge. Apart from that, his practice consisted mainly of routine conveyancing and probate work. There was plenty of conveyancing to do. I became very familiar with the root of title to the marquess of Zetland's estate. Anything more difficult tended to be parked on the floor of his office until he could work out what to do about it. The junior partner, Ralph Waggett, was a totally delightful man who took a great deal of trouble to teach me how to do things, trouble which paid off when I chose to take the conveyancing option in the Bar Final examination. Many years later, he also played an important part in my reintroduction to Richmond life: he re-established the ancient Company of Fellmongers (dealers in skins) of Richmond, one of the thirteen craft guilds which had flourished in the town in the Middle Ages, and now devoted to fellowship and good works. I was proud to serve as its master in 2017–18. It was easy to see what a lovely life these solicitors had: a secure income doing not very taxing work in a beautiful setting. But all those irritatingly entitled young men in Cambridge had taught me to aim a little higher than that.

The next long vacation I spent time as an intern with one of the 'magic circle' London firms. It could not have been more different. The vast majority of their work came from corporate clients. There was still the odd wealthy private client: I remember being very shocked by a man whose wife was on the brink of death: he seemed more worried about reducing her wealth in order to avoid death duties than about losing her. There were also some entertaining clients, such as the Clay Pigeon Shooting Association who were anxious to suppress a rebellion in their ranks. But by and large it was corporate business which, though lucrative for the firm, lacked human interest. Nevertheless, they were kind enough to take the risk of offering me articles, although I do not think that they had had a woman articled clerk before.

But with my final examinations looming I was less and less attracted, both by the prospect of articles in the City of London and by the thought of immediately having to cram for yet another set of exams. Mrs Jolowicz, my director of studies, suggested that I might get an academic post in another university: those were the days when the shortage of law lecturers was such that it was possible to get a post immediately on graduating with a good enough degree. So I applied for assistant lectureships and both Bristol and Manchester offered me a post. Which to choose?

Fortunately, despite the pouring rain on the day of the interview (and I was laughingly told that this was a good day for Manchester), I chose Manchester. I now know only too well what an agreeable place the University of Bristol is: one of my tasks as its chancellor, between 2004 and 2016, was to award medals to people who had served the university for forty years – ranging from gardeners to Nobel Prizewinners. Had I gone there, someone else would probably have handed me a long-service medal and I would not have had the life that I have had. There were two main reasons for preferring Manchester. First, it had famous professors: we had studied family law from Peter Bromley's textbook and civil liberties from Harry Street's *Freedom, the Individual and the Law*. Second, they wanted me to qualify as a barrister and do some part-time practice as well as my university teaching. There was a large and thriving Bar in Manchester and also in Liverpool: the Bar on the Northern Circuit, which covers the north-west of

England, was then and still is larger than the whole of the Scottish Bar. So that is what I did.

I had first to join an Inn of Court. I chose Gray's Inn because I knew people who were members there. These included a fellow lecturer called John Hoggett, newly returned from researching for his PhD in the University of Michigan, and beginning to show an interest in me. The interest soon became mutual. Here at last was someone who was extremely clever himself and not put off by the thought that I might be almost as clever as he was. It cost the princely sum of £120 to join the Inn, which I borrowed from the bank. In those days, this was a scary thing for someone like me. We were not used to credit (credit cards had not yet been invented) nor were we obliged to borrow to fund our university studies.

Next, I had to pass the Bar Final exam. This was not very demanding. I could study for it by buying a self-tuition correspondence course from the College of Law. This consisted of 'nutshells' in each of the subjects, model exam papers and model answers. I swotted in my little attic flat over the summer of 1967 and took the exam in September. I didn't get a first, but I did get an upper second and came top of the list. Given that all the subjects were new to me, apart from the half-paper in divorce, I was not unhappy. It just shows how easy the Bar exams were in those days, compared with the solicitors' exams. I came away with a prize of books from the Council of Legal Education and a scholarship from Gray's Inn. But then I had to complete my thirty-six dinners. They had recently changed the rules, so that I could be called to the Bar after eating two years' worth of dinners and do the remainder the following year.

So it was not until July 1969 that I was called to the Bar, along with John Hoggett. We had married on 28 December 1968. We did not approve of the whole bizarre process, as I wrote to my mother:

> In the evening, John dressed himself up in white tie and tails, I put my new black dress on, and we paraded conspicuously through the streets to Gray's Inn. There we had a quick 'snifter' to keep our courage up, and then joined the queue in the Games Room. We all lined up in order of joining the Inn, so John, who joined ages ago, was quite near the head of the line, while I was seventh from the end. The line filed

into Hall, and then waited for the benchers – and the end of the queue was still in the Games Room, sitting down, so I didn't see John called. Being called consists of bowing to the treasurer, having a formula murmured over one, shaking hands and bowing again. We also all received a little book on the 'Duty and Art of Advocacy', which I imagine they can't get rid of any other way. After the ceremony, we had the usual dinner, slightly better, in the middle of which the benchers toasted us. Then after the meal, the benchers as usual retired to their vintage port and brandy, and the barristers in Hall toasted us again. We then <u>all</u> had to reply one by one. As there were eighty-three of us, this took ages, and most of the speeches were either boring or in extremely bad taste – and in any case, they couldn't be heard, either because of constant interruptions or because they weren't very well 'projected'. It was all most boring and embarrassing (some of them got pretty drunk and rowdy) and most of the people round about were pretty putrid, so that at the end of it all John and I were feeling quite depressed ...

I must admit to having as yet little respect for the early stages of becoming a barrister ... the activities leading up to [it] are expensive, irrelevant, and either boring or embarrassing! Seems a pity. Still, it's nice to have it all over, and if anyone else read that last paragraph, I would probably be disbarred!

Much had changed by 2017, the year when I was treasurer of the Inn (monarch for a year), some things for the better and some not so. For the better is what the Inn does. The thirty-six dinners were replaced by twelve 'qualifying sessions' taken in a single year, some involving dining or other social events, but all having an educational element. Students could choose from a menu of possible sessions, to meet their timetable and their budget. The Inn also provides advocacy training from experienced practitioners. Especially popular are the weekends at Cumberland Lodge in Windsor Great Park, which combine intensive advocacy training with group discussions of ethical problems and more light-hearted events such as an impromptu concert on Saturday nights (my party piece was getting everyone to join in the chorus of 'On Ilkley Moor Bar t'Hat', Yorkshire's national anthem). The Call ceremony is now a proper degree ceremony, which family and friends can attend, and in my year as treasurer we actually allowed them to clap!

For the worse is the cost of the training course. The course itself has become much more demanding, a combination of technical knowledge and practical advocacy skills, assessed by examination and observation. This is a good thing, but it costs a great deal of money to provide. And, for some reason, opening it to commercial as well as not-for-profit providers has gone hand in hand with a steep escalation in the price, up to as much as £18,000 for the nine-month course. The Inns of Court offer scholarships, and some barristers' chambers fund the students to whom they have offered pupillages, but this is a lot to ask of students, most of whom are already burdened with the debts taken on to fund their university courses (and, if they are non-law graduates, the graduate diploma in law). There is a real worry that the greater diversity of entrants to the Bar, achieved over the decades since I was called, will suffer as a result. Efforts are now being made to find a cheaper way of delivering the course, but we shall never get back to the days when I could qualify by studying alone in my attic flat.

After the exams, one had to do a twelve-month pupillage learning from an experienced barrister how things are done. Like everything else in those days, mine was arranged through personal contacts. Rhys Davies, a Manchester law graduate who was doing very well at the Manchester Bar, persuaded John da Cunha, a senior member of chambers at 43 King Street, to take me on. There were thirteen barristers crammed into five shabby rooms with another room for the clerks and a single (very fast) typist. They were used to having academics as part-time members. They charged members a percentage of turnover, which meant that the high earners subsidised the less high earners and made part-time practice affordable. They also had a woman tenant, Monica Stalker, to whom I am eternally grateful for not pulling up the drawbridge after her or frightening the horses.

I sat at a desk in my pupil master's room. His practice was mainly high-value personal injury claims but he also specialised in complex fraud crimes and had a sideline in divorce cases, usually involving Roman Catholics, as he was one. My job was to do a first draft of the 'pleadings' – a statement of claim or a defence, a reply to a request for further and better particulars, or a divorce petition; or to sift through a mass of papers in a complicated case and prepare a note summarising the story and the issues for him; and to take a note for him in court (he would not allow me to carry his robes bag, another job for pupils). Most memorable was a defended divorce where he acted for a husband who claimed that his wife had committed adultery in the local family planning clinic – 'one can scarcely conceive of a more suitable place', he declared. Obviously, he had never been there.

He was a delightful but very conservative man. Rumour had it that he did not approve of women at the Bar. Halfway through my pupillage, I plucked up courage to ask him whether this was true. He said that it was. I expressed surprise, because his wife practised as a doctor along with bringing up their five children. Ah, he replied, medicine is a caring profession and women both can and should do caring work; but the Bar is a fighting profession and women neither can nor should fight. In his view, they were either too obstinate or too yielding. He had never settled (compromised) a case against a woman. Despite this, he had taken me on, and I think he may have modified his view when I appeared in front of him after he had become a judge. He was wrong about women – we can and do fight just as well as men – but he was right about the Bar. He made me think about whether I really had what it takes to succeed. You do have to have the judgment to know which cases you should fight and which cases you should compromise if you can, together with the courage to fight those which you have to fight. The Bar is a scary profession and stage fright is – or should be – inevitable.

After six months' pupillage a fledgling barrister is allowed to appear in court. Our clerk, the redoubtable Vincent Hemingway, took pride in finding a brief for the very first day. Thus it was that, soon after being called, I found myself arrayed in wig, bands and gown, getting to my feet in the Manchester Crown Court, before the recorder (the top criminal judge in the city), to ask for bail pending trial. The result was a foregone conclusion – bail would be granted – but that did not make it any less terrifying, waiting my turn, going over and over what I had to say, worrying whether the judge would have difficult questions for me, how stern or how merciful he would be. From there I moved on to the standard diet of people starting out at the provincial common-law Bar in those days – criminal and matrimonial cases in the magistrates' courts, civil claims and undefended divorces in the county courts, and an occasional appearance in the Crown Court or even the High Court. In one memorable case, I secured the acquittal of a fireman accused of indecent exposure by persuading the justices' clerk that it was not indecent unless the penis was erect. I was not so lucky defending the same fireman against the same charge when he did the same again.

Matrimonial cases in magistrates' courts were not so amusing. The usual ground for complaint was persistent cruelty – wives had to prove, not only that they had been badly treated, but also that it was persistent. Often there was a long itemised list of assaults and excessive sexual demands. Yet the magistrates still had to begin the proceedings by asking whether there was any chance of a reconciliation. It was bad enough that the court was obliged to send out the terrible message that wives were expected to put up with this sort of behaviour; it was worse still when the couple did sometimes reconcile. I began to realise, contrary to what we had been led to believe in Cambridge, that family law was not always good to women.

Undefended divorces in the county courts were not supposed to be difficult. There were senior barristers who made a good living out of conducting large numbers of them. They had recently been transferred from the High Court to the county courts, where the fees were lower, causing some resentment from the Bar and even from the bench. Early on, I was instructed in two undefended divorces where the petitions had been drafted by a solicitor. The judge made my life as difficult as he possibly could, finding all sorts of technical faults in the petitions, before doing the inevitable and granting the divorces. I dread to think what my clients must have thought, having such a solemn moment in their lives treated like a game. Afterwards he called me into his room and complained about the quality of the solicitor's work. He was, of course, apologising for giving me such a hard time, but without actually saying so. I hope that, when I became a judge, the memory of the badly behaved judges I had encountered long ago made me do better.

Another dreadful divorce experience was very soon after the Divorce Reform Act 1969 came into force. People against whom no matrimonial fault could be shown could now be divorced against their will after the couple had lived apart for five years. I was instructed to resist a claim for costs against such a blameless spouse – it was monstrous that the claim should ever have been made, so I was all fired up to oppose it. But the senior barrister who had included the claim announced at the beginning of the hearing that my presence was unnecessary because he was not going to pursue it. I have never forgiven myself for not leaping to my feet and applying for his side to pay my client's costs. That is another thing about the Bar – there is a moment to ask a question or make a submission which has to be seized. If you miss it, it is gone forever.

Meanwhile, of course, the main reason for my coming to Manchester was to teach in the Law Faculty there. It was quite a change from Cambridge. Most of the staff lived in the suburbs or outside Manchester altogether, so there were very few around in the evenings or at weekends. Not realising this, I managed to get locked into the Law Faculty building on my first Saturday in town. The students were more diverse than in Cambridge, with a higher proportion of women, and a lower proportion of public schoolboys. More of them were local and living at home. The great majority planned to become solicitors. Very few planned to become barristers.

Teaching law in Manchester was hard work. The teaching methods were much the same as in Cambridge but the students were expected to learn the law in much more detail than we had done in Cambridge and junior lecturers were required to teach several subjects. We were also put to teaching 'law for … ' courses in other departments. This could be a terrible chore, but I was lucky enough to be asked to do the law for students training to be child care officers. They were mainly experienced and mature people who were already working in local authority children's departments or for voluntary organisations. They were in many ways more challenging than the bright young things in the Law Faculty. I learned a lot from them – not only about their own lives and work but also about their clients' lives. The course expanded in 1970, when social work went 'generic' and the students had to know about mental health law as well as child care law. In those days, no one knew much about mental health law: the whole idea of the Mental Health Act 1959 had been to take the law out of the compulsory treatment of mental patients. Of course, this cannot be done when mental health professionals are given the power to lock people up in hospital and treat them against their will: there have to be legal standards and legal safeguards. When one of the leading law publishers decided to commission a series of books on social work and the law, *Mental Health* was an obvious subject to tackle, because there wasn't a textbook designed for mental health professionals. This was my first book, published in 1975.[1] A second in the same series, *Parents and Children*, followed in 1976.[2]

In my second year as an assistant lecturer, I was given the lecture course in constitutional and administrative law. At least this was something I knew a little about, having been fascinated by constitutional history from an early age and very well taught the modern law by Geoffrey Wilson in Cambridge. He had concentrated on how the constitutional principles did or did not work in practice, with concrete examples: one of them was the story of the Crichel Down affair mentioned in the first chapter. It was an enjoyable course to teach, but it is not really a suitable subject for a young lecturer. It needs years of experience and exposure to the ins and outs of how our unwritten constitution actually works. It did, however, lead to my first publication: two well-received chapters on 'The Impact of Community Law on the Law of the United Kingdom', in *The Law of the Common Market*, edited by our senior professor, Ben Wortley. Much later, of course, I was called upon to adjudicate upon many important constitutional issues and my earlier efforts may not have been wasted.

I did not set out to specialise in family law, nor was I forced into it. But it did seem to me that the subject should not be dominated by men. In the 1960s, the approach of the law to the traditional gender roles of homemaking wife and bread-winning husband was very favourable to the husband. Professor Bromley might declare, in his leading textbook, that they were now 'joint, co-equal heads of the household'. Yet a homemaking wife had no claims over the family's assets and few opportunities for acquiring any assets of her own; had only limited financial claims if they separated; and had no rights and authority over her children unless and until her husband died or there was a court order giving her 'custody' or 'care and control'. I was, therefore, delighted when Professor Julian Farrand, then dean of the faculty, persuaded Professor Bromley that it was not good for the students if the author of the leading textbook not only gave the lectures but also set the examinations. They would not be tempted to think and write critically about the subject, which all good students should do. And so I took over the lecture course in 1972. This was an exciting time in family law, because the balance between the gender roles had been radically altered by recent legislation.

The time had also come to choose between practice and academia. It was not possible to develop my practice and take on longer cases while I had to be there for my students on fixed days and times. It was not possible to devote much time to research and writing outside the demands of my teaching when I was spending so much time in court. The chambers at 43 King Street were splitting up – some of the most successful barristers were joining with barristers from other chambers to form a brand-new set. Donald Hart, the leader of the breakaway group, told me that they would be glad to have me with them, but only if I was prepared to come full-time. Professor Farrand told me that I would have to give up practice if I wanted to make progress in the university.

It was a tough choice. I loved doing both. There is a wonderful camaraderie about the Bar – fighting hard in court one minute and going off for a drink together the next. The Law Faculty in Manchester was also a very friendly place. But they were right. After much debate, I chose to leave the Bar and concentrate on the university. There were three good reasons for this. First, and least important, my husband John had started at the Bar at roughly the same time as I did and we had narrowly avoided being on opposite sides of the same case a little too often for comfort. As junior members of chambers, there was often nothing in the diary for the next day, but if you were there around 6 p.m., briefs would come in, either because there was a genuine emergency, or because the solicitor who had planned to do the case himself found that he had better things to do, or more often, because the barrister who was due to do the case was double-booked and had to 'return' the brief. Several times, we got home in the evening to find that the other had almost been given the brief on the opposing side.

Second, and more important, university teachers may not be very well paid compared with successful barristers – even quite junior ones – but at least they are paid. A salary comes in regularly each month. There are other benefits, like sick leave, paid holidays and pensions. Barristers have to provide all those for themselves and it can take a very long time for them to be paid for the work they have done. This was especially true in those days, when barristers' fees were not legally enforceable and the universal 'fear of the empty diary' made many of them reluctant to alienate their instructing solicitors by pressing too hard for payment. It seemed prudent, therefore, for one of us to have the regular salary of a university lecturer while the other forged his career at the Bar. We need not have worried, because John quickly became very successful in the comparatively lucrative field of town and country planning, but we weren't to know that then.

Third, and most important, we wanted to have a family. There were women at the Manchester Bar, notably Joyanne Bracewell and Helen Grindrod, who managed to combine a successful practice with having a family, but it was obviously a great deal easier to combine academic and family life. The dates, times and places of teaching, meetings and other commitments were fixed long in advance: no more getting a brief in the evening to go to Carlisle the following morning. It would be possible to arrange the teaching into two or three days a week and to work from home on the other days.

But if I'm honest, there was probably more to it than that. I hope that it wasn't stage fright. John fell in love with the Bar the moment he started his pupillage. Once he was on his feet, he could not imagine doing anything else. I cannot claim to have fallen in love with the Bar in quite that way. I enjoyed it most of the time and people told me that I was good at it, but I also enjoyed the students, the teaching and the legal research needed to do it. Doing both had suited me fine but it was time to move on. And in moving on it never occurred to me that I might one day become any sort of judge. It would have been an odd ambition in any event. Elizabeth Lane was appointed the first woman county court judge in 1962. She was promoted to the High Court in 1965. But in 1972 she was still the only one (among seventy-two).

So in 1972 I gave up the Bar and concentrated on the university and in 1973 our daughter Julia was born. This was not straightforward. There was an early scare when it was feared that the pregnancy might be ectopic and I was sent off from Stepping Hill hospital in Stockport to St Mary's hospital in Manchester to have a scan. There was then only one machine in the area. The radiographer was straight-faced. I was handed a sealed envelope to take to my next appointment with the consultant at Stepping Hill, which was two weeks later. Obviously, there was no emergency. But I am so law-abiding that I did not open the envelope. The consultant assumed that I had. All was well. But at six and a half months I developed toxaemia of pregnancy – evidenced by raised blood pressure – and was admitted to Stepping Hill hospital for bedrest – then the only known way of treating the disease. After six weeks in hospital, my blood pressure went sky-high and they decided to induce the birth.

My daughter was born after a normal delivery. But she did not cry and the midwife whisked her away, so I did not know that she was alive until the midwife put her head round the door and asked 'What are you calling the baby, Mrs Hoggett?' John and I had not dared to discuss this since I went into hospital, so I came up with the first name that entered my head – Julia, after the leading lady in *Brideshead Revisited* – not yet a famous television series but a compelling novel, recently read. Julia was only four weeks premature but she was eight weeks immature, because of the oxygen starvation brought about by the toxaemia. She was seventeen inches long and weighed three pounds four ounces. An aubergine-coloured shrimp. Nowadays that would not be a problem. Even then, everyone was optimistic – premature girls did better than boys. In those days, parents did not stay in hospital with their babies. I went down to the Special Baby Care Unit every day to look after her for six weeks until she was discharged. One day, the nurses told me that 'your daughter, Mrs Hoggett, has a mind of her own'. How right they were!

But it was an anxious time when she came home. The hospital paediatrician told me to expect her to develop normally. But of course she was two months immature, so things took longer than the baby books said they would. Then the paediatric follow-up suggested that I might expect her to have learning difficulties. By then, I was doing multidisciplinary child care work with local practitioners, including Frank Bamford, consultant paediatrician at St Mary's hospital. We travelled together to a residential seminar on the adoption of 'hard to place' children and I told him of my worries about Julia, then aged two. He went out of his way to drive me home. Julia was waiting up, dressed in her cherry-red dressing gown, and promptly showed off to the company with a series of somersaults down the living-room floor. Frank phoned me up the next morning: 'Brenda, the only question is whether it's a first or a two-one.'

The Stepping Hill gynaecologist, when discharging me after the birth, had been blunt. My condition was not bad enough to suggest immediate sterilisation, but I should not consider having another child for at least two years. So I did not. But after two years, I sought advice. A kindly gynaecologist told me that it was not inevitable that toxaemia would recur. But I should ask myself whether having another child would be in Julia's best interests, or in John's best interests, or in mine. And then give double weight to mine. That made it even, so I felt that I had been given permission not to have another child, even though being one of three had meant so much to me.

Part of my thinking was that, by then, I was beginning to get my academic show on the road. After Julia was born, I had three months' sick leave and then three months working part-time before returning to full-time work. However precious my daughter, I could not imagine becoming a full-time mum. John did not expect me to. We were lucky enough to be able to employ a trained nanny for the first two years: she lived with us during the week but went home to her family at weekends. This meant that we had to be hands-on parents and could not leave it all to her. After she left, we employed young women who came in during the day, so one of us had to get home for bedtime, and it was almost always me: after all, the reason I had left the Bar was that it would be easier – though never easy – to combine my career and my family. Julia would get ready for bed and sit at her bedroom window in her cherry-red dressing gown to see me come over the hill from Glossop into Little Hayfield in the Peak District in Derbyshire, where we lived in an old stone house.

Nowadays, all academics are expected to research and publish regularly as well as to teach and examine students. In those days it was possible to get by without doing much beyond teaching (the picture of academic life in the arts department of a provincial university, as a relaxed occupation with little pressure to publish, painted by David Lodge in his novel *Changing Places*, has more than a grain of truth in it). But having left the Bar, I wanted to make a success of my academic career. I was still a speccy swot. Julia remembers going to sleep to the sound of my typewriter. And it so turned out that almost everything that I did as an academic led one way or another to a public appointment.

Norman Lees, a Manchester barrister, was chairman of the Mental Health Review Tribunal for the north-west of England. He read my book on *Mental Health* and in 1979 he proposed me as a part-time legal member of the tribunal. This was my very first judicial appointment. It was fascinating work. The tribunal for each case consisted of a lawyer, who presided, a psychiatrist, who examined the patient and reported his or her findings to the tribunal, and a layperson, often in those days a magistrate. We would go to the hospital where the patient was detained and hold a very informal hearing, interviewing the patient, the psychiatrist, the nearest relative and sometimes a social worker from the home local authority. Then we would have to decide whether the legal grounds for continuing to detain the patient were made out (technically in those days the patient had to prove that they were not, but we tended to look at it the other way about). As with judging in family cases, it was all about predicting the future, assessing the risks and deciding whether it was safe enough to take them. The patients whom I saw were not dangerous: they were sad, not bad. There was one middle-aged woman who made a great nuisance of herself to her neighbours. A layperson might well describe her as 'bonkers' or 'mad as a hatter' but the psychiatrists struggled to find a diagnosis: 'she must be some sort of schizophrenic', they said, but she didn't fit the textbook definitions. We decided to discharge her and agreed that the main problem had been putting her in a house next door to some house-proud neighbours.

I was sorry to have to give up the work after only a year because of my next public appointment, to the Council on Tribunals. This came out of my work in social welfare law, a new branch of law dealing with the relationship between the welfare state and the people it was there to serve. The legal publishers Sweet & Maxwell decided to produce a new learned periodical, the *Journal of Social Welfare Law*, to be jointly edited by a lawyer and a social worker. I was chosen as the first lawyer. Among the distinguished people we persuaded to join the editorial board was Professor Kathleen Bell, an expert on social policy who was a member of the Council on Tribunals. The council was set up in 1958 to oversee the myriad tribunals which had been established to resolve disputes, usually between the citizen and the state about such things as taxes and welfare benefits, but sometimes to police schemes to protect employees from their employers or residential tenants from their landlords. Its mission was to reinforce the tribunals' independence from their sponsoring government departments and ensure that their procedures were fair while remaining informal and user-friendly for people without legal representation. When Professor Bell retired from the council in 1980, she proposed me as her successor – not as a prominent lawyer but as someone who knew something about welfare law and mental health. After my interview with civil servants in the Lord Chancellor's offices in the House of Lords, there were 'some comings and goings' (as one of them put it – meaning that I wasn't their first choice). At thirty-five, I was very much the youngest of the people they were considering. But eventually I was offered the appointment and so had to give up sitting on mental health review tribunals.

Strangely, I did not feel an imposter when I started at the council. Part of our job involved sitting in on all sorts of tribunals and reporting back on how things went. This was great fun. I learned the acronyms taken for granted in tribunals dealing with war pensions. I saw how industrial tribunals (now employment tribunals) were becoming more and more like courts. I enjoyed travelling to Wales to sit in on a mental health review tribunal where everyone kept switching between Welsh and English during the hearing. It was difficult to believe that the mild-mannered middle-aged patient had done the terrible things that had landed him in a secure psychiatric hospital. But judging soon teaches you that things are not always as they seem.

The council brought me to the attention of the Lord Chancellor's officials. In those days almost all judicial appointments were done by a 'tap on the shoulder'. The officials took 'soundings' to discover possible candidates and then approached them with a proposal, presumably with the approval of the Lord Chancellor, who made or recommended all appointments to the court-based judiciary. Early in 1982 I got a mysterious invitation from Derek Oulton, who was then head of judicial appointments. I went down to London to meet him in the Lord Chancellor's offices. He explained that they wanted to diversify the bench by appointing a few academics with practical experience as assistant recorders and would I like to be one? Assistant recorders sat for a few weeks a year in the Crown Court trying criminal cases and in the county courts trying civil and family cases. We talked it over and at the end of our meeting he said, 'Well, Brenda, having now met you and had this conversation, is there anything you would *rather* do?' It felt as though I had failed the interview, but of course I said that I'd like to try. I had learned by then that, however daunting a new opportunity might be, the only thing to do was to go for it. Two of my professors were very negative – it would be a distraction from my academic work. The other two, Professor Harry Street and Professor Julian Farrand, were very positive – they both spent a lot of time sitting on a variety of tribunals, so they knew how interesting judging could be.

So off I went, later that year, for the baby judges' induction course run by the Judicial Studies Board (JSB). It was intentionally alarming. The centrepiece was a mock trial in which absolutely everything which could happen did happen – from applications to sever (split) or amend the indictment, questions of admissibility of evidence, to contempt in the face of the court. We all had to play a part. I was the main prosecution witness, a fourteen-year-old girl, the victim of an alleged assault by frightening. This raised the legal question of whether such an offence existed. But there was also the question of whether a fourteen-year-old girl could give evidence, and whether on oath or not. We were not as used to young children giving evidence then as we are now. Being a bit of an actress, I decided to put on a broad Yorkshire accent. Eventually, counsel for the prosecution, an old friend from the Manchester Bar, was so entertained that he gave up asking me questions. So I 'dried': a good lesson for advocates doing an examination in chief, where you have to get the story out of the witness in a coherent way without asking leading questions: make sure that you interject a question often enough to keep the witness going. As well as the mock trial, there were sentencing exercises and guidance on preparing a summing-up. The JSB had recently developed model versions of the standard directions which have to be given by a judge to a jury in any jury trial. This was to avoid appeals having to be allowed because of silly slip-ups. Invaluable for novices like me.

As well as the induction course, I spent time sitting in with the recorder of Manchester, Arthur Prestt QC, and the recorder of Liverpool, Sanderson Temple QC, and other local judges, more time than others because I had been away from the courts for ten years. There were also visits to a variety of prisons in the region. The one thing that visiting any prison tells you – especially closed 'local' prisons like Manchester's Strangeways, remand prisons as HMP Risley then was, and above all women's prisons like Styal – is that prisons are no place to be. They are not holiday camps. However well run, they are nasty, dangerous, smelly places. And there are many people in prison who should not be there, especially people with mental disorders or disabilities and women who are the victims of all kinds of abuse. But for a judge, there is often no alternative and you have to harden your heart.

The training took time, so I did not begin to sit as a judge until 1984: another imposter moment. After more than ten years away, I had returned to the courts. But by then my life had changed dramatically in other ways, because I had been appointed a Law Commissioner. This was in large part due to a pioneering academic publication, *The Family, Law and Society: Cases and Materials*, co-authored with David Pearl, in 1983.[3] But just after I went to the Law Commission, I co-authored with Susan Atkins a book entitled *Women and the Law*.[4] This is where feminism comes into the story.

6 A Feminist, Frank and Fearless

This is how Dinah Rose QC, undoubtedly a frank and fearless feminist herself, described me at the valedictory ceremony to mark my impending retirement from the Supreme Court on 18 December 2019. She meant it as a compliment but there are many others, both men and women, who would not regard it as such. I have lost count of the number of able professional women who have declared that 'I am no feminist ... ' Why are they so anxious to deny it, when they clearly believe that women are, or should be, equal to men in dignity and rights, and that the experience of leading women's lives is as valid and important as the experience of leading men's lives? That is what I mean by feminism. That is its primary meaning according to the *Oxford English Dictionary*: 'the advocacy of women's rights on the ground of the equality of the sexes'. There can be additional meanings. I have great sympathy for some, such as the belief that women should not feel obliged to conform to male expectations of their dress or appearance: why should professional women feel obliged to wear pencil skirts and very high heels when their male colleagues can wear comfortable suits and shoes? I have no sympathy for other meanings, such as antipathy to men. There are many men who are feminists in my sense and many women who are not. I have never been afraid to call myself a feminist – albeit a soft one – and to stand up for those beliefs. But I have not always been popular for doing so.

In 2018 we celebrated the centenary of the Representation of the People Act 1918, which for the first time gave some women the right to vote in parliamentary elections. In 2019 we celebrated the centenary of the Sex Disqualification (Removal) Act 1919, which gave women the right to join the learned professions, to go to university and to enter public life, as magistrates and eventually as judges. Yet it is easy to forget how very slow progress was for at least the first fifty of those hundred years. In Parliament for example, just twenty-six out of the 641 Members of Parliament elected in the general election of 1966, were women: a mere 4.1%. The proportion of women did not get above 10% until the 1997 election, when there was a leap to 18.2%. In the 2019 election they were 220 out of 650, just over a third, the highest proportion ever. A great deal has changed in Parliament, in public life and the law, over the years since I graduated.

Back in 1966, there were built-in quotas for places in selective schools and in Oxbridge: there were fewer grammar schools and academically strong boarding schools for girls; there were only three women's colleges in Cambridge and five in Oxford; women were not admitted to the prestigious Cambridge Union Society until 1965. There were also quotas in medical schools. Other universities did not have quotas, but the percentage of young women going to university was less than half that of young men. In 1960, only 444 of around 19,000 practising solicitors (2.3%) and only eighty-four of around 1,900 practising barristers (4.4%) were women. A decade later, the proportions had risen to 3.3% and 5.8% respectively but were still minuscule. While there were many women serving as lay magistrates, there were very few professional women judges. Sybil Campbell was the first, appointed a metropolitan stipendiary magistrate in 1945; Rose Heilbron QC was appointed recorder of Burnley in 1956; but the first woman who could call herself a judge was Elizabeth Lane QC, appointed a county court judge in 1962 and promoted to the High Court in 1965.

In 1966, many sets of barristers' chambers had yet to have a woman either as a pupil or as a tenant. Women found it hardest to break into the top-flight commercial chambers in London, where not only was the most money to be made but also many High Court judges were recruited. Very few chambers, even in relatively progressive Manchester, had more than one woman. The courts in England and Wales were organised into six regions, or 'circuits', and barristers had to be a member of the circuit in order to practise there. So women had to be allowed to become members of the circuit. On the Northern Circuit, they were elected at a dinner at which most of the women being elected were expected to climb onto the table. I was spared this, perhaps because I wasn't young or pretty enough, or perhaps because my husband John was being elected on the same occasion.

But women were not allowed to become members of the 'Bar mess': a tradition of dining together once or twice a week during the legal terms, dating back to the days when the High Court judges travelled round the circuit and the barristers travelled with them. There were special 'ladies' nights' once a term, which Rose Heilbron QC refused to attend on principle. In 1969, shortly after I had joined, there was a 'business court' to decide whether women should become full members of the mess. I was prosecuting in Bolton Crown Court on that day and anxious to get back for the meeting, and luckily so was the judge. The meeting was hilarious. Barrister after barrister got up to protest that letting women join their dinners, especially the principal one known as 'Grand Court', would ruin their traditions, i.e. spoil their fun. But it looked as if a compromise proposal, whereby we could become members of the mess but not go to Grand Court, might get through. So the naysayers pressed for a postal vote, which was agreed. This was disappointing, as I wanted to go to the mess that night, because my pupil master, John da Cunha, was to be congratulated on becoming a judge. So I plucked up courage to ask whether it would be possible for me to attend. The sympathisers pointed out that the circuit 'junior', Giles Wingate-Saul, had power to declare the mess to be a special ladies' night. The naysayers protested that, in exercising his discretion, he should bear in mind that men had signed up for the mess in the belief that there would be no women present. Undeterred, Giles did declare it a special ladies' night. The result of the postal vote was, of course, that sense prevailed and women became full members of the mess. My guess is that the after-dinner speeches at Grand Court became even wittier as a result. But the whole sorry tale shows how, even in 1969, things had not changed much since 1919.

Everyday discrimination was rife. There was a bar in Manchester where we would sometimes meet for a drink after leaving chambers. It served pub lunches. Naively I assumed that if I could go there for a drink in the evening I could go there for lunch at lunchtime. I was turned away. In 1968, we were joined in the Law Faculty by our first woman professor, Gillian White, a distinguished international lawyer, then unmarried. She wanted to buy a house in Manchester. She was unable to get a mortgage without having a man to guarantee the debt. The only man she could offer was her father, a retired local government officer in his eighties. His credit was acceptable while hers was not. Soon after that, an able student of mine, who had decided that she did not want to go into the legal profession, told me that she had been offered a job by an insurance company at two-thirds of the salary which a man would get for doing exactly the same job. None of this was against the law: the Sex *Disqualification* (Removal) Act 1919 was not the Sex *Discrimination* (Removal) Act. It took until 1975 for that to come in.

But the 1960s should be famous for more than the Beatles, flower power and the student rebellions of 1968. It was the decade when 'women's liberation' was born, when classic polemical texts such as Betty Friedan's *The Feminine Mystique* (1963) and Germaine Greer's *The Female Eunuch* (1970) were written. It was the decade when women began to be able to control their fertility, with the Abortion Act 1967 and the growing availability of contraception. It was the decade when women began to believe that they could 'have it all'. Is that the reason for the very different lives which the three Hale sisters have lived? My elder sister Jill graduated from Nottingham University with a good degree in Spanish and Portuguese but went off to train as a secretary. For this she had to learn shorthand, which she loathed. She also loathed being a secretary, where her brain and her talents were not put to good use, so she turned to teaching. Fortunately, she had already met the love of her life, Mike McCarthy, who qualified as a chartered accountant and then went into industry. He was a good man, and proud of his clever wife, but he wanted her to be there when he came home for lunch every day, to keep an immaculate house, to help in the garden, and to dress smartly. All of these she enjoyed doing, so it was no hardship. But it was not until her two daughters had gone to university that she was able to re-enter public life, as a magistrate and Citizens' Advice Bureau organiser.

My younger sister, Frances, took a different path. She too graduated from Nottingham University, with a good degree in English; then went off to do Voluntary Service Overseas, teaching English to university

Richmond and its castle in early autumn.

The Hurworth Hunt meets outside Scorton Grammar School and Leonard Robinson's old house, 1930s.

Watercolour drawing of Scorton village green in 1860 by Juliana Ewing, a well-known children's author, frontispiece to 'Mrs Gatty and Mrs Ewing' by Christina Maxwell.

Staff and pupils of Scorton Grammar School in 1949, including Joe the handyman and Mrs Botterill the cook, as well as Mr Hale the headmaster and Mrs Hale.

Portrait of Grandpa Godfrey when he was headmaster
of Mansfield Grammar School.

Kiplin Hall, saved from destruction by sand and gravel.

Aunt Mary Godfrey, my mother's more beautiful sister.

My parents, Marjorie Godfrey and Cecil Hale, in their wedding outfits, 1936.

Brenda, Jillian
and Frances
Hale in 1946.

Frances (*left*) and
Brenda (*right*) in
matching outfits
with sister Jill.

Brenda, Joan and Claire, best
friends at Richmond High School.

Richmond High School for Girls, an outstanding
example of modern school architecture,
built in 1939.

St Mary's Church, Bolton-on-Swale.

Brenda receiving the
Freedom of Richmond, 2018.

Master of the Company of Fellmongers
of Richmond, Yorkshire, 2017.

Watercolour of Girton College, Cambridge,
by its architect, Alfred Waterhouse.

Brenda in a home-made ballgown at
Sidney Sussex College May Ball, 1965.

The Lhotka family at home
near Klosterneuburg,
Austria, 1963.

The European Schools Day prize-winners in Strasbourg, 1962.
Ursula in the front row, on the right.

Mother and baby, 1974.

Julia and children admiring the view
while out walking in Swaledale,
2016.

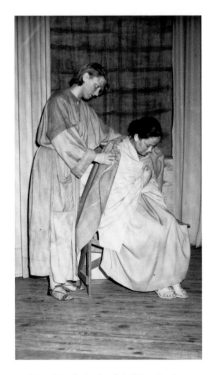

Mrs Noah in André Obey's play
Noah, 1961 – she goes mad.

'Strange Adventure' – Kate in
The Yeomen of the Guard, Cambridge University
Gilbert and Sullivan Society, 1966.

Anya in *The Cherry Orchard*, Manchester University Stage Society, 1969.

Mae West has all the best lines,
A Night at the Cinema Gray's Inn
Miscellany, 2014.

'Am I not your Lord?' thunders
Julian as Oberon. 'I have Lords
enough about me', declares Brenda
as Titania, to general merriment.
*Shakespeare Inn Love, or A Miscellany
of Errors*, Gray's Inn, 2016.

students in India (where she could pass as a local if she wore a shalwar kameez); then returned to do a PhD on English novels about India, and to meet and marry a Norwegian architect, Håkon Mannsåker. She went into academic life, first as a teacher and later as an administrator, ending a highly successful career as a pro-vice-chancellor at the University of Lincoln. She had one son but did not stay married to his father. A trajectory not unlike my own.

We all had such similar abilities, such similar drive and determination, such a similar desire to excel at whatever it was that we were doing, so why the difference? Perhaps because Frances and I lost our father at a young age, which encouraged us to value the independence which our careers gave us. Perhaps because Frances and I were children of the 1960s, the decade when so much changed. Or perhaps because we all liked doing what we did.

The 1960s was also the decade when women workers began to fight for their right to equal pay and win. In 1968, the women sewing machinists making car seat covers at the Ford Motor Company's plant in Dagenham went on strike: a pay regrading had rated their work as less skilled than the men's and awarded them 15% lower wages. Car production came to a halt after three weeks because there were no seat covers and no one else knew how to make them (thus proving that there was skill involved). A deal was brokered by Barbara Castle, Secretary of State for Employment and Productivity, and the women agreed to go back for 8% less than the men were paid, rising to the full amount the next year. But it took until 1984 and another strike for their work to be recognised as equally skilled.

In 1970, Barbara Castle piloted the Equal Pay Act through Parliament. This gave women a contractual right to equal pay for 'like work' or 'work rated as equivalent', as long as the material circumstances were the same. This solved the problem of my student working for an insurance company. It did not solve the problem of the Dagenham machinists and others like them, segregated into 'women's work' which was routinely paid less than the work done by men. Perhaps worse, the Act was not due to come into force until 1975, to give employers time to adjust. Some may well have used that time to organise even more job segregation than there already was. Only in 1984, with an action against the United Kingdom in the European

Court of Justice, was the Act amended to require equal pay for work of equal value.

Equal pay for men and women had been one of the fundamental principles of the Treaty of Rome which established the European Economic Community back in 1957. But there is not much point in requiring equal pay if a woman can be refused the job simply because she is a woman. The Sex Discrimination Act 1975 was the logical next step. This went further than Europe required and prohibited the suppliers of employment, training, accommodation, goods, facilities and services from discriminating on grounds of sex – treating people less favourably because they were a woman or a man as the case might be. This sounds simple enough. Nevertheless, the courts sometimes struggled to understand what treating a person less favourably meant.

Three examples will illustrate the problem. The courts held in a series of cases that discrimination against pregnant women was not sex discrimination under the 1975 Act: discrimination required a comparison between a man and a woman in the same circumstances and there was no male equivalent to a woman with child.[1] Alternatively, a pregnant woman should be compared with a sick man, so that if her pregnancy meant that she was off work for a length of time which would lead to the dismissal of a sick man, she was not being treated less favourably.[2] But the House of Lords was sufficiently dubious to refer the case to the European Court of Justice, which resoundingly rejected both excuses and held that incapacity because of pregnancy could not be compared with incapacity because of sickness: dismissing a woman because she was pregnant was sex discrimination.[3] The House of Lords gave in, eight years after Mrs Webb had lost her job.[4]

Much worse was Mrs Coleman's case, in 1981.[5] Mr and Mrs Coleman were employed by the same company. The employer wrote to Mrs Coleman saying 'Regretfully I have come to the conclusion that it would not be fair to your husband in his position to keep you employed in a similar capacity.' The tribunal awarded her £1,000 for injury to feelings, the Employment Appeal Tribunal reduced this to £250, and the Court of Appeal to £100. Lord Justice Shaw thought that her 'complaint was trivial and banal even when topped up with much legalistic froth' and that 'when she had dried her tears she would have had to look for new employment and to count herself lucky to find it'. He would have awarded her 1,000 pence (£10). Yet what had been done to her was outrageous – how would the judges have felt if the employer had sacked her husband because his wife was in a similar position?

It took a case with which the men really could empathise for the penny to drop.[6] Tess Gill (a barrister) and Anna Coote (a journalist) complained that they were not allowed to buy drinks and stand at the bar in El Vino on Fleet Street. The trial judge took the view that this was too trivial to be a detriment. The Court of Appeal held that that wasn't the question. The question was whether they had been treated less favourably than men in the provision of a facility. Lord Justice Griffiths waxed lyrical:

> El Vino's is no ordinary wine bar, it has become a unique institution in Fleet Street. Every day it is thronged with journalists, solicitors, barristers exchanging the gossip of the day … Now if a man wishes to take a drink in El Vino's he can drink, if he wishes, by joining the throng which crowds round the bar and there he can join his friends and pick up, no doubt, many an interesting piece of gossip, particularly if he is a journalist. Or, if he wishes, he can go and sit down at one of the two tables that are on the right immediately behind the main door of the premises. Thirdly, if he wishes, he can pass through the partition and enter the little smoking room at the back, which is equipped with a number of tables and chairs. But there is no doubt that very many men choose to stand among the throng drinking at the bar. But if a woman wishes to go to El Vino's, she is not allowed to join the throng before the bar. She must drink either at one of the two tables on the right of the entrance, or she must pass through the throng and drink in the smoking room at the back. There is no doubt whatever that she is refused facilities that are accorded to men, and the only question that remains is: is she being treated less favourably than men? I think that permits of only one answer: of course she is.

Thus did His Lordship display his personal knowledge of the bar in question! But of course it did not matter that El Vino was 'no ordinary wine bar'. The answer to the Manchester bar which had refused to serve me all those years before would have been the same.

The 1970s also saw the growing recognition that 'domestic' violence was not a private matter between husband and wife or cohabiting partners but something against which the law should provide effective protection. While at the Bar, I had been shocked that wives were still expected to stay with their violent husbands and by how difficult it was for them to escape. Part of this was the psychological dominance of men who not only held the purse strings but could also threaten to keep the children if the mother left. Other women, including me, could tell them that this wouldn't happen, but they didn't believe us. Erin Pizzey gave a searing account of the problems they faced, in her groundbreaking book *Scream Quietly or the Neighbours Will Hear* (1974). She also provided a practical solution by setting up the first women's refuge. The House of Commons published reports on *Violence in Marriage* (1975) and *Violence in the Family* (1977). The lawyers began to develop new remedies to prohibit molestation and exclude an abuser from the home.

As an academic, I could play a small part by lecturing about these on lawyers' training courses. Steadily, legislation was passed to improve the remedies available (Domestic Violence and Matrimonial Proceedings Act 1976; Domestic Proceedings and Magistrates Courts Act 1978) and, more important, to require local authorities to provide housing for homeless people who were pregnant or had dependent children (Housing (Homeless Persons) Act 1977). But this only applied if the woman had not become intentionally homeless by leaving a home which it was reasonable for her to continue to occupy. Once again, the courts did not distinguish themselves. They thought that it might be reasonable for a victim of domestic violence to continue to occupy the family home if she could apply for an injunction to get the abuser out.[7] But getting such an injunction, especially for an indefinite period, was by no means a foregone conclusion. The House of Lords veered between the view that the 1976 Act was designed to prioritise personal safety over property rights[8] and the view that it actually restricted the courts' discretion to interfere in property rights.[9] Ousting a property owner or tenant from his home was regarded as a 'draconian' step, even though failing to do so meant that the victim and her children were ousted from their home. As Susan Atkins and I wrote in *Women and the Law*, 'The woman may thus be caught in a "catch 22", where the authorities refuse a home because she could get an injunction and the courts refuse an injunction because she could be rehoused by the authorities.'

In 1972, Anthony Lester and Geoffrey Bindman had published a groundbreaking book, *Race and Law*. The editors of a series of books on Law in Context wanted to commission a similar book on women and the law. They approached me because I had been teaching an extramural course on the subject for some time. I would concentrate on women's private lives and a colleague would concentrate on their public lives. I spent a good deal of time during the 1970s reading the growing academic feminist literature which explored the reality of women's lives, such as Ann Oakley's *The Sociology of Housework* (1974) and *Becoming a Mother* (1979) and Hannah Gavron's *The Captive Wife* (1966); numerous studies of violence in the family; and of how the criminal courts dealt with rape and other sexual offences. This was the decade when sociolegal studies – that is, studies of what the courts actually do and the impact upon the people involved – became accepted as an academic discipline in its own right. Another important influence was Professor Herma Hill Kay, of the University of California, Berkeley, who visited Manchester in 1976. In 1969 she had co-authored, along with Ruth Bader Ginsburg and Kenneth M. Davidson, the massive tome *Sex-Based Discrimination: Text, Cases and Materials*, the first book of its kind. What was so impressive about Herma, apart from her charm, was the depth of her scholarship, the clarity of her thought and the firmness of her convictions. I well remember a seminar in which she firmly rejected a senior colleague's suggestion that the prospective father might have a right to veto an abortion: it was the woman who was pregnant and it was the woman who had the right to choose. This was the approach of the Supreme Court of the United States in the landmark case of *Roe v Wade*[10] very different from the medicalised approach of the UK's Abortion Act of 1967, which focused on risk to the life or health of the pregnant woman.

Our *Women and the Law* project was delayed until the early 1980s, when I teamed up with Susan Atkins, then a young lecturer at Southampton University. Our approach was not to look at how each area of law – family, tort, contract, employment, property, crime and the constitution – looked at women, but to look at the various aspects of women's lives – work and employment outside the home, sexuality, motherhood, roles within the family, power and violence in the home, marriage and cohabitation, the welfare state, taxation and citizenship – and take a holistic view of how those laws interacted with each aspect. As it turned out, the delay from when the book was first proposed was beneficial. There was a great deal of optimism in the 1970s, when there was so much legislation which aimed to improve women's lives. The research, thinking and legal developments over the years which followed showed that those reforms, or their implementation by the courts, still left much to be desired. It was undoubtedly a radical text at the time: Sue and I were surprised and delighted that it was shortlisted for the Fawcett Society's prize for non-fiction. We enjoyed the prize-giving dinner at London Zoo, but were disappointed when the judges described our innovative book as 'solid'. We didn't win.

In the preface, we acknowledged that our views might change should the Law Commission come to consider reform of the law on any of the topics we discussed: but if our analysis were to contribute to the reform of the law, 'so much the better'. Others may judge from later chapters how far our analysis fed into my proposals for law reform and my judicial decisions: whether, to quote Dinah Rose once more, I have been an 'antidote to the ubiquitous male lens through which the law has traditionally been viewed'.

One noticeable omission from the book's section on 'women in public life' was any discussion of women in the judiciary. Yet the situation in 1984 was staggering. Sixty-five years after the Sex Disqualification (Removal) Act 1919, there had only ever been four women on the High Court bench: Dame Elizabeth Lane, Dame Rose Heilbron, Dame Margaret Booth and Dame Elizabeth Butler-Sloss. All were assigned to the Family Division, although only Margaret Booth had been a family-law practitioner. When I was appointed a High Court judge in January 1994, I was only the tenth woman ever. Perhaps worse, it was not until 1992 that Dame Ann Ebsworth became the first woman in the Queen's Bench Division, where the most serious criminal, commercial and public law cases are tried, and 1993 that Dame Mary Arden became the first woman in the Chancery Division, which deals with property, tax, company and insolvency cases. Proudly, five of the six women High Court judges in 1994 had practised on the Northern Circuit and the sixth was the daughter of a Liverpool solicitor.

The view commonly held by the senior judiciary in the 1990s was that there were so few women judges because so few women had joined the legal profession in the 1960s and earlier; that now they were joining in much larger numbers, they would in time 'trickle up' into the judiciary. The politicians, on the other hand, realised that there was a deeper problem and were trying to find ways of solving it. It was not until the twenty-first century that the senior judiciary woke up to the fact that there were systemic barriers which had to be tackled before women could play their full part in the justice system.

The Association of Women Solicitors and the Association of Women Barristers (of which I became president in 1994) had been pressing for change for years, along with organisations such as JUSTICE (the UK section of the International Commission of Jurists). In 2002 they organised a meeting in Committee Room 10 in the Houses of Parliament, attended by legal bigwigs including the Lord Chief Justice of England and Wales, Lord Woolf. The speaker was Beverley McLachlin, chief justice of Canada from 2000 until she retired in 2017. A concerted effort by the legal profession, the judiciary and the politicians in Canada had succeeded in increasing the proportion of women judges at all levels to over a third. She thought that having more women on the bench had made her court a happier place. Not only that. She gave four principled reasons for wanting more women in the judiciary. They go something like this.

The first is democratic legitimacy. Our constitution is founded on the rule of law: the idea that society is governed by laws and not by the diktat of individual men and that everyone, the governors as well as the governed, is subject to the law. This means that the law must be there to serve every member of society, not just one section of it: the women as well as the men, the ethnic minorities as well as the white majority, the gay as well as the straight, the poor as well as the rich, and so on and so on. Everyone must be able to feel confident that the law is there for them if they need it. Everyone must feel confident that they will get a fair hearing if they come before the courts. This means that our courts, and the lawyers who serve their clients in and out of court, must be as reflective as possible of the society they serve. Women make up half of that society.

The second is closely linked to that. The guiding principles of our law are justice, fairness and equality. Three hundred years ago, we would not have included equality among those guiding principles, but the eighteenth-century Enlightenment brought with it the 'value that every human being is entitled to equal respect and to be treated as an end and not a means. Characteristics such as race, caste, noble birth, membership of a political party are seldom, if ever, acceptable grounds for differences in treatment.'[11] Gender was added to that list in the twentieth century. In one way or another, that notion of equality is reflected in all the modern human rights instruments and in many written constitutions. It is also reflected in our domestic law. Those values of justice, fairness and equality ought to be visibly embodied, not only in our laws, but also in the lawyers who administer them. Our absence – and that of other under-represented groups – means that they are not.

Third, and leading on from that, there is equality of opportunity. This benefits not only the individuals concerned but also society, so that we don't waste the talents that are available to us. We were wasting them in 2002 and, despite recent improvements, we are wasting them still. There is a noticeable falling out of (or with) self-employed practice as a barrister or a solicitor after between fifteen and twenty years. Such attrition is found in other professions, but it is particularly noticeable in the law. Women – and for that matter men – should feel free to put their family responsibilities before their own professional advancement if they want. But many of them want to do both and find this increasingly hard because of the way much private practice is organised. Even in academic life, where one is much freer to organise one's time conveniently and can do such a lot of one's work at home, the career expectations and trajectory are structured around the life of a person without demanding responsibilities outside work. In private practice it is much worse. Increasingly, it is motherhood rather than gender which holds women back. All those able young women who go into the law should be enabled to stay in it, and not be forced out by the long-hours culture in some parts of the profession. But if they do take a break from self-employed practice

or, more commonly, step sideways into some other area of legal
practice, such as the government legal service, local authorities, regu-
latory bodies or in-house counsel in commerce, finance or industry,
they should not for that reason alone be regarded as less worthy of
judicial appointment. We should be looking for judicial potential
wherever it can be found – not just amongst people in self-employed
legal practice.

Those are all good reasons enough to fight for a more diverse
judiciary. But might there be another one? Might not judicial
decision-making be enhanced by greater diversity amongst its practitioners? I used to be sceptical about this and many senior women
lawyers still are. We are all servants of the law and true to our judicial
oath 'to do right to all manner of people after the laws and usages
of this realm, without fear or favour, affection or ill will'. In most
cases, as Mary Jeanne Coyne, on the Supreme Court of Minnesota,
put it, 'A wise old woman and her wise old man reach the same conclusions.' But of course the law is not, or at least not always, neutral
or clear-cut. Choices have to be made. As Chief Justice McLachlin
argued in Committee Room 10 that day: 'jurists are human beings,
and, as such, are informed and influenced by their backgrounds,
communities, and experiences. For cultural, biological, social and
historic reasons, women do have different experiences than men.'

In short: 'We lead women's lives: we have no choice.' And the
experience of leading those lives should be just as important in shaping
the law as is the experience of leading men's lives. This is all the more
important in a legal system like ours, where the principles are deduced
from the decided cases, rather than the cases deduced from a codified
set of principles, and the law is developed incrementally, building from
case to case. As Oliver Wendell Holmes Jr, justice of the Supreme
Court of the United States, explained, 'The life of the law has not
been logic; it has been experience.' The experience of being a woman
may have made a difference in a Supreme Court case about the customs
duty payable on the import of a mastectomy bra.[12] If it was an item
of clothing, the duty was 6.5%. If it was an 'appliance worn to compensate for a defect or disability', there was no duty. Reading the
description, it did not seem very different from an ordinary bra. But
I asked to see one. In the flesh, it was obvious that no one would

spend money on such a device unless she needed it to hold a breast prosthesis to compensate for the absence of a breast. There will be other examples in later chapters of the difference which the experience of leading a woman's life can make to the development of the law.

I believe that that meeting in 2002 was something of a light-bulb moment for the senior judiciary. But there were political forces at work too. Judicial appointments were in the hands of a senior polit- ician, the Lord Chancellor. More modern and egalitarian recruitment practices had been introduced for the junior judicial appointments, but the higher appointments still relied heavily on the traditional 'tap on the shoulder' method. This depended on knowing whose shoulder to tap. And for that the Lord Chancellor still relied mainly on the views of the senior judiciary and the leaders of the legal professions. The high-ranking officials who did the work were advised that they should join the Garrick Club, to which many barristers and judges belonged, so that they could get to know them and even pick up names. The Garrick Club did not and still does not admit women. There were growing calls for an independent Judicial Appointments Commission which would use open and transparent recruitment methods. The Lord Chancellor, Lord Irvine, although well disposed towards diversity, was reluctant to give up control. But for other reasons the prime minister, Tony Blair, came to see the Lord Chan- cellor and his department as an obstacle to the reform of the justice system, in particular the criminal justice system. Without consulting the senior judiciary or the Lord Chancellor's Department, it was decided to dismantle the threefold role of the Lord Chancellor, as Speaker of the House of Lords, head of the judiciary and minister in charge of the justice system and legal services. In June 2003, it was announced that the post was to be abolished. This proved legally impossible, but the role was indeed dismantled. An independent Judicial Appointments Commission was established to recommend who should be appointed to all judicial posts.

Originally, it was planned that the new commission would have a duty to try and secure a more diverse judiciary, one which was more truly reflective of the communities it served. The Judicial Appointments Commission already established in Northern Ireland did have such a duty, although this was aimed at reassuring the nationalist and unionist communities in Northern Ireland rather than at gender or other kinds of diversity. But the suggestion, which was obviously designed to benefit women, raised the typical outcry: we cannot promote diversity at the expense of 'merit'. This is an exceedingly irritating diversion. It assumes that those traditionally appointed are, as a group, more meritorious than any more diverse candidates might be. Yet this required to be proved and could not be. Many of those traditionally appointed were indeed highly meritorious, scoring highly on what I call the four 'in-' quotients necessary for judges: intelligence, industry, independence and incorruptibility. But many were not. It also assumes that there is a commonly agreed definition of 'merit' which owes nothing to the gender, ethnicity, professional background and socio-economic status of the candidates or those appointing them. This again required to be proved and was not. There is a well-known psychological tendency to recognise merit in 'people like us' and to fail to see it in others. And it assumes that those making the appointments know how to recognise 'merit' amongst those they are considering for appointment: in those days, usually done with one hand tied behind their backs because they relied on recommendations and 'secret soundings' rather than a properly designed application process. The result of the outcry was that the Judicial Appointments Commission has a duty to 'have regard to the need to encourage diversity in the range of people available for selection for appointment', but this is expressly subject to the requirement that 'selection must be solely on merit'.[13] The comparable provisions for Scotland and Northern Ireland were amended accordingly.

I had been thinking and writing about the problem of women in the judiciary for some time before Chief Justice McLachlin's visit. In September 2000, I gave a lecture to academic lawyers on 'Equality and the Judiciary: why should we want more women judges?'[14] I suggested three reasons: equal opportunities, making a difference, and democratic legitimacy. The first and the third were very powerful: they argued for fairness to individual candidates and fairness to society. As to the second, while we should not expect individual judges to make a difference, we could hope that a more reflective judiciary would make a difference. I quoted Ruth Bader Ginsburg quoting Judge Alvin Rubin: this would bring 'a distinctive medley of view influenced by differences in biology, cultural impact and life experience'. Since then I have written and spoken on the subject many times. I considered it my duty, when I became the most senior woman judge in the country, to speak out. I could not be accused of furthering my own ambitions. Other women judges might be deterred, fearing either that accusation or the inevitable unpopularity that speaking out would bring.

It is a fact of life that, if the number of appointments remains roughly the same but more of them are filled by women, or other traditionally less advantaged groups, then fewer of them will be filled by the white men who have previously been appointed. Equal opportunity for the women brings an end to unequal – i.e. more favourable – opportunity for the men. There is also a persistent fear that appointing more women will bring with it a reduction in the status and financial rewards of the job. No wonder, therefore, that those who had traditionally been regarded as the most meritorious candidates should insist that merit be the only criterion. But another problem with 'merit' was the assumption that the best barristers make the best judges. This assumption is also open to challenge. As Helena Kennedy QC explains, 'The pleasure of working with a jury is hard to describe and for those who are addicted to it there is nothing like it. It is one of the reasons why good advocates often make lousy judges ... they continually want to step into the ring and spar with one side or the other.'[15] Even outside the battlefield of jury trials, according to David Pannick, 'to have the ability to argue a proposition is not necessarily to have the qualities required fairly to decide the same issue according to law'.[16] Sir Stephen Sedley summed up the problem neatly: the greatest of the arts of advocacy is 'reasoning from a given conclusion': in other words, advocates start with the best result they can expect for their client and then work backwards to a way of achieving it from the evidence and the law.[17] Judges, of course, should do the reverse: start with the evidence and the law and work forwards to the right result. Assuming that the best barristers make the best judges also disadvantages women because of the systemic disadvantages they suffer in making a career at the Bar: even in 2020, only 32% of barristers with fifteen years or more post-qualification experience and only 17% of practising Queen's Counsel were women (and the latter had been going up at roughly one percentage point a year for the past ten years, which shows how recent even this is). I have been arguing for years that we need to rethink the traditional assumptions about who gets what sort of judging job.

This is not an argument for positive discrimination, that is, choosing a woman candidate who is not as good as a male candidate just because she is a woman. But it is an argument for affirmative action to try and improve the selection criteria and processes. Yet even this has been opposed on the ground that it will put off both the best women and the best men. The best women will be put off, it is argued, because they do not want it said that they have been appointed only because they are women. The best men will be put off by the fear that they might suffer discrimination. The best women should not be put off. For one thing, if they are indeed the best, that is why they have been appointed. And for another thing, as Dame Sian Elias, chief justice of New Zealand, has said, even if you do fear that you have been chosen because you are a woman, it is your duty to step up to the plate and prove that you can do as good a job as a man. Nor should the best men be put off: if women had been put off by the fear that they might face discrimination, we would never have got anywhere.

There has been a good deal of progress since the Judicial Appointments Commission began its work. In April 2020, 32% of the judges sitting in the ordinary courts were women, though only 26% in the High Court and Court of Appeal. But 47% of the judges sitting in tribunals were women: indeed, the tribunals judiciary now largely reflects the proportions of women and members of ethnic minorities of the same age group in the working population as a whole. This is a major achievement and shows what can be done. I believe that the disparity has a good deal to do with the wider professional pool from which tribunal judges are appointed.

As late as 2004, I was the first woman to be appointed to the highest court in the land, until 2009 the appellate committee of the House of Lords and from then the Supreme Court of the United Kingdom. I remained the only woman until 2017, when Lady Black was appointed, and we were joined by Lady Arden in 2018. I did worry that I was doing something to put them off having another woman. The recent progress may have been helped because there were so many vacancies in the Supreme Court that (at my suggestion) we were able to fill them in groups of three. Then we are not pitting one individual against another. Their different merits can be appreciated. When I retired in January 2020, we were not able to appoint another woman among the three upcoming vacancies, but at least we were able to diversify the court in other ways, by appointing Lord Burrows, whose main career has been as an academic.

I always tried to do as much as I could to encourage women judges. In 2002, a few of us attended the biennial World Conference of the International Association of Women Judges (IAWJ) in Dublin. We were inspired by the gathering of so many women judges but shocked that so few women had crossed the sea from Great Britain. In 2003, I convened a meeting at the Royal Courts of Justice to which all the women judges were invited and many of them came. We resolved to set up a United Kingdom Association of Women Judges (UKAWJ), open to judicial office-holders at all levels in the system. We debated whether men should be able to join. Some women felt so alone amongst their male colleagues that they wanted a place which would just be for them. But we decided that we would be an inclusive organisation, open to all who were interested in what we were interested in – equality and human rights, with an emphasis on issues affecting women. Only a few men were interested in joining an organisation where they were outnumbered by the women. Membership of the UKAWJ brought with it membership of the IAWJ and we managed to send a respectable party to world conferences in Sydney (2006), Panama (2008), and Seoul (2010), before staging our own in London in 2012, when I was president of the IAWJ. We held this in Church House, Westminster, wondering what the church leaders who had resisted women priests for so long would have made of the famous round conference room filled with women. Church House did us proud and the conference was a great success. I was very grateful for the support which the Lord Chief Justice, Lord Judge, and other legal luminaries gave to us. The IAWJ has grown from strength to strength. The UKAWJ is also going strong under the leadership of Lady Justice Asplin.

But feminism is not always popular. As a Law Commissioner, I was pilloried in the press as one of the 'legal commissars subverting family values'. When I went to the House of Lords, I was said to be 'The most ideological, politically correct judge ever to have been appointed' – that cannot have been the case, given the politicians who had been appointed to high judicial office in the past. I was also said to be a 'hard-line feminist' apparently intent on destroying the institution of marriage – this was because I had suggested that marriage was such a good thing for the children and the economically less advantaged spouse that some of its benefits should be extended to unmarried relationships. Those same commentators didn't notice years later when I defended the institution of marriage in *Radmacher v Granatino*.[18] My appointment as a Law Lord was said to epitomise 'the moral vacuum within our judiciary and wider establishment'. Why a commitment to gender equality at home and at work was thought to be a moral vacuum has never been clear to me, unless this was a not-so-subtle attempt to defend the status quo. But others were also troubled by my appointment. Lord Hope, one of the two Lords of Appeal in Ordinary from Scotland (Lord Rodger was the other) recorded in his diary for 31 December 2003:

> A new team of Brenda Hale (Monday 12 January will be 'Hale Day' says Alan Rodger), Bob Carswell and Simon Brown will inject a different atmosphere into the corridor ... Of the three, Simon will keep up the spirit of good humour. Bob will drop neatly into Brian [Hutton]'s shoes as our man from Northern Ireland, *and Brenda will be a source of some anxiety until we adjust to the very different contribution she will make.* [My emphasis.]

I have got some good laughs out of quoting that in lectures and talks, but in reality it is no laughing matter. It is an unusually frank confession of the unease which even the most intelligent and otherwise fair-minded people can feel when confronted with a feminist and her 'agenda', as he called it. I do not think that that anxiety was ever entirely allayed.

7 Public Life

Manchester had been very kind to me, but after eighteen years, it was time to move on, if I could. I had been turned down for professorships in three universities which were within a reasonable travelling distance from our home on the edge of the Pennines. How glad I now am! If any had accepted me, I would not have had the life that I have had. Then, late in 1983, two vacancies for Law Commissioners were advertised – one in property law and one in family law. A friendly colleague remarked that there were two excellent candidates for them on the Manchester staff. He meant Professor Julian Farrand and me.

This was an exciting thought, because the Law Commission had been responsible for the revolution in family law which took place in 1971. But despite my colleague's encouragement, I did not apply. It was a full-time post in London. My daughter Julia was then aged ten, in her penultimate year in the prep school of Manchester High School for Girls. My husband John did plan to apply to become Queen's Counsel, which he hoped would lead to his joining planning Chambers in London, but he decided at the last moment that it was too soon to do so. So I did not apply for the Law Commission. But soon after the deadline had passed, I had a phone call from Dr Stephen Cretney, the family-law commissioner: it had been noticed that I had not applied – was this a firm decision against it or could I be tempted? I could indeed be tempted.

I was invited for interview on Friday 13 January 1984 (an auspicious date). Among the other candidates interviewed was Professor Julian Farrand, who had applied for the property-law vacancy. Neither of us was optimistic. They wanted one academic and one solicitor – Julian was a solicitor but had not practised for years. Worse still, the academics appointed had almost always been from Oxford or Cambridge.

Two from the same provincial university was surely unthinkable. Nevertheless, after the interview, I wrote to the Lord Chancellor's Department asking them to treat me as an applicant. But I heard nothing more for several weeks. Then one day Julian's secretary came to my office and told me that he wanted to see me. I found a very happy man, who told me that, not only had he been offered the appointment, but so had I. This was news to me. Because I had not put in a formal application, the Lord Chancellor's Department had written to my old home address.

My appointment caused a small stir, because, at thirty-nine, I was the youngest ever and the first woman commissioner. I was even prepared to describe myself as a feminist, although I managed to avoid declaring any position on the women then encamped outside the Greenham Common airbase: an early lesson in coping with press interviews. I caused a smaller stir at the Law Students' annual dinner, when I told them that 'Professor Farrand and I are running away to London together.' The joke took seven years to come true.

Julian had already negotiated with the university that the appointment would be such a feather in the university's cap that he could have leave of absence for the full five-year term. The university had to do the same for me, even though no one had contemplated that we might both be appointed. Thus it was that we turned up together at the Law Commission's offices, then on the corner of John Street and Theobalds Road, overlooking the Gray's Inn 'walks'. Looking back, it must have been irritating for our fellow commissioners. Although not in the slightest bit romantically entangled, we had known one another for years, were good friends, and being away from home during the week, we regularly teamed up for meals and outings and on train trips (by the Manchester Pullman) back home. We often thought alike on law reform issues and of course we discussed things. Not surprisingly, we were called 'the Manchester Mafia' or 'the Piccadilly line'.

But what is the Law Commission? It (along with its Scottish coun-terpart) was set up by the Law Commissions Act 1965. The role is 'To take and keep under review all the law, with a view to its systematic development and reform ... and generally the simplification and modernisation of the law.'[1]

The thinking was that there were many rules of law, especially the common law that is made by the decisions of judges, which were outdated, unjust or simply in a mess. These were in areas like property law, of contract, tort, criminal law and family law: what is known as 'lawyers' law'. They matter a lot to ordinary people and businesses, they are the day-to-day work of the courts, but they are not the immediate concern of government departments.

There are five full-time commissioners, senior lawyers who are independent of government and serve five-year renewable terms. The chair has always been a High Court judge and these days it brings automatic promotion to the Court of Appeal. The others are supposed to be representative of the barristers', solicitors' and academic professions. The barristers have usually been senior QCs who could expect appointment to the High Court bench. The attractions for solicitors are less obvious and it has sometimes been difficult to fill that slot. The attractions for academics are many: the opportunity to promote the reform of one's own subject in a way which stands some chance of actually happening; the opportunity to contribute to the development of the law in other areas; a higher salary than most academics can earn; and the prospect of returning to academic life with a reputation enhanced.

Decisions are made collectively: the idea is that if five distinguished lawyers from different branches of the profession can agree on what is wrong with the law and how to put it right, their views will carry more weight than if they were acting individually. A large part of my job was persuading the other commissioners to agree with what the family-law team were proposing. When I arrived, there was talk of 'blood on the walls' in past commissioners' meetings. I can remember some hairy moments but no blood. One commissioner during my time was an excellent lawyer and conversationalist but fundamentally opposed to reforming the law in any meaningful way. It was a real struggle to get him to agree, for example, to opening the Land Register to public inspection. But mostly they kept their hands off 'Brenda's weird child law', as one of them called my principal project.

As well as the commissioners, there are the legal staff, civil servants either seconded from government departments or recruited directly, able young research assistants on short term contracts and sometimes consultants hired for particular projects. But the most striking thing about the commission is that it has parliamentary drafters seconded to it. The commissioners therefore have the unique privilege of being able to instruct them to draft a bill without having to get the approval of Cabinet. This means that their reports usually have a draft bill attached which can easily be picked up by Parliament. Compared with much of government, it should give the commission a running start towards actually getting things done.

From the start, the commission had an ambitious programme in family law. In the first five years, it produced reports on the grounds for divorce;[2] the financial consequences of divorce;[3] the grounds and consequences of annulling a marriage;[4] and recommending the abolition of the actions for breach of promise of marriage, restitution of conjugal rights, and interfering between husband and wife.[5] These were all implemented by legislation which came into force on 1 January 1971.[6]

The sole ground for divorce was now that the marriage had irretrievably broken down (although this could be proved only by showing that the other had committed adultery; or behaved in such a way that the petitioner could not reasonably be expected to live with him; or deserted for two years; or that they had been separated for two years and the other agreed to the divorce; or that they had been separated for five years, irrespective of whether the other agreed). On divorce, the courts could share out the present and future income and assets of both parties, irrespective of who owned what, in a way which was designed to minimise the loss which each would suffer from the breakdown of the marriage: I called this the 'equal misery' principle. The law no longer made any attempt to oblige the couple to live together. The law was now much kinder to the homemaker. Previously, unless she could show that her husband was to blame for the break-up, she stood to lose her home, her livelihood and even her children. Now she could expect a fair share of the family's assets and there was a good chance that she and the children could keep their home.

The commission later published reports improving the courts' powers to redistribute property after a death to provide for the deceased's dependants[7] and improving the powers of magistrates' courts to award maintenance and give protection against domestic abuse.[8] These too became law.[9] In less than a decade, the law of marriage was transformed – towards making marriage a genuine partnership of equals, whatever the roles the couple chose to adopt.

However, the commission had less success with two family-law projects upon which it spent a great deal of time and energy in the 1970s. One was to simplify the bewildering complexity of the law relating to getting married.[10] One obstacle was the special position of the Church of England, which is there to provide baptisms, weddings and funerals for everyone, whether or not they are members of the church. Another recommended automatic joint ownership of the matrimonial home and household goods. The commission proposed this in principle in 1973, when enthusiasm for the equality of the sexes was at its height.[11] But it took another five years to work out the conveyancing details, by which time enthusiasm had waned.[12] There were many, especially in the Lord Chancellor's Department, who were implacably opposed to anything remotely smacking of continental-style community of property.

My theory about all this is that the successful projects mostly involved remedies which gave the courts a broad discretion about what to do. The unsuccessful ones would have laid down hard and fast rules. It is much more difficult to devise hard and fast rules which will do justice to everyone than it is to give the courts power to do what is fair, just and reasonable in the circumstances of the individual case. Not only that: the successful projects mostly involved the ending of family relationships. In those days, this could still be seen as the exception to the norm: the married men in the Lord Chancellor's Department did not expect to be divorced but neither did they expect to have to share the ownership of their homes with their wives unless they wanted to.

There was another successful burst of family-law activity while Stephen Cretney was a commissioner and when he left it was decided to continue the family-law programme. Thus it was that I arrived at Conquest House in May 1984, with Julian Farrand and a strong attack of imposter syndrome.

The 'Manchester Mafia' were tested, and imposter syndrome suppressed, very early on. One strand of the commission's programme of work on criminal law was to examine the few remaining criminal offences which were defined by the decisions of judges rather than by Act of Parliament, with a view to abolishing them or replacing them with a modern statutory offence. Amongst these were blasphemy and blasphemous libel and other offences against religion and public worship. Blasphemy protected Christianity from insult or vilification, indeed possibly only protected the doctrines of the Church of England. The Church of England agreed that protecting only one religion could not be justified in today's multi-faith society. There had been no prosecutions between 1922 and 1977. But in 1977, Mrs Mary Whitehouse brought a private prosecution against the publisher of *Gay News* for printing a poem entitled 'The Love that Dares not Speak its Name', recounting the homosexual fantasies of a Roman soldier as he removed the body of Christ from the cross. The case went all the way to the House of Lords which held, by a majority of three to two, that there was no need to prove an intention to insult: it was enough to intend to publish the insulting material.[13]

In 1981, the commission published a consultation paper examining the criticisms of the offence, and the pros and cons of replacing it with something else, but provisionally proposing that the offences of blasphemy and blasphemous libel should be abolished without any replacement.[14] Then two members of the commission left and the new commissioners tipped the balance towards a different view. They decided to recommend replacing the common law with a new statutory offence of injuring religious feelings, but without defining what was meant by religion. A report was drafted, but its publication was held up because the parliamentary drafters had not found time to draft a bill. Then another two members of the original commission left and were replaced by Julian Farrand and me.

One of the first things to land on our desks was the draft report. Julian could be expected to disagree with it, as he had been brought up a convinced atheist and could not accept that religious feelings were any different in character or more worthy of legal protection than any other sort of feelings. But I had been brought up in the Church of England. If anything, however, my opposition to the proposal was even stronger: it seemed to me a broad and vague interference with freedom of expression which was likely to bring both the law and the religions that it was trying the protect into disrepute.

It was decided to wait until another member of the original commission had left and see what his replacement (a practising solicitor,
Trevor Aldridge) thought. He joined us in September 1984 and was
firmly in the Farrand and Hoggett camp.

So the report was published in 1985, the majority recommending
abolition without replacement, the minority recommending a new
offence, and a bill simply providing for abolition.[15] Of course, nothing
was done: successive governments saw little if anything to gain by
abolishing blasphemy and perhaps something to lose. However, never
say never in law reform. More than twenty years later, Lord Avebury
and Dr Evan Harris MP moved amendments to what became the
Criminal Justice and Immigration Act 2008, abolishing the offences
of blasphemy and blasphemous libel, and these were accepted.[16] They
joined Julian and me at a very jolly 'bye-bye blasphemy' party held
by the National Secular Society. Ian McKellen read the offending
poem – technically still an offence because the law had not yet come
into force. It is not a very good poem, but in 2008 it seemed more
loving than shocking.

My first main task was to decide what the family-law team should
do next. I had no doubt – and had said at my interview – that the
priority was the law relating to the care and upbringing of children.
Now that greater equality between spouses had been achieved, it was
high time to think about the children. Child law is 'weird' because
it is all about trying to plan a better future for the child rather than
compensating for past misdeeds. There are two branches – the allocation of responsibility for looking after children between their
parents and other individuals (known as the 'private' law), and the
responsibilities of the state for looking after children and protecting
them from harm (known as the 'public' law). These operated completely separately from one another and both were in a mess. The
private law was 'lawyers' law' which the Law Commission could
tackle as part of its family-law programme. The public law was the
responsibility of what was then the Department of Health and Social
Security (DHSS).

Soon after my arrival, the House of Commons Social Services
Committee published a report on *Children in Care*.[17] This recommended
a comprehensive review of child care law. There was a bewildering

array of routes by which a child might be compulsorily removed from home and put into the care of a local authority, some with very precise criteria and some with very vague ones. The distinction between these compulsory processes and the services which local authorities could provide to help children in need and their families was blurred. And the procedures were not well designed to give a fair hearing either to the children or to their parents.

The DHSS had suggested this review but had no idea how they would be able to do it, so the Law Commission's enthusiastic secretary, John Gasson, offered our services. The result was an innovative way of working for the commission and one which involved us in social policy decisions to a much greater extent than previously. It also meant that I did not have to persuade my fellow commissioners of the wisdom of our proposals. An interdepartmental working group was set up, with representatives from the DHSS policymakers, legal department and social workers, the Home Office, the Lord Chancellor's Department, and me. The commission's chairman took some convincing that we should be offering our resources to a project led by a government department (and chaired by a visionary civil servant, Rupert Hughes, who had a lower Civil Service grade than my notional one). The donkey work in the Law Commission was done by an energetic and far-sighted staff lawyer, Peter Graham Harris, and a brilliant, scholarly and seriously industrious research assistant, Jonathan Whybrow. They quickly formed a good working relationship with the policymakers and lawyers on the DHSS side. I supplied a long background in the subject, a commitment to the Law Commission's mission to modernise, simplify and codify the law, and a determination to make the law better for some of the most disadvantaged children in the country. Within a year, the group produced twelve consultation papers and a report.[18] Even more unusually, Rupert Hughes continued to involve the Law Commission team in developing the next steps, beginning with a White Paper in 1987.[19]

Meanwhile, in parallel with the child care law project, the Law Commission was examining the private law – guardianship, custody and access, and wards of court. Traditionally there had been one law for the rich in the higher courts and another law for the poor in the magistrates' courts, so the rules and remedies were different. Custody and access were outdated and confusing concepts, suggesting a winner and a loser, deterring parents from sharing the care of their children. There was a reluctance to allow them to make their own arrangements without the courts' approval.

When we started, the law still discriminated against children whose parents were not married to one another. The commission had published a report on illegitimacy in 1982[20] which aimed to give them the same rights as the children of married parents. But the bill attached to the report still insisted on applying an adjective to the children – calling them 'non-marital'. This could easily develop into an insult. It was also quite unnecessary. All the law had to do was to refer to parents who were not married to one another. Fortunately, the Lord Chancellor, Lord Hailsham, did not like 'non-marital', so we were asked to redraft the bill. This became the Family Law Reform Act 1987. I am particularly proud of its first section. Stripped of its legalese, it means that mentions of children, offspring or family relationships in legislation and legal documents are to include everyone, whether or not their parents or the parents of anyone through whom the relationship is traced were married to one another (unless they are excluded). A gift to 'my nephews and nieces' includes my sister's children, even if our parents were not married to one another or she was not married to their father. There is no need for an adjective.

Meanwhile, the government kept promising to introduce a bill to implement the child care White Paper, but kept on putting it off for more urgent things. Then along came the Cleveland child abuse scandal. In the 1970s and early 1980s there had been a string of scandals where children had been killed by their parents, despite being known to the social workers: Maria Colwell was returned to her family after being in care but had died soon afterwards; Jasmine Beckford, Kimberley Carlile, and Tyra Henry had not been removed despite clear evidence of abuse. But in the late 1980s, paediatricians in Cleveland diagnosed a remarkable number of cases of child sexual abuse and it was realised just how easy it was to remove children from home without having to show even a reasonable suspicion of abuse. In 1988, Dame Elizabeth Butler-Sloss produced a report which (among much more) supported our recommendations.[21]

The government decided that it must act. Rupert Hughes had a brainwave. Why not get the parliamentary drafters at the Law Commission (led by Edward Caldwell QC) to draft a comprehensive bill which brought together the government's public law recommendations with the private law recommendations of the Law Commission in a single coherent scheme? This would be so much better than the usual 'quick fix' of the most obvious problems.[22] And so the Children Act 1989 came to be.

It is still the framework for our child law today. All the statute law relating to the care and upbringing of children could now be found in one place. The same set of orders and principles applied in all the courts hearing cases about children. Cases could be transferred to the court for which they were most suited – whether the magistrates' courts, the county courts or the High Court. 'Custody' and 'access' were replaced with more flexible 'residence' and 'contact' (now the even more flexible 'child arrangements'). Sharing care was encouraged. Interfering unnecessarily in what the parents had agreed was discouraged. Orders could be made in favour of other family members. The duties of local authority social services were codified, bringing together the services for disabled children and the services for children who needed protection from harm or other forms of support. The aim was to work in partnership with families who needed help rather than in opposition to them. A clear distinction was drawn between the voluntary provision of help for disadvantaged families who wanted and needed it and compulsory intervention to protect children from harm. The grounds for compulsory intervention were simplified and clarified: children could be removed from home only if they suffered or were at risk of suffering significant harm as a result of their parenting *and* if removal would be in their best interests. Courts were to decide upon the allocation of parental rights and responsibilities, local authorities were to provide services and look after children.

Of course, the Act wasn't perfect. The grounds for removing children from their families had to be interpreted by the House of Lords and Supreme Court on several occasions. Better laws do not always make for better practice: children such as Victoria Climbie and 'Baby P' were killed by their families despite being well known to both health and social services. Social workers became more and more risk-averse, less inclined to try to work in partnership with families. The number of care cases rocketed, putting a major strain on the family justice system, and reducing the resources available for preventive and rehabilitative work with families. The courts became more and more reluctant to relinquish control to the local children's services authorities and the proceedings became more and more elaborate and protracted. But it was a groundbreaking piece of legislation, which has largely stood the test of time, and was the result of a groundbreaking way of working for the Law Commission.

Meanwhile, the team was busy with projects on the ground for divorce[23] and domestic violence.[24] Both had a rockier road in Parliament than the Children Act had done. Our bill on Domestic Violence and Occupation of the Family Home at first attracted little attention in the House of Commons. It was in its final stages in the run-up to the end of the parliamentary session of 1994–5 when the *Daily Mail* published a series of articles attacking it and me personally. I was by then a High Court judge, so these could be illustrated by an unflattering picture of me in a full-bottomed wig. On 23 October 1995, there was a front-page article by Paul Harris, 'Anger at Bill to "sabotage" marriage', and an article by William Oddie, 'How could MPs fail to spot this blow to marriage?'. On 27 October 1995, there was a front-page article by Steve Doughty, 'Live-in lovers bill is shelved', another article 'When a live-in lover becomes a cohabitant', an article by John Torode, 'A master of morality who found himself trying to prop up permissiveness', attacking the Lord Chancellor for having 'fallen among trendies' and the 'fashionable liberals who run the Law Commission', and a *Daily Mail* Comment on 'Marriage, the family and Tory principles'. On 1 November, there was another article by William Oddie, 'Legal commissars subverting family values', claiming, among other things that, 'the hundreds and thousands of child victims of divorce in Britain may wish that [she] had kept her views on marriage to herself'; there was another by John Torode, 'Twice-married feminist behind radical new laws', which pursued the personal attack.

Far more distressing than the personal attacks upon me was that all these articles were based on a complete misunderstanding, both of the existing law and of what the bill actually did. They thought that the existing law gave no protection to unmarried victims of domestic abuse, which was wrong. They thought that the bill gave the same property rights to the unmarried as it gave to the married, which was also wrong. The *Daily Mail* Comment claimed that 'the bill would effectively sabotage the whole institution of marriage, by giving radical new property rights to live-in lovers'. It did no such thing. And where had they got their ideas that I was opposed to marriage or indeed to family values?

It must date back to a paper that I delivered in 1979 at the world conference of the International Society on Family Law in Uppsala, Sweden, entitled 'Ends and Means – the Utility of Marriage as a Legal Institution'.[25] In this I demonstrated that marriage law had shifted from protecting the dynastic ambitions of the rich and powerful to protecting the more vulnerable members of the family, usually the wives and the children, from poverty and abuse. I asked, therefore, whether similar protection might also be needed by unmarried cohabitants and their children. It was a much less radical paper than the one contributed by Professor Eric Clive of Edinburgh University,[26] under the title 'Marriage – An Unnecessary Legal Institution?'. Much later, while I was at the Law Commission, Relate, the marriage and relationship counselling organisation, held a series of seminars on various aspects of relationships, at which I gave an updated version of my Uppsala paper. The press were present. No doubt the reports of my paper contributed to the sensational comments in the *Daily Mail*. But these did not reflect what I had actually written.

The *Daily Mail* campaign provoked enough concern in Parliament for Lord Mackay, the Lord Chancellor, who was an enthusiastic supporter of our work, to withdraw the bill. But he is not a man to be intimidated by pressures which he believes to be unwarranted. In the next session of Parliament, he reintroduced its provisions, with a few modifications, as Part IV of what became the Family Law Act 1996. It is still the law today.

Part II of the same Act was supposedly based on our recommendations for reform of the ground for divorce. Our proposal had been simple. The law required a divorce petitioner to prove that the marriage had irretrievably broken down in one of five ways. Three of these depended upon how one of the parties had behaved during the marriage, which was often seen as demeaning and unjust. Two involved long periods of separation which were difficult for many of the neediest and most vulnerable to achieve. We would have replaced this with a requirement to state on day one the belief (sole or shared) that the marriage had irretrievably broken down and, if still wanted, a second requirement to state on day 365 that it had indeed broken down. In between, there would be space and opportunity to work out the arrangements for the children, the home and the finances, so that people would know where they stood before they were actually divorced. Unfortunately, the government, while accepting the basic idea, introduced some complications into this simple scheme and even more were inserted as it went through Parliament. The *Daily Mail* returned to the attack. On 26 April 1996, an article by David Hughes was headed 'Divorce plans at mercy of Labour', alongside a huge picture of me in judicial robes, complete with full-bottomed wig, and a piece entitled 'Architect of a marriage wrecking measure' by Geoffrey Levy. He managed to persuade one of my schoolteachers, a college friend, and my second husband's first wife, Winnie, to speak on the record. He developed a picture of a loner and school swot, whose childhood was traumatised by the removal of the male figure, and impressed with 'a strong philosophy of independence bordering on feminism' by the teachers at school: not inaccurate you may feel, but he didn't mean it as a compliment. Winnie, as always, was generous and friendly.

My view at the time, and now, is that some good, well-meaning people opposed the bill because they thought that it would make divorce easier and that preserving the need to prove bad conduct or to separate for a long time somehow preserved the moral framework of marriage. We had explained in detail why this was not so, but few people would have read the full report. But there were also less well-meaning people who knew perfectly well that the bill would, if anything, make divorce harder and certainly take longer to achieve. They valued the ease with which a divorce could be obtained quickly under the present law, leaving the financial and other consequences to be worked out months, if not years, later. The irony is that the Divorce, Dissolution and Separation Act 2020 has introduced a scheme remarkably like the one which we proposed, but with a much shorter waiting period, and has attracted very little of the criticism which we faced. Never say never in law reform.

Not all our projects needed legislation to succeed. The criminal-law team and the family-law team jointly produced a working paper entitled *Rape within Marriage* in October 1990.[27] The law then was that a woman gave her consent to intercourse on marriage which was revoked only if the couple were separated by formal agreement or court order. We examined the arguments for preserving this rule in great detail and made a powerful case against it. Some criminal lawyers had been afraid that removing the immunity would endanger the institution of marriage, but the family lawyers were able to explain that it would not. As it happens, in July that year, a High Court judge had already ruled that a man could be guilty of raping his wife if she had withdrawn her consent to intercourse, whereupon the defendant pleaded guilty to attempted rape. In March 1991, the Court of Appeal dismissed his appeal, and in October 1991, the House of Lords did the same.[28] Nowhere in their learned judgments did they refer to the Law Commission's working paper, but it is difficult to believe that they had not read it. In January 1992, all our report had to do was confirm that consultation had supported that result and tidy up a few details.[29] I regard that as another win for the Law Commission.

The last big project for my team was on mental incapacity – how to make decisions on behalf of adults who are unable to make decisions for themselves. We started this in 1990, encouraged by the Law Society, by parents with mentally incapacitated adult children, by adult children with mentally incapacitated parents, and by healthcare professionals. What to do when serious or sensitive decisions had to be made, like whether to resuscitate a desperately ill patient or whether to sterilise a seriously mentally disabled young woman? Or even when there were disagreements about more mundane matters, such as whether an elderly person with dementia should go into a care home? The House of Lords had decided that no one, including the next of kin, had the legal right to make decisions on behalf of an incapacitated adult, and also that the courts had no power to do it for them.[30] All the court could do was make a declaration – a solemn pronouncement – that a proposed course of action would, or would not, be lawful. It would be lawful if it was in the best interests of the person concerned.

If lawful, it could be done, but there was no compulsion to do it. We published a series of discussion papers[31] and held extensive meetings with focus groups of healthcare professionals, families and voluntary organisations, and lawyers. The final report[32] was published in 1995, after I had left the commission, but it was very much my project and the product of the team which I had been leading.

We were anxious to retain the principle that healthcare professionals and other carers could continue to do what was necessary in the best interests of the person concerned without having to go to court or have some formal declaration of incapacity. A person was to be presumed to have capacity rather than the other way about. Capacity was decision-specific rather than global and could fluctuate from time to time. We provided a definition of when a person was unable to take a decision for himself or herself. We devised a scheme for making decisions, either in advance by the person concerned, or by carers, or by people to whom the person concerned had given a lasting power of attorney, or by a court. We emphasised that decisions had to be made in the best interests of the person concerned, but that the person's known wishes and feelings and values were an important component in deciding what would be best for him or her. All of this was meant to respect the dignity of each individual and preserve as much autonomy for them as possible. The Lord Chancellor's Department then conducted a further round of consultation and came up with proposals which were much the same as ours.[33] And in 2005, the Mental Capacity Act was passed, only ten years after the Law Commission's report. It bore a striking resemblance to the bill annexed to the report. Never say never in law reform.

My work at the commission was enriched by many contacts with the 'real' world. I was sitting for a few weeks a year as a part-time judge, increasingly hearing family cases. I was in frequent contact with family-law practitioners and academics. But I also became closely involved with other organisations. One was the National Family Conciliation Council (NFCC), as it was then called. Conciliation is not about trying to get a couple back together. It is about helping them to resolve the practical issues arising from their separation and divorce as amicably as possible without fighting in court. Services with professionally trained staff were springing up in the voluntary, not-for-profit sector. The NFCC was their umbrella body, providing professional training and accreditation, insurance, and a code of practice. In 1987, I was asked to chair their management committee. This was a challenging task, as the services struggled, not only for funding, but also to discover where they sat: were they part of the counselling and similar services for separating couples, or were they part of the growing array of alternative dispute resolution services (ADR)? Eventually, they aligned themselves with ADR and the NFCC transitioned into National Family Mediation (NFM). There was also a turf war with the solicitors' profession, who had established their own body to offer family mediation, but our aims and values were the same, even if our methods were different. Added to this, the courts were showing increasing enthusiasm for court-based procedures aimed at getting the parties to reach their own agreements rather than fighting in court. Debate raged over whether this was as effective in helping them to reach lasting agreements as were the less authoritarian 'out of court' services. All of this kept me in close touch with what was going on in the family justice system and in the lives of the people it was there to serve.

Sociolegal research in family law was also developing fast. Some of this was done in specialist academic centres, and some by non-governmental organisations. Much was funded by the Nuffield Foundation, set up in 1943 by William Morris, Lord Nuffield, who had made an enormous fortune in the motor car industry but had no offspring. Its mission was and is to advance social well-being and education through research and experiment. It has taken a special interest in access to justice for a long time. It has also taken a special interest in child protection and family law.[34] I was appointed one of the seven trustees in 1987 and served for a thoroughly enjoyable fifteen years. Once again, I don't think I was their first choice. I was invited to lunch with the trustees in the foundation's beautiful premises in Bedford Square, along with another legal luminary. Unbeknownst to me, this was an interview. At a later meeting one of the trustees inadvertently let the cat out of the bag that the other 'candidate' had turned it down. The trustees' role was to decide which projects got funding: there is no more exhilarating task than giving away someone else's money for research and practical projects in which you believe.

For example, the foundation was responsible for putting family mediation on a proper professional footing. More recently, it has funded a large research project which clearly demonstrated what was wrong with the law of divorce.[35]

In 1990, I became a founder member of another public body, the Human Fertilisation and Embryology Authority (HFEA). This was set up by the Human Fertilisation and Embryology Act 1990, following the recommendations of a committee chaired by Dame Mary Warnock, to regulate the fast-developing provision of fertility services for parents who wanted but were unable to have children in the ordinary way. The treatments covered were artificial insemination by donor and *in vitro* fertilisation, together with the storage of sperm, eggs and embryos. The HFEA licensed the clinics offering these services, which had to comply, not only with the regulations (for example, as to the length of time for which sperm, eggs and embryos could be stored and the consents needed for their storage and use) but also with the HFEA code of practice. I was asked to chair the committee which devised this. Numerous puzzling questions had to be decided at lightning speed. What was the maximum number of embryos which could be implanted in a woman at any one time? What was the maximum number of children that a sperm donor could be allowed to father? What was the maximum age for a woman to be offered treatment? How were the clinics to comply with their statutory duty to take due account of the welfare of any child who might be born as a result of the treatment? What, in particular, should be their approach to same-sex couples?

For the first time in my life, I belonged to a body which had equal numbers of men and women. This was refreshing, having spent so long in a male-dominated environment, trying to reform laws which had been devised by men. Though some of those men were very forward-looking, their views were shaped by their experience of life, just as the views of judges are shaped. Members of the HFEA came from a wide variety of disciplines – embryology, obstetrics and gynaecology, psychiatry and child psychiatry, theology and ethics, law, journalism – as well as users of both the fertility and adoption services. The actress Penelope Keith was there as an adoptive parent. Many of the issues we had to discuss involved complex scientific, moral and legal arguments. We could all agree on the need for safety: for example, sperm had to be frozen and stored for months, to allow for testing for HIV and other infections which might otherwise be passed on, and laboratories had to be properly equipped and staffed. But there was a fundamental philosophical divide. Some saw the services as treating their patients for the 'disease' of infertility. Others saw them as enabling people to have children who would not otherwise have been born. The former tended to put the interests of the patients first. If they wanted to pretend that the child had been conceived in the usual way, then they could. The latter tended to put the interests of the children first. They should have the same rights to know about their origins as adopted children had. We decided to call the service-users 'clients' rather than 'patients', which also emphasised the commercial basis upon which most clinics then operated.

There were two particularly controversial issues. First, sperm donors were conventionally paid a small sum for their donations. They were often students who found this a useful addition to their incomes. But should such payments be banned and only altruistic donations be allowed? Second, the HFEA was collecting information which would enable the link between the donor and the child to be traced. The 1990 Act placed strict limits on when this could be done. It also provided that the donor was not to be treated in law as the father of the child. Should a child resulting from donor sperm or donor egg have the same right to discover his or her identity as every other child? After a vote was forced upon the reluctant chairman, the authority voted narrowly in favour of a right to know. Eventually the law on both issues was changed. But the inevitable result has been a shortage of sperm donations. This in turn has led to more people buying sperm from abroad rather than going to licensed clinics. This is a problem faced by many regulators: the more you strive for best practice amongst the services you regulate, the more people may be tempted to go elsewhere to get what they want.

The code of practice has gone through several versions since the first which my committee produced, but the fundamental principles are still recognisable. The issues – along with new ones raised by advances in treatment – are just as live now as they were thirty years ago. It was exciting to be involved at the very beginning and to work with some remarkable people: I still treasure the 'fan letter' which Penelope Keith sent me when our draft code of practice was adopted.

Julian too led many successful projects at the Law Commission and also chaired the Lord Chancellor's conveyancing committee. Contrary to all expectations, this agreed to recommend the establishment of the new profession of licensed conveyancers. Despite this, Julian was told at the end of 1988 that 'the Lord Chancellor was not minded to renew his appointment' (what the Lord Chancellor knew about this, I do not know). Julian had told me on the way down to the Law Commission that he wanted to be an ombudsman. So he went off to become the insurance ombudsman, then a voluntary body set up by the insurance industry, but now the financial services ombudsman and a massive operation. After five years there he became pensions ombudsman, a statutory office which he found much more congenial.

The personnel officer at the insurance ombudsman's office was Daphne Vandersteen. As a bit of fun, she administered a short word-association personality test to us both. I have kept the results of mine, as an antidote to vanity. For example, under 'Self-Image', it reports that

> This person is friendly, personable, assertive, mobile and alert. He/she has a strong self-image and is often seen as verbally aggressive and unconventional ... This person is extremely competitive but will in normal circumstances work within the rules and parameters of the organisation ... This person likes the limelight and wants authority and the respect that goes with it. He/she is a self-starter who can turn an idea into a practicality ... Socially aggressive in every respect, a good leader, promoter and enthuser. This person has lots of energy and can be somewhat impatient with less energetic people ... A good communicator with natural leadership abilities. This person needs to be careful that his/her tendency towards verbal aggression does not offend others, particularly superiors.

Only others can judge how accurate this was. I do remember Miss Thornton saying that I could sometimes appear 'pert', but 'verbally aggressive'? I remember more occasions when I should have spoken out and did not than the other way about.

All in all, the Law Commission years were some of the happiest and most fulfilling of my career. When asked about my proudest achievement, I am torn between the Children Act 1989 and one or two of my decisions in the highest court in the land. Bit by bit, my centre of gravity moved from Manchester to London. My daughter Julia decided that she wanted to go to a London secondary school. We entered her for four of them and it suddenly occurred to me that we were not in charge: it would be up to her whether she tried to pass the exams and interview well. She was firmly of the view that it was her right to choose which school she went to. And she did. The Law Commission years also led to great happiness in my private life, as Professor Farrand and I did eventually run away together and we were married on New Year's Eve, 1992.

8 Onto the Bench

It was late 1993 and I was approaching the end of my term at the Law Commission with nowhere else to go. I had been there for more than nine years. My original five-year term had been extended three times and was due to run out at the end of the year. It would not be extended again. I had burnt my boats with the University of Manchester. They had kindly promoted me to professor during my five years' leave of absence, but they could not extend my leave forever. When it expired, King's College London had appointed me a professor and given me a year's leave of absence. But when I accepted another extension at the Law Commission, I had to resign without ever taking it up. My best move, I thought, would be to try to combine some practice at the Bar with some academic work. So I approached three of the leading family-law sets of chambers in London and 1 KBW (King's Bench Walk) took me on. Perhaps James Townend QC, head of chambers, or David Dear, their senior clerk, had sources of information that I did not?

When I was first appointed to the Law Commission, there had been some loose talk at the Manchester Bar of my going on the High Court bench – loose, because it was usual for the QC commissioners to be appointed to the High Court but not for the academics. I had been sitting as a judge for nine years, first as an assistant recorder, then as a recorder, and latterly as a deputy High Court judge. The imposter syndrome I had suffered when I first started had long gone, especially in civil and family cases. I really did want to become a High Court judge. But most part-time judges are never approached to join the High Court. One of the Lord Chancellor's top officials had sounded me out about becoming a circuit judge, but I had told him (politely I hope) that I was not interested. Academics have, or should have, a deep understanding of the law and legal principles, together with the capacity to think about how they might be developed to meet changing social circumstances. The law is made in the High Court and above. Circuit judges do from time to time have to decide points of law, but their decisions are not authoritative. Their main task is to try cases, often very serious and complicated cases, to direct juries in criminal cases or in civil and family cases to find the facts for themselves. It is on the circuit bench, particularly in the Crown Court, that long experience in court may be most helpful (although it also has its dangers). Curiously, however, while several academics had been appointed to the circuit bench, none had been appointed to the High Court. Many High Court judges had experience of teaching law early in their careers, some had even been full-time academics, but all had then concentrated on developing a quality practice at the Bar. Cynics might suggest that those in a position to influence appointments, almost all of whom either were or had been elite barristers themselves, were interested in preserving the High Court appointments for their own kind: why otherwise only appoint academics to the circuit bench? Be that as it may, I had also burnt my boats as a potential circuit judge and maybe anything else.

The Lord Chancellor's Department did take an interest in the future of Law Commissioners, because it would not look good if they had nowhere else to go, but it did not undertake to find anywhere for us. One Friday morning in November 1993, I was due to see Robin Holmes, a senior official in the Lord Chancellor's Department, to discuss what I might do next. I was also due to see the Lord Chancellor, Lord Mackay, in the afternoon. I told myself that this would be to discuss the Ground for Divorce project, which his department was then actively taking forward. So I went along to Southside, the office block beside and on top of the House of Fraser store on Victoria Street, and spent an hour discussing my plans with Robin Holmes. He did so with a completely straight face, endorsing my strategy as the right plan. After our meeting, I ambled slowly along Victoria Street and went into St Margaret's Church for a touch of quiet contemplation, before turning up at the pass office through which visitors have to go to enter the House of Lords. My name was not on the list of those due to see the Lord Chancellor that afternoon. Then the officer exclaimed 'Oh, there's someone coming about a judicial appointment!' and let me through. So that is how I found out that the Lord Chancellor was going to offer me appointment to the High Court bench.

A wise old bird indeed, Lord Mackay warned me to take care in the early days. He meant not to frighten the horses. He knew that he was taking something of a risk with me. But he was not afraid to take risks. That year, he had also appointed the very first solicitor to the High Court, Michael Sachs. The year before, he had appointed Stephen Sedley QC, a notable left-wing lawyer, and John Laws, of a rather different persuasion, both of them extraordinarily able constitutional and administrative lawyers, thinkers and writers, thereby showing a fine sense of balance and the value of diversity of thought on the High Court bench.

I learned later that the decision had been taken many weeks before but of course I was the last to know. Returning home that Friday afternoon, my euphoria was seriously deflated: a large part of the plaster ceiling in the first-floor drawing room of our Islington house had collapsed, covering the whole place with a ghastly grey dust. Julian was away for the weekend, training to be an arbitrator, so I spent the whole weekend trying to clear it up. That put me firmly in my place.

Summoned for a secret meeting with the president of the Family Division, Sir Stephen Brown, before my appointment was announced, I was asked what I wanted to be called as a High Court judge. It struck me that this was a golden opportunity to revert to my maiden name of Hale. I thought that this would be welcomed both by my former husband, John Hoggett QC, and by my present husband, Julian Farrand. But this was not what the president meant. Mary Arden, the first woman in the Chancery Division of the High Court, was campaigning not to have to call herself '*Mrs* Justice Arden', because Arden is her maiden name. But the president was pleased – if the name got out, no one would know who the new Mrs Justice Hale was.

So on 12 January 1994, I was sworn in by the Lord Chancellor as Mrs Justice Hale. I had been a member of 1 KBW for all of eleven days. This arrangement has been to our mutual benefit ever since: we have both taken great pleasure and pride in the connection without my ever having held a brief from there (though I do have some concrete evidence that there were people who would have liked to brief me). Next day came the meeting of all the High Court judges, chaired by the Lord Chief Justice, Lord Taylor, in his court at the Royal Courts of Justice. This is the headmaster's pep talk. There were six women present among around one hundred men. We were invisible in our dark suits. Mary Arden brought up her proposal that the women should no longer have to call themselves 'Mrs Justice'. She was supported by Mrs Justice Bracewell and Mrs Justice Hale, both married women using their maiden names professionally. But what was the alternative? Did we all have to call ourselves the same? 'Miss' or 'Mrs'? 'Ms' was unthinkable. (Many people then associated it, wrongly, with an aggressive form of feminism.) It was incorrect to use 'Dame' with our surnames. How about all of us, men and women, becoming simple 'Justice'? Oh no: as one judge solemnly declared: 'I was sworn in as Mr Justice X, I was introduced to my sovereign as Mr Justice X and Mr Justice X I shall always be.' So the men voted on what the women should be called and opted for the status quo. Twenty years later, on 13 January 2014, Alison Russell QC was sworn in as Ms Justice Russell without (much of) a murmur.

It is quite a performance, becoming a High Court judge. The appointment itself is made by letters patent under the great seal: a magnificently inscribed and illustrated document on parchment, to which is affixed a large circle of sealing wax impressed with the image of the monarch's seal. Along with it comes a typewritten writ of attendance at Parliament. This commands the recipient (waiving all excuses) to be 'personally present with Us and the with the rest of Our Council to treat and give your advice upon' 'certain arduous and urgent affairs concerning Us the state and defence of Our United Kingdom and the Church'. The accompanying note, however, explains that 'no action is to be taken on receipt of the Writ. The need for the judges to attend Parliament to give their advice disappeared with the creation of the Lords of Appeal in Ordinary in 1876'. Why, more than a century later, we were still getting the writ is a mystery.

The top judges and a random selection of High Court and Court of Appeal judges are, however, expected to attend the State Opening of Parliament at the beginning of each parliamentary session. They sit, arrayed in all their finery, on the woolsack immediately in front of the throne. As luck would have it, my name came up for the State

Opening in 1997, shortly after the Labour victory in the general election. There was a noticeable ripple of excitement on the woolsack when Her Majesty announced that Her Government would bring forward a bill to turn the rights protected by the European Convention on Human Rights into rights protected by UK law. We did not yet know how that would be done, but we did know that it would bring a whole new dimension to the relationship between the individual citizen and the state, a dimension which would bring new responsibilities to the judiciary.

There were five sets of robes to go with the office. Most magnificent were the full ceremonial robes: a red woollen dressing gown edged in ermine; an ermine cape; a large academic style hood also in ermine; all worn with a lace jabot and bands in front, a black rosette at the back, black slip-on shoes with gold buckles, white gloves, and a 'black cap' – the square of black silk placed on top of the judicial wig when passing sentence of death. This last is another anachronism as the death penalty has not been imposed since 1964 and was finally abolished in 1997. The whole, of course, topped off by a full-bottomed wig. The practice then was for each judge to be given a grant with which to buy the robes, usually from one's predecessor. So it was that I acquired my robes from Dame Margaret Booth, who had acquired them from Dame Elizabeth Lane, the very first woman High Court judge. When I went to the Court of Appeal, they were passed on to Dame Jill Black. The robe-makers had saved the best of the Russian ermine for Dame Elizabeth and they are magnificent. They have also had four careful lady owners. It is fitting that they should now be in the gallery of judicial costume in the Royal Courts of Justice. With the robes, Dame Margaret was also kind enough to give me the full-bottomed wig which had belonged to Joseph Jackson QC, her first husband and doyen of the Family Law Bar for many years. I hope that I absorbed a little of his wisdom through it. The red robe, without the hood and mantle, is worn for criminal trials in winter. There was a red woollen robe faced with pink silk (they didn't match), worn for criminal trials during the summer. There was also a summer and a winter version of the robes worn in civil cases, black with ermine facing for winter, and navy blue with turquoise silk facing for summer. Finally, there were the usual QC's robes – a black silk gown, 'court' jacket, collar and bands – which were worn in the Family Division when we sat in open court and in the Civil Division of the Court of Appeal. If we sat in robes in court, however, we did not wear a full-bottomed wig, but a short 'bench' wig, rather like a barrister's but with tighter curls.

I have never made any secret of my dislike of wigs. The story (possibly apocryphal) goes that most gentlemen gave up the habit of wearing wigs early in the nineteenth century. Only the clergy, the barristers and the judges continued to do so. Then there was a heatwave and everyone gave them up. When the heatwave passed, the clergy did not go back to their wigs, but the judges and the barristers did. They have proved remarkably difficult to shake off ever since. They are firmly fixed in the public image of a criminal trial. Such evidence as there is suggests that, not only the public, but also the defendants, see them as a symbol of a 'proper' trial. Many barristers practising in the Crown Court would feel naked without one. So much so that solicitors appearing in the Crown Court also wanted to wear wigs, because otherwise they might be seen by judge and jury alike as second-class advocates. Wig-wearers also think that they bring some anonymity, which is a protection for judges and advocates in very serious cases. I am sceptical about this. The only judge in this country who has been murdered by a disgruntled defendant always sat in the Crown Court wigged and gowned. A determined and vengeful person has ways of finding his victim out. The people who have most to fear are the magistrates. They are the first to take away a defendant's liberty; they are members of the local community; and they never sit in robes. In civil cases, there has never been much of a case for wearing wigs and they have now been abandoned: unfortunately, the new civil robes which came with the change are scarcely dignified, flattering or attractive, although they may be more comfortable. The problem with wigs is not only that they are anachronistic, insanitary and uncomfortable: they are also men's wigs, thus denying the female barristers and judges the right to assert their gender. Extraordinarily, when the first women were called to the Bar in 1922, it was decided that they should wear men's wigs but with skirts. We were not allowed to wear trousers until the 1990s.

Apart from at swearing-in and the State Opening of Parliament, the only time that High Court judges get into their full ceremonial dress is for church services. As near as possible to 1 October every year, the judiciary of England and Wales process into Westminster Abbey, in order of seniority, to ask for God's blessing on their endeavours. The Lord Chancellor and the Lord Chief Justice read the lessons. The sermon is usually given by someone with a connection to the law. The choir sings beautifully and the congregation sings lustily, especially when we get to the second verse of the national anthem: 'May she defend our laws, and ever give us cause, to sing with heart and voice [ouch], "God Save the Queen".' After the service, we process out, again in order of seniority, bowing to thank the dean for his hospitality, and cross the road into Westminster Hall for the 'Lord Chancellor's Breakfast'. It is a great spectacle but it does produce the press photos of a collection of judges in their full-bottomed wigs which the media like to trot out when writing about them – thus contributing to the picture of the judiciary as old-fashioned, out-of-touch, old men. Other places hold legal services too – and none more splendid than the one in York Minster, where we process from the old Assembly Rooms preceded by the pikemen, to be greeted by a fanfare from the police trumpeters as we enter the minster.

Readers will notice how much about judicial life is ruled by seniority. We process in order of seniority. We choose rooms in the Royal Courts of Justice and in judges' lodgings in order of seniority. Cases are listed in the daily cause lists in order of the judges' seniority. Even flu jabs are timetabled in order of seniority. I have been told that this is a very male thing. There has to be a pecking order and knowing one's place in that pecking order is more important than where that place is.

Along with the robes comes a title. It was, and still is, automatic for the men to become knights bachelor and the women to become dames of the British Empire. Most such honours are conferred at large investitures to which the recipients can bring guests. The new judges, however, had the privilege of an individual audience with Her Majesty. I was nearly late for mine. My clerk, a retired police officer, drove me to the palace, but we got caught up amongst the changing of the guard. He was told by the policemen at the gate to drive as close to the palace as he could get and then just keep on going. Sure enough, without breaking step, the guardsmen seamlessly avoided us and we made it into the inner courtyard just in time. Her Majesty presented me with the insignia of a DBE – 'What a pretty prefect's badge!' exclaimed my daughter Julia when she saw it – and we sat down in her private drawing room for a fifteen-minute chat. I must not say what it was about, but Her Majesty was charm itself: I look back on that meeting as one of the greatest bonuses in my unexpected life. Being a dame, on the other hand, is not such a bonus. People seem to know how to address a knight of the realm, as Sir John or Sir Henry or whatever, but they don't know that a dame should be addressed as Dame Brenda rather than Dame Hale. Dame is hardly ever on the menu of possible titles on any website. Nor are people particularly impressed by it, while knighthoods seem capable of attracting favours in certain quarters. I am not sure which I disapprove of more – the sexism or the favours.

The High Court sits in the Royal Courts of Justice in the Strand. The Family Division sits in two buildings: the Victorian Gothic West Green building with high ceilings, carved wooden furniture and pan-elling, and a judge's bench 'halfway up the wall'; and the Queen's building, built in the 1950s. I sat in the Queen's building and it is hard to imagine courtrooms less suitable to hearing intimate details of unhappy family lives – large, with the judge well-distanced from everyone else, and with furniture and panelling in plain dark wood. Very gloomy.

High Court judges in the Queen's Bench and Family Divisions also go out of London 'on circuit' regularly. This dates back to the reign of Henry II when His Majesty's judges toured the country in an effort to make sure that the same laws were being applied everywhere (this is one meaning of the 'common' law). In the Family Division, each of us would spend three weeks, a quarter of the term, sitting in some major provincial centre, hearing the High Court cases listed there. We would also be on 'firefighting' duty for another three weeks, ready to go out of town to hear a particular case which needed us. I had some memorable times on firefighting duty in Oxford (a case about a baby's head injuries), in Lincoln (a case about a toddler's multiple fractures), and in Hereford (a case about fabricating a baby's illnesses). Lincoln was especially memorable. The court sat in the castle and the judges' lodgings were just outside the castle gates so I could walk to court. The case was a real whodunnit: the child had suffered several fractures at different times and all natural explanations had been ruled out. But had they been caused by the mother, the mother's present boyfriend, or her previous boyfriend, the child's father? The large courtroom was crowded: there were counsel for the local authority bringing the case, leading and junior counsel for the mother, the boyfriend and the father, and for the child. Most unusually, counsel for the local authority opened the case by saying that he knew that I would have read the papers, so he was not going to tell me what the case was about, as is normal practice, and proceeded to call his first witness. Having heard all the evidence, I decided that it showed that the boyfriend had done it. Also unusually, I was later proved right: the local authority took the risk of returning the child to the mother, who undoubtedly loved him dearly but was still living with the boyfriend. The child suffered two more fractures and her children had to be permanently removed. It is important to hear these cases as close as possible to the community where the events took place, quite apart from the benefits to the judges of getting away from the hot house in the Strand.

For my regular stint I tried to go to Leeds or Newcastle: our cottage in Richmond was roughly halfway between them. We were expected to stay in judges' lodgings (even if we had a home nearby). I was thought to be letting the side down by commuting daily to Oxford and saving the enormous cost of opening up the Oxford lodgings just for me. These lodgings were and are small country houses or large suburban villas, able to accommodate between two and five judges and their clerks (socially segregated of course). They were run, I was told, like an upper-middle-class household between the two world wars (not that I really knew what that meant). There would be a butler, a housekeeper and a chef, as well as domestic staff. The judges would eat breakfast, lunch and dinner there. The style was set by the senior judge, but it was standard practice to dress for dinner: smoking jackets for the men on the days when we were not entertaining and black tie and dinner jackets when we were. The junior judge would say grace. I remember puzzling even the classical scholars amongst my fellow judges by reciting the Girton grace, which uses the feminine forms of adjectives and nouns in place of the familiar masculine. It was a real luxury to be in lodgings on one's own, as I was in Lincoln.

It was, and is, expected that the High Sheriff of the county will entertain the judges to dinner and that the judges will reciprocate. This kept us particularly busy in Newcastle, where there were the High Sheriffs of Northumberland, Tyne and Wear, and Durham. High Sheriffs hold office for a year. They used to be involved in enforcing court orders, but that is now done by others. They now do lots of good work supporting local public and voluntary organisations, usually connected with the police, the prisons and the justice system generally, as well as looking after the visiting judges. They are selected from names put forward by the present High Sheriff to serve in five years' time. This means that they come from a particular social circle, but this does vary from place to place. In Tyne and Wear, for example, they tended to be doctors, university teachers or other professionals. In Northumberland, they were landed aristocracy: one could meet the duke and duchess of Northumberland at dinner (before the duchess became famous for the Alnwick Garden and Alnwick Castle became famous as Hogwarts School for wizards). In Durham, they tended to be the descendants of the magnates who had made big money in shipbuilding, mining, industry or brewing.

These dinner parties were usually very entertaining and we met some interesting people. But there was a problem. The rule book had been written in the days when there were no women on the High Court bench and for that echelon of society in which it was customary for the ladies to withdraw at the end of the meal, leaving the men to gossip and smoke over their port and brandy. No doubt that was still the custom for many, if not most, High Sheriffs and they had surely been told that the judges expected it. But what about the women judges? Were we to be treated as women or as judges? The answer was that we were women first and judges second. I should have made a fuss right at the beginning, but was reluctant to frighten the horses. So I went along with it, politely I hope, but sulkily certainly. There was one terrible evening in the Birmingham lodgings when the men were kept in the dining room for an hour before joining us. This was hugely embarrassing, as I had invited a male university professor as my guest and of course we wanted to talk.

However, I rebelled one evening in the Newcastle lodgings when we were entertaining not just the High Sheriff and his wife, but also the young woman barrister who was 'junior' of the North-Eastern Circuit, an important role in circuit life. I was affronted that she should be expected to leave. So I sat tight when the meal ended. Eventually the senior judge, Sir Michael Morland, whispered to me that the High Sheriff's wife would like to leave, so I said that of course she could, but I told the junior that she and I were staying put. We both stayed until the men decided to 'join the ladies' soon afterwards. After that, High Sheriffs tended to ask what I would like when inviting me to dinner. The senior judges were also becoming more relaxed, either not insisting or joining the ladies after only a minute or two.

But the story has a small sting in the tail. Many years later, after giving a talk about my life and times in Richmond, I was greeted by a woman who had brought her young daughter to hear me: she had been the junior that evening. She explained what a difficult position she had found herself in – here was I telling her not to leave but perhaps she risked offending the male judges in the room before whom she might have to appear. I cannot believe that she did offend them – they were more fair-minded than that (although not all their guests were). Sir Michael was always very kind to me – when I went to the Court of Appeal, he wrote that he would 'miss the opportunity of enjoying your sparkling and mischievous personality in lodgings'. We both knew what he meant.

There are many happier memories of circuit life. One of my proudest possessions was presented by the lord mayor of Newcastle upon Tyne on 21 March 1996. It is a silver sixpence dated 1578 from the reign of Queen Elizabeth I. In the olden days, when Her Majesty's judges finished their sitting in Newcastle, the lord mayor would attend upon them at their lodgings and deliver the following address: 'My Lords, we have to congratulate you upon having completed your labours in this ancient town, and have also to inform you that you travel hence to Carlisle, through a border county much and often infested by the Scots; we therefore present each of Your Lordships with a piece of money to buy therewith a dagger to defend yourselves.'

This was 'dagger money' and a modern lord mayor had generously revived the custom, even though we no longer travelled from Newcastle to Carlisle and the Scots were no longer the danger they once had been.

The other great benefit of going on circuit was that, if the list of family cases collapsed, I could do some civil cases to fill the gaps. These were usually procedural appeals from district judges, who cannot have relished having their decisions overturned by a Family Division judge, but sometimes there were proper trials. The variety made a welcome change from the otherwise endless diet of family cases, which can be extremely wearing, and also prepared me for the variety of work which I would later find in the Court of Appeal.

Quite rightly, High Court judges are asked to do things which part-timers are rarely if ever asked to do. Whole days are spent doing 'applications' – urgent matters which often have to be decided without the benefit of hearing the other side of the story. There are even some practitioners who will try out such applications on a newly appointed judge in the hope that she or he will be more receptive than an older hand would be. Very soon after my appointment, I was confronted by an application for what was then called an 'Anton Piller' order:[1] basically, an order allowing one party to a case to organise a private search of the other party's premises. This was a jealous husband who was obsessed with the completely unfounded idea that his wife (from whom he was separated) was having an affair and wanted an order to search her home. I had to retire to do some quick research and gather my thoughts: this always involved doing my best to work out what the other side would say if they were there. I refused the order.

But what did the work of a Family Division judge usually involve?

9 Family Life in the Family Division

The Family Division of the High Court was created in 1970 and deals with all the High Court cases having anything to do with family law. In practice, most of the cases are about children or the financial settlements in 'big money' divorce cases and many of them have an international element. When I was there, the judges tended to specialise in either money or children, but I tried to do as much of both as possible. Even so, most of my case load consisted of international child abduction, serious physical or sexual abuse of children, and intractable disputes between parents over contact with their children. Looking back when I left the division, it seemed to me that I had spent most of my time oppressing women, specifically mothers: sending them back around the world to the country from which they had escaped, bringing their children with them without permission; or taking their children away from them and into the care of the local authority, often to be adopted later; or making them encourage and facilitate their reluctant children's visits to their fathers.[1] Justified oppression, maybe, but oppression certainly.

Most child abduction cases are brought under the Hague Convention on the Civil Aspects of International Child Abduction of 1980, implemented in UK law by the Child Abduction and Custody Act 1985. The object of the Convention was to get a child, who had been wrongfully removed from his home country, back there as quickly as possible, without a long-drawn-out inquiry into whether this was in his best interests. When the Convention was drafted, the typical case was thought to involve the parent with whom the child was not living, usually the father, spiriting the child away (there was much talk of the 'school gates') or refusing to return the child after a visit. It works very well in cases like that. But by the 1990s, most cases involved the mother, the child's primary carer, leaving the family home with the child but without permission, sometimes against a background of domestic abuse, and often coming back to her 'own' country. The pursuing father did not usually want to look after the child himself – he wanted to preserve his right to see the child (and sometimes, it has to be said, his power to dominate and control the mother). The Convention draws a clear distinction between 'rights of custody' – the right to decide where the child shall live – and 'rights of access'. Breaching the former involves an immediate, few-questions-asked return; breaching the latter does not. But in many Hague Convention countries, both parents have the right to veto foreign travel and this is now recognised as a 'right of custody'. The distinction between custody and access has virtually disappeared.

The abducting parent has very few grounds for resisting return: the consent or acquiescence of the 'left-behind parent'; a 'grave risk' that the child's return would expose him or her to 'physical or psychological harm or otherwise place the child in an intolerable situation'; or the child's objections to return. The English courts prided themselves on their strict approach to these grounds. They insisted on a risk of 'grave' harm to the child and did not at first recognise that one parent abusing another parent could be harmful to the child. They distinguished between a child's 'objections' to return and a mere desire to stay here. They devised ways of softening the blow of return, extracting undertakings from the 'left-behind' parent about what would happen when the children came back with the abducting parent; but these undertakings were not recognised or understood in many other countries. They were reluctant to hear oral evidence (video hearings were then in their infancy and Zoom was unknown) because the whole point was to avoid the left-behind parent having to come all the way here. The abducting parent was usually at a serious disadvantage in court. The left-behind parent was given automatic legal aid without a means test and the services of expert solicitors and barristers instructed by the Child Abduction Unit. The abducting parent had only non-automatic means-tested legal aid and often went to a high-street solicitor with little experience of this specialised work.

Because the issue was not what would be best for the child, most of our attention was focused on whether one of the limited exceptions to return applied. Most difficult were the cases where the mother had fled domestic abuse, and return would probably not be in the child's best interests, but would it lead to a grave risk of harm? The most striking example was a case I heard in the Court of Appeal in December 2000. There were three children from New Zealand, aged nearly fifteen, thirteen and nearly ten. Their parents had separated in 1990. The oldest, K, had not seen her father for ten years and adamantly refused to see him. Her priority was to stay with her mother, preferably in England. The middle child, A, loved both his parents and wanted to retain a relationship with them both. He too wanted to live with his mother, but had said that he wanted to go back to New Zealand. The youngest, KI, had had very little contact with his father since leaving the father's home when he was six weeks old. He did not really know who his father was. Their mother had remarried and they had a half-brother aged six. The mother brought all four children to England in March 2000 without telling the father, or her second husband, and therefore in breach of their rights of custody. The first husband brought proceedings under the Hague Convention. She claimed that there was a 'grave risk' that the children would suffer 'physical or psychological harm or otherwise be placed in an intolerable situation' if returned. The reason for this was that her second husband was guilty of very serious domestic violence towards her and towards the children. The children had suffered much as a result. She feared that he would come after her and punish her for leaving him and that the New Zealand authorities would not be able to protect her, because he was devious and manipulative and, as an ex-policeman, would be able to circumvent any court orders. All this was having a serious effect upon her mental health. The children were all extremely distressed, K and KI at the prospect of returning to New Zealand, A because he was torn between his feelings for his father and his mother and his fear of her second husband.

In the Family Division, the trial judge accepted that the 'grave risk' exception was made out and refused to order return. By a majority of two to one, the Court of Appeal allowed the father's appeal and ordered the children's return. I was the one. I did not think that we should interfere with the very careful judgment of an experienced Family Division judge. The risks to the children stemmed from a combination of serious psychological and economic pressures. A protection order, even supposing it to be readily available, would not solve all of their problems. The majority held that the mother would be sufficiently protected from her second husband by the New Zealand authorities, so she had no good reason not to return.[2]

The mother did not obey the order and there was a second Court of Appeal hearing, before a different panel, in which she argued that fresh evidence about her mental health and the children's views meant that the first order should be overturned. That court held that the circumstances were not sufficiently exceptional for them to do that. Temporary arrangements could be made for the children in New Zealand if the mother refused to return with them.[3] The mother still did not obey the order. Eventually, the High Court tipstaff was ordered to arrange for the children to be collected by the police and taken to the airport. The children barricaded themselves in the bathroom saying that they had a knife. The officers had to give up.

It was cases like that which had made me comment in 1999 that 'it sometimes looks as though we are punishing the mother for her clandestine behaviour rather than saving her children from the evils of abduction'. There has since been a greater recognition, both of the importance of listening carefully to the children's views, and of the harmful effect of domestic violence upon the children who witness or suffer it, but the problem of what to do about mothers who flee with their children because of domestic abuse remains insoluble. There was such concern about this that some countries threatened to withdraw from the Convention. Then there was talk of amending it. Instead, the Hague Conference on Private International Law, which had produced the Convention, set up a working group to advise on a guide to good practice in applying the 'grave risk of physical or psychological harm' exception. I was for a time the UK representative. It was not a happy experience. There was a deep divide between two camps: those who wanted some explicit recognition of the harm that can be done to children by experiencing violence and abuse towards their parent, as well as the damage to parenting capacity that fear of abuse can cause; and those who were afraid that any relaxation of the strict approach to return would cause irreparable harm to the objectives of the Convention. The resulting guide owes more to the second than to the first camp.

Child abduction cases took up a lot of court time because there were usually several orders to be made before the case came on for hearing – trying to extract information so that the child could be located and making sure that the child stayed where he or she was until the hearing. But the hearings themselves were usually quite short because the issues were so limited. Perhaps because these cases are so difficult for the abducting parent to win, they have generated a lot of appeals raising clever legal points. But once they are over and the return ordered (or not), that is usually that, unless the child adamantly refuses to go.

Child abuse cases were different. Those that came to the High Court were often a genuine 'whodunnit' or 'who-done-what'. There was complex and conflicting scientific and medical evidence which could take many days to hear. What was the cause of head injuries to a very young baby – a fall, a bang on the head or severe shaking? What was the cause of multiple fractures suffered by a toddler – brittle bones, another rare disease, or repeated assaults? Why was a child being presented to so many different hospitals with so many different complaints – were these real or was the mother either inventing them or even causing them herself? Why was a child behaving in a sexualised way long before this would be normal? Why was a child persistently running away?

I tried many such cases but one stands out in my memory. The father was a doctor qualified in Pakistan who had come to the UK to study for membership of the Royal College of Physicians. His wife held a Master's degree in Pakistan. They were both devout Muslims. When they came to this country, it was decided that the wife would go into full purdah while they were here: this meant that she wore not only a long black loose-fitting garment and an Islamic headscarf, but also a veil which covered her nose and mouth, and a further net veil which covered her whole head and upper torso. They had three children, one of them a young baby boy. He had suffered serious head injuries. The medical profession left no stone unturned in the search for possible natural causes for the injuries. They found none. But the parents denied that either of them had injured the child.

Parents can be compelled to give evidence in care proceedings. I was clear that the mother would have to give evidence and that to do so she would have to take off her veil so that I could see her face. But how could this be done, consistently with her religious beliefs? Fortunately, it was not difficult. In those days care proceedings were routinely held in private with only the parties and their lawyers present. The judge was a woman. Counsel for the local authority bringing the case was a woman. The child's guardian, an independent social worker appointed to protect the interests of the child, was a woman and so was her counsel. The only men involved in the case, apart from the father, were the QC and his junior who were representing the parents. It was agreed that a screen would be put up so that they could not see the mother while she was giving evidence. It must have been a very strange experience for them. But for me it made all the difference to be able to see the mother's face. She lit up when she talked about her children and it was obvious how much she loved them. She was straight-faced as she recited the parents' account of the events leading up to the discovery of the baby's injuries. There is much debate about how much one can tell from the 'demeanour' of a witness when giving evidence. Good liars can often be good witnesses. Truthful people can often appear to be bad witnesses. But in this particular case I had little doubt when the mother was telling me the truth and when she was not. I found that the baby had been harmed by one or other of his parents. I did not have to decide which of them had done it.

This was and is one of the most difficult aspects of these cases. If a child has been sexually abused, it is usually not too difficult to work out who has done it. But with physical injuries it is different. Either or both of the parents (or parent-figures) might have done it. The child must still be protected and it is not necessary to decide who did it in order to make an order removing the child from the family. But it is important to decide if one can: the consequences of not doing so are terrible. If the couple stay together, the child cannot be safely returned. If they separate, it may still not be safe to return the child. Not only that, and especially if an abused child has died, it may not be safe to let the mother keep a later child by a new partner.

Social workers have a hard time. They are often criticised for failing to spot obvious signs of child abuse or for failing to take action when they do. Yet, as the Cleveland child abuse crisis of 1988 showed, they may sometimes be too ready to remove children from home. And should we really be removing children from home because of the risk that they will suffer emotional or developmental harm at some time in the future? We ought not to expect ideal parenting, merely 'good enough', but how do we tell what will be good enough? Generally speaking, social workers are more likely to be criticised for doing nothing than doing something. This has led to a culture in which they are risk-averse and the number of cases brought to court has rocketed.

My view, then and now, is that it is for the social workers to bring the cases before the courts and it is for the judges to decide what the risks are and whether they should be taken. We are there to protect the child but we are also there to protect the family from the well-meaning but overmighty state. Both the Universal Declaration of Human Rights of 1948 and the International Covenant on Civil and Political Rights of 1966 assert that '[t]he family is the natural and fundamental group unit of society and is entitled to protection by society and the State'.[4] This is taken up by the Preamble to the United Nations Convention on the Rights of the Child of 1991: '[T]he family, as the fundamental group of society and the natural environment for the growth and well-being of all its members and particularly children, should be afforded the necessary protection and assistance so that it can fully assume its responsibilities within the community.' Many of the Convention's articles reflect this proposition. As the Supreme Court has pointed out:

> There is an inextricable link between the protection of the family and the protection of fundamental freedoms in liberal democracies ... Individual differences are the product of the interplay between the individual person and his upbringing and environment. Different upbringings produce different people. The first thing that a totalitarian regime tries to do is to get at the children, to distance them from the subversive, varied influences of their families, and indoctrinate them in their rulers' view of the world. Within limits, families must be left to bring up their children in their own way.[5]

In our law, that limit is reached if the child is suffering or is likely to suffer significant harm as a result of a lack of reasonable parental care.[6] But even if this is shown, the court cannot make an order allowing or requiring the state to intervene unless this will be in the best interests of the child.[7] There are judgments to be made about what has happened or is likely to happen. There are also judgments to be made about what will be best for the child. Those judgments now have to be made against the need to protect the family from unjustified state interference.[8]

Some of the hardest cases are those where the child has been physically or sexually abused by the mother's partner and the mother has failed to protect the child. Sometimes, there can be little sympathy: the mother has chosen to cover up for a dangerous partner. But at other times, her inability to protect her children stems from her own vulnerability or the abuse she has suffered. Whatever the reason, the child has to come first. But the mother who suspects that her child is being abused is in a difficult situation. If she does nothing, and the truth comes out, she may be accused of failure to protect. If she does tell social services, she will probably be advised to exclude or leave her partner and deny all contact. But if he then applies to the courts and her suspicions cannot be proved, she is in an even worse position. She may be regarded as a wicked woman who has made it all up to get rid of him (and there are indeed such wicked women). If she persists or runs away, she may lose the child, either to social services or to the person she has accused. If she stays put, she will be expected to facilitate the relationship between them.

Contact disputes were the third type of children's case to come our way.[9] It is taken for granted[10] that it is in every child's best interests to develop a meaningful relationship with both parents unless this would be harmful to the child. Most of these cases are dealt with in the county or magistrates' courts (now the family court). They might come to the High Court, either because there were difficult factual issues, such as allegations of physical or sexual abuse, or because of what was known as 'implacable hostility': where the mother (it was usually but not invariably the mother) had shown herself so adamantly opposed to contact between the children and their father that she would refuse to comply with the court's orders. The lower courts seemed to think that we had magic powers which they did not. We did not. Enforcing contact orders is difficult for any court. Sending the mother to prison, or fining her, is not going to help the child. Changing the child's residence from mother to father is the 'nuclear option', but it is not always practicable.

The most troubling contact case I encountered involved the ten-year-old daughter of a married couple who had separated because the father (whom I shall refer to as 'she') was changing sex. She was living as a woman for the two years required before undergoing surgery. She appeared in court elegantly dressed each day. The feelings of all were complicated. The father was desperate for her transition to be validated by the court and accepted both by the mother and by the child. Indeed, she may well have hoped to assume a maternal role in due course and this fear may have added to the mother's anxieties. She wanted a generous level of contact. The mother was devastated by the father's wish to become a woman. She was angry, bitter and afraid. She believed that it would be damaging for the child to see her father dressed as a woman and even more damaging once the father became a woman. The child was saying that she did not want to see her father 'who was changing into a woman before her eyes'. Proceedings in the High Court merely served to heighten the emotions of all concerned. There was a contact order in place but contact was not happening. I was persuaded (by counsel for the Official Solicitor, who was representing the child) to attach a 'penal notice' to the order, warning the mother that failure to observe it was a contempt of court which could lead to a prison sentence. This cannot have been helpful. Fortunately, when the case came on for trial before another judge, she opened the proceedings by announcing that she had no intention of sending anyone to prison. Her aim was to reach some form of compromise which would mean that the child did not form an unhealthy view of her father and regard her as a danger – she had to have some contact, however minimal. A cautious approach was essential, lest any possibility of a future relationship was destroyed. Her order involved the mother having several meetings with the father's gender-identity consultant, so that she could understand the father's course of treatment and be in a better position to explain things to their daughter, coupled with one or two sessions of supervised contact which could be extended if they were successful. Neither of us knows what happened next.

The case troubled me for two reasons. There was no doubt that this child did not want to see her father, understandably enough, even though there were good reasons why she should. How far should we go in forcing a mother to persuade or even force a child? And selfishly, why had I allowed myself to be persuaded into putting a penal notice on the order, a threat to send the mother to prison? Everyone needed professional help, not threats of prison. The trial judge handled a difficult situation with greater sensitivity and common sense than I had done.

One consequence of the Children Act 1989 was to recognise that family cases are a multidisciplinary effort – between social workers, doctors and other healthcare professionals, as well as the lawyers and the courts. One of my jobs, when I was Family Division Liaison Judge for London, was to organise multidisciplinary conferences where we could all get together to try and understand one another's perspectives. Another job was to visit all the courts hearing family cases in London, to meet the judges and to discuss what was bothering us. At one of these conferences we began to tackle the growing recognition that violence and domestic abuse between the adults is also harmful to their children. Previously, the courts had tended to see it as something which affected only the adults and was irrelevant to whether and how the children should have contact with the abuser. This was one area where, as a judge, I could help to bring about the sort of change which it had been possible to promote at the Law Commission.[11]

Contact remains a fraught area. Over many years, fathers had become increasingly frustrated, because they felt that the courts were ineffective in helping them to maintain a fatherly relationship with their children. The promise of the Children Act, to encourage parents to share the care of their children and to avoid the 'winner takes all' impression given by the old orders for 'custody' or 'access', was not being kept. These fathers undoubtedly had a point. The courts had a tendency to keep putting the case off in the hope that feelings would calm down and both parents would see sense. But some members of one organisation for frustrated fathers, Fathers 4 Justice, resorted to totally unacceptable tactics to try and get their point across: one Family

Division judge, for example, had non-drying paint thrown on his doorstep and slipped on it, suffering serious injury. Sometimes their stunts demonstrated only too clearly why they had been denied contact with their children. But the basic problem remained. The courts now have additional powers designed to 'Make Contact Work'.[12] These could in theory be used, not only to oblige the parent with whom the child is living to comply with an order for contact with the other parent, but also to oblige that other parent to have the contact which the court has ordered: many lone parents would dearly like the other parent to take a greater interest in the children and share some of the responsibility for looking after them. But traditionally enforcement has been all the other way.

My conclusion in 1999 was that we expect a great deal of our children's primary carers, mostly mothers, and it was my job to enforce and reinforce those expectations. If that sometimes felt like oppressing them, particularly at the behest of controlling or vengeful men, then that was how it had to be. But the cases we saw were exceptional. Child abduction cases are very rare. Most parents do not harm their children. Most separating parents can work out their own arrangements for their children and their finances, particularly if they have help. Family Division judges get a very partial picture even of the few cases which do come to court. They rarely see the cases where men are ordered to stay away from their homes and families, or the run-of-the-mill financial arrangements where the courts try hard to preserve the home and something to live on for the children and their primary carer, cases where it is often the men rather than the women who may feel oppressed.

If a couple separate, they have to decide where they will live, where the children will live and what they are all going to live on. These various issues are usually dealt with separately: the divorce itself if they are married (usually the most straightforward part); orders to protect against violence and abuse or to settle who is to stay in the family home for the time being; arrangements for the children; arrangements for the family's property and finances. This means that the court does not get the full picture, even though the issues are so obviously interrelated. I have long been arguing that we should have a 'one stop' approach: one application form on which the applicant can ask for whatever remedies he or she feels right for the case, one form on which the respondent can reply and indicate what is and is not agreed, and one set of witness statements and other evidence. I understand the historical reasons why this has not been done in the past, but I do not understand why it cannot be done now.

Women did comparatively badly in 'big money' cases because, until the House of Lords' decision in *White v White*,[13] they were limited to their 'reasonable requirements' rather than a fair share of the couple's accumulated assets. That case laid bare the underlying sexism of this. The husband and wife were both farmers who had worked hard to build up the family business and there were two farms which could have been shared between them but the wife had been limited to a lump sum while the husband kept the farms. The House of Lords established a principle of fair sharing with a starting point of equality, but in most 'big money' cases, the richer party is still looking for reasons to depart from this.

The financial cases which came my way tended not to be the multimillionaires, where the question was usually quite simple (although tracing the assets might not be): how many of 'his' millions should she have? My cases tended to involve couples who had been comfortably off while they were together but had assets which it would be difficult to divide without damaging their value: such things as a family farm or other businesses. And once they were divided, neither party would be able to live as comfortably as they had done before. That is, of course, the sad truth about most divorces, but in these High Court cases, the couple had been used to thinking of themselves as quite well off. The other problem with financial cases is that, unless the couple can agree a solution quite early on, the court proceedings can be very expensive, out of all proportion to what is at stake.

This is because our law takes a similar approach to the financial arrangements as it does to the arrangements for the children. In children cases, the court has very flexible powers to decide what the arrangements will be; the welfare of the child is the paramount consideration; and there is a long list of relevant factors for the court to take into account in deciding what will be best for the child. In financial cases, the court also has very flexible powers to rearrange the property and finances of each party: it can order the transfer or resettlement of property, it can split pensions, it can award lump sums, or periodical payments, or a mixture of them all. It is required to take all the circumstances of the individual case into account, giving first consideration to the welfare of any minor children, but including in particular a long list of relevant factors. There are no hard-and-fast rules, for example that each should walk away with a half-share of the assets built up during the marriage. Such a rule is well known to disadvantage wives who have devoted more of their time and energy to looking after their husbands and families than to building a successful career: half the assets will not supply the earning capacity which she does not have and he does have. The object is a tailor-made solution which will be best for this particular family. But that costs money, particularly if one party (usually the husband) is determined to conceal his assets or avoid his responsibilities. English law takes a highly individualistic approach to money and property during the marriage: neither spouse is entitled to know what the other earns, makes or has in the bank. But then it expects them to sort out their fair shares when they divorce.

Other countries take a different approach: which brings me to the first of my two most memorable cases in the Family Division. One Friday in September 1994, I was faced with a most unusual application. It concerned a gentleman named Ernst Schwitters. He was born in Germany in 1918, the son of the now world-famous artist, Kurt Schwitters. Kurt had trained as a painter and continued to paint throughout his life, but he is famous for what he called 'Merz' art: collages of fragments of paper and other rubbish. The Nazis regarded his art as degenerate and father and son had to flee to Norway and then to Great Britain after the Germans invaded Norway. They were interned here for a while as enemy aliens. Kurt eventually made his home in the Lake District, while Ernst returned to Norway and became a Norwegian citizen. He married his present wife in 1945 and they had a son, Bengt, in 1947. Ernst was a photographer who travelled the world on various projects. His wife suffered from ill health and did not go with him but he returned to the family home after his travels and there was no question of divorce. He had become a very rich man, having bank accounts in Switzerland, properties in Norway and Tenerife, and a large quantity of books, pictures and photographic material, most of this derived from his father, who had not been recognised during his lifetime but was now a major figure. In 1989 Ernst met a lady referred to as Mrs A. They became friends, she began to accompany him on his travels, and he bought a house for her in Leicester. In March 1993, after a family row, Ernst moved into her house. In September 1993 he suffered a major stroke, resulting in right-sided hemiplegia and severe impairment of his communication skills. He was admitted to a private hospital in Leicester. Mrs A paid the bills from one of his Swiss bank accounts over which she had power of attorney. In mid-1994 his consultant decided that he no longer needed hospital care and should be moved to a nursing home. The consultant discussed this with the Norwegian family and a place was found for Ernst in a nursing home near Oslo. On 10 September 1994, it was arranged that Bengt would collect him in a hired ambulance, take him to the airport and fly him by private jet to Oslo. Only the consultant knew about this and the usual hospital discharge procedures were not followed. After the ambulance had left, the matron was so concerned that she rang the police. The police stopped the ambulance and Ernst was taken back to the hospital. They also informed Mrs A's lawyers, who obtained a court order over the telephone to prevent Bengt taking him away. A fortnight later, the case came on for hearing before me.

It was bristling with legal difficulties. There was not then a comprehensive set of powers to make decisions on behalf of people who were unable to make them for themselves: that had to wait until the Mental Capacity Act 2005.[14] No individual had the power to make such decisions, not even the next of kin. If there was a dispute, the High Court could declare what would be in the person's best interests. It would then be lawful to do that, although the court could not order it to be done. But could Mrs A bring such proceedings? I held that she could.[15] The family promptly appealed to the Court of Appeal, which upheld me.[16] So the case came back to me to decide, firstly, whether Ernst did indeed lack the mental capacity to decide for himself, which Mrs A had at first denied, and secondly, what would be best for him if he did. By the time I heard the case, it was agreed, in the light of overwhelming medical evidence, that he did not have the capacity to decide: as well as a total loss of language he had lost a great deal of his powers of comprehension and of thought, although he could still feel pleasure and pain. Indeed, a distinguished Norwegian neurologist told the court that he had only ever seen one patient with brain damage so severe: that patient was King Olav. In the meantime, the Norwegian authorities had appointed a young woman lawyer as 'curator' to look after Ernst's interests, so the next question was, did she have the right to make decisions about him which would be binding on an English court? Relevant to that was whether he was still domiciled in Norway or was now domiciled in England. I held that he was still domiciled in Norway and that the curator did have the right in Norwegian law to make the decision. However, that was not binding on the English court, although her views were worthy of great respect. She was clearly horrified that he was still in a lonely hospital bed rather than in a bright and welcoming nursing home. After hearing all the evidence, I concluded that it was in Ernst's best interests for her to make the decision and the arrangements about where he was to live in the few months remaining to him.[17] So back he went to Norway where he lived for another seventeen months, longer than expected.

There were many striking things about the case, quite apart from the legal complexities. Both sides had warm feelings for Ernst but also thought that if they had the body they were more likely to have the riches as well. It was a mystery, which was never explored, why either of them should think that. If he had not made a will in favour of Mrs A it was too late for him to do so now. The power of attorney she had over one of his bank accounts was probably ineffective once he lost capacity[18] but in any event could only be used for his benefit or as he directed. We discovered during the hearing that Mrs A was planning to sell the house which Ernst had bought for her and buy a hotel, which rather cast doubt on her declared desire for him to come home to the house he had shared with her. We did not explore Norwegian matrimonial property law, but his wife might well have had unassailable rights to some if not all of his wealth. She was a feisty woman who gave her evidence with great dignity. She clearly thought herself entitled to know everything about her husband's property and affairs: a far cry from an English woman, who is not.

The Family Division is not the Old Bailey. Courtroom dramas of the television sort are rare. But every case is its own drama, its own story of one family's life, and as Leo Tolstoy said, while 'all happy families resemble each other, each unhappy family is unhappy in its own way'. I am not sure about the first proposition, but I am certain of the second. We saw many very sad stories, but perhaps none sadder than the story of Dayne Kristian Childs. He was born in Brisbane in 1972 to Cheryl Buchanan, a young unmarried mother of Aboriginal origin. The records contained a form, apparently signed by the mother four days after the birth, consenting to his adoption. The baby was removed to a children's home when he was a few weeks old. His first adoptive placement did not work out, but at the age of two he was placed with an English family who were living in Australia. They had one natural son and another adopted son, of mixed heritage. The adoption went well; they were a 'close, loving and open-minded family'. They came back to England when Dayne was about six and he went to school and grew up here. Then, in 1991, out of the blue, the Childs family received a phone call from Australia, answered by Dayne's brother, saying that Dayne's birth mother wanted to be in touch. At that time, Dayne was not interested in speaking to her. But she was given their address and in 1996 Cheryl Buchanan's mother and partner visited England with an Aboriginal football team and did get in touch. They invited Dayne to visit Australia and he did so.

The visit was extremely unsettling for him. He was treated as one of the children 'stolen' from their Aboriginal parents by the Australian authorities. From the mid-nineteenth century until the 1970s, many indigenous children, particularly those of mixed descent, had indeed been removed from their families by compulsion, duress or undue influence, as a matter of deliberate policy. The Report of a National Inquiry into the separation of Aboriginal and Torres Strait Islander children from their families was published by the Australian Human Rights Commission in 1997. This laid bare the abuses which had gone on and for which the government of Queensland apologised to the Aboriginal people only the day before I gave judgment. Dayne's visit was publicised as one of a 'stolen son'. This astonished and frightened him. He was no longer the 'cool and carefree' young man he had been before. He died in a road accident in July 1998, only eight months after he had returned from Australia. He left no will (what young man does?) but he did leave behind a daughter, Hollie, born in July 1997, her mother, Kirsten Milton, to whom he had proposed marriage shortly before he died, and his adoptive mother, Annette Childs. Their plan was to cremate him and bury the ashes next to those of his adoptive father, who had died two years before.

Very properly, though, the family told the Australian family about this. The instant response was that cremation was not acceptable in Aboriginal culture; he must be laid to rest in the place where he had been born. Thus it was that I had to decide what should become of his mortal remains.[19] Technically, it was a dispute about who should be granted letters of administration of his estate, because it is the administrator's duty to arrange for the disposal of the remains. Hollie, his daughter, was the person entitled to be appointed, and because she was a child, that meant the person with parental responsibility for her, her mother. But in 'special circumstances' if 'necessary or expedient' the High Court can appoint someone else.[20] Cheryl Buchanan applied for me to do that. What would you have done?

I decided that the circumstances were sufficiently 'special' for the power to arise. The context was, of course, the transracial placement of an Aboriginal child at a time when the law facilitated the rapid separation of mother and child. I was not, in the end, asked to decide whether Dayne had indeed been 'stolen'. But in the United Kingdom we would not have regarded a mother's consent, given only four days after the birth and treated as irrevocable after thirty days, as a valid consent. Such a law was certainly capable of being abused in pursuit of a racist policy, whether or not it had been in this case. Then the Queensland law had gone to the other extreme and allowed the birth mother to trace the child without any prior warning or counselling. The suggestion that Dayne had been 'stolen', which may have carried the suggestion that his adoptive parents were to blame, was deeply upsetting and confusing for him.

But it was certainly not 'necessary' to exercise the power. Was it nevertheless 'expedient'? There was no law to guide me, but I decided that there were several interests to be considered: first, the views of the birth family and the imperative of their religious beliefs, in the context of their fight against colonial oppression and racism; second, the views of the adoptive family, who were in no way to blame for any of this and who had given Dayne a loving and nurturing home – Mrs Childs was in every modern sense his mother; third, the interests of Hollie, who needed the knowledge of her father and his concern for her – she also needed to know and accept the Aboriginal part of her heritage, but she should not be exposed to the sort of pressures to which Dayne had been subjected; and fourth, the wishes of the deceased – there was no evidence that he would wish to be buried in Australia; he did not identify himself as a member of the Aboriginal community and had certainly not rejected the family, the culture and the values in which he had been brought up.

Balancing these four factors as best I could, I decided that the English family should not be displaced as administrators and that they should decide on the appropriate funeral and burial arrangements. They had already agreed that he should be buried, not cremated, and I hoped that they might be prepared to let the Australian family perform appropriate funerary rituals and to view the body.

When I tell this story in talks about my life, I often ask the audience what they would have done, before telling them what I decided. There is always a clear majority in favour of my decision. But I do wonder how I might have decided had I been an Australian judge, where sensitivity to the history and cultural context is now so acute. And would it have made a difference whether I was deciding it in Brisbane or in Western Australia, which for practical purposes is as far away from Brisbane as is England? I have always tried *not* to start with a foregone conclusion, but to listen carefully to the evidence and arguments, to weigh them up and then reason to a result which matches both the facts and the law. When I asked a question, it was because I wanted to know the answer, and not because I was trying to give an indication of what I thought the result would be. Counsel didn't always understand this, so I expect that some other judges were different. But however true to the facts and the law you may be, the context cannot be forgotten.

The sorts of decisions which family judges have to make are quite different from the decisions made in criminal and civil cases. There, it is mostly about finding out what went on in the past and imposing the appropriate punishment for a crime or the appropriate compensation for a breach of contract or a civil wrong. It is not usually about managing the future relations between the parties. In family cases, it may be necessary to find out what went on in the past, but this is always as a preliminary to managing the family's future. It is necessary to be sensitive to the whole family context, its religious and cultural background, as well as the personalities of each of the people involved, including their children. It is necessary to be sensitive to what the children are saying, although this is usually learned through a court officer or social worker rather than by direct interaction with the child. It is necessary to try and create an atmosphere in court which reduces the tension rather than ramps it up, making it more rather than less likely that agreements can be reached. It is necessary to smile.

10 My Lady, Lord Justice

The Court of Appeal for England and Wales was created in 1873 to hear appeals from trial judges in civil and family cases. A separate Court of Criminal Appeal was created in 1907. The two were amalgamated in 1966, but there is still a Civil Division and a Criminal Division. It is based in the Royal Courts of Justice in the Strand. The courtrooms mainly used by the Criminal Division are grand Gothic affairs. The courtrooms mainly used by the Civil Division are more modern, light and bright. Is there some symbolism there? The judges were known as Lord Justices of Appeal and, until Dame Elizabeth Butler-Sloss joined them in 1988, they were all men. She is an example to us all. She was called to the Bar in 1955, married another barrister in 1958, had three children, and was appointed a registrar (now a district judge) in the Principal Registry of the Family Division in 1970: it was easier to combine bringing up children with being a judge than with practising at the Bar. In 1979, she was promoted to be a High Court judge in the Family Division – leaping over the middle rank of circuit judge. This raised some eyebrows at the time, but she proved more than equal to the task. She also completed the report into the Cleveland child abuse scandal in double-quick time (and is now an effective cross-bench member of the House of Lords).

It cannot have been easy being the first woman in the Court of Appeal. The Master of the Rolls, Lord Donaldson of Lymington, was not enthusiastic. His wife had been the first woman lord mayor of London and he favoured the women doing what the men did rather than adapting the rules to accommodate both sexes. The Supreme Court Act 1981 (echoing its predecessors dating back to 1873) declared that the judges of the Court of Appeal 'shall be styled Lord Justice of Appeal'. Hence Dame Elizabeth was 'My Lady, Lord Justice Butler-Sloss' until Lord Donaldson's successor, Lord Bingham, declared that she could be known informally as Lady Justice Butler-Sloss. She tells me, perhaps in jest, that this was because I was soon to join them and would not put up with anything else. The formal legal position caught up in 2003. Her intellect, her charm and her no-nonsense common sense had won over the doubters.

In 1999 she became the first woman president of the Family Division of the High Court. This meant that there was a vacancy in the Court of Appeal, but would it be filled by a family-law specialist? The volume of family work had fallen from over 300 cases in 1995 to under a hundred in 1999. Not every High Court judge wants to leave the drama of trial judging and move on to the more abstract and cerebral work of the Court of Appeal, reviewing what the trial judge has done. But there were three of us in the Family Division who definitely did want it: not only would it be a big step up the ladder, but we all enjoyed deciding difficult points of law. Which one of us would it be? On the last day of the summer term, I was summoned back to London from sitting in Chester to see the Lord Chancellor, Lord Irvine of Lairg. We had half an hour of inconsequential conversation at the end of which he said that he was *thinking* of recommending me for the Court of Appeal. I did not feel that I had distinguished myself in our conversation, so left feeling that it was another interview which I had failed. But in fact the die was already cast. I was to move to the Court of Appeal in October after five and a half years in the Family Division. What may have swung it for me was the breadth of my knowledge and experience of the law, stemming from my university and Law Commission days, so that I was thought (or so Dame Elizabeth kindly wrote to me) to be able to turn my hand to anything. If I had a sneaking suspicion that my gender might have given me the edge, I did not let that put me off. If we think that we can do the job, we are letting the side down if we do not grasp the opportunities which come our way.

I was bold enough to think that I could do the job because I had already been sitting in the Court of Appeal as often as the opportunity arose.[1] Though the work of the Family Division is fascinating and challenging at a personal level, it rarely is at a legal level. I relished having to decide a point of law. I also relished exposure to the multitude of different areas of the civil law, from personal injuries, to shipping contracts, to intellectual property disputes, to judicial review of the actions of government and public authorities. But I expect that it was partly ambition. I wanted to prove both to myself and to others that I had it in me to become the second woman in the Court of Appeal. It was about time there was one.

On 1 October 1999 I handed over four of my five sets of robes, including the red robes made for Dame Elizabeth Lane, to their fourth careful lady owner, Dame Jill Black, who had taken the Family Division vacancy created by my appointment. The fifth, the black QC's robe, was worn in the Civil Division of the Court of Appeal. There was also a splendid black and gold robe with a train, which was, and still is, worn for ceremonial occasions. Unlike the High Court robes, this belonged to the court. The only two available had been worn by very tall men. One of them had to be taken up several times for me.

It is, in fact, a privy counsellor's robe. All members of the Court of Appeal are made privy counsellors so that, if necessary, they can sit in the Judicial Committee of the Privy Council, the final Court of Appeal for a dwindling number of Commonwealth countries. So on Wednesday 24 November 1999, I took another trip to Buckingham Palace to be sworn in. Careful attention to the instructions was requested. The new privy counsellors were lined up with the Lord President of the Council, Margaret Beckett MP, and two others. The president called my name, I knelt on my right knee on one footstool and took the oath of allegiance, then rose and moved forward to kneel on another footstool to kiss Her Majesty's hand, very nervous that I would not be able to get up again. I then returned to my position in the line to take the privy counsellor's oath standing up. This oath includes a solemn promise to keep secret the business discussed in council. The business itself was very short and formal but, even if I could remember what it was, I am sworn not to reveal it (or, of course, any of the deliberations of the Judicial Committee of the Privy Council).

It was an exciting time to be joining the Court of Appeal. The Human Rights Act 1998 was due to come into force in October 2000. This made a momentous change to the relationship between individuals and enterprises and the state. It was a brave thing for any government to do and not universally popular. It made the rights protected in international law by the European Convention on Human Rights into rights protected in United Kingdom law, so that victims could have a remedy in the courts here rather than having to bring a case against the United Kingdom in the European Court of Human Rights in Strasbourg. Victims can now complain if a public authority has acted or proposes to act in a way which is incompatible with their Convention rights (unless an Act of Parliament means that the authority has no choice but to act incompatibly). The courts, and everyone else, have a duty to 'read and give effect' to Acts of Parliament and regulations in a way which is compatible with the Convention rights, if it is possible to do so. If a regulation is incompatible, it can be ignored. But if an Act of Parliament is incompatible, the courts have no power to strike it down. It remains valid. However, the higher courts can make a formal declaration that it is incompatible. This sends a clear message to government and Parliament that the court thinks that if the victim complains to the European Court of Human Rights that the United Kingdom has violated his or her rights, the United Kingdom will lose. Government and Parliament then have a choice: take a fast-track route to putting it right; promote a new Act of Parliament to put it right; or do nothing. So far something has always been done.

The Human Rights Act has enabled many ordinary people to protect their fundamental rights – to life, to liberty, to freedom of thought, speech and assembly, to respect for their private and family lives, and not to be tortured, degraded, treated inhumanely or enslaved, among others. Most cases which come to court are about the meaning of those rights and whether there is a good reason for interfering in them.[2] But the first case to come my way was about the much more difficult question of what it means to 'read and give effect' to an Act of Parliament in a way which is compatible with those rights. The Children Act 1989 had deliberately removed the power of the High Court, when placing a child in local authority care, to give directions to the local authority about how the child should be looked after and to require regular reviews in court. But what if the local authority's decisions were an unjustified interference in the Convention right to respect for family life? The plan might have been to reunite the child with her family, but the authority might have failed to do this. The plan might have been to find a new 'family for life' for the child, but the authority might have failed to do this. Could we 'read and give effect' to the Children Act in such a way as to require the case to be brought back to court if the rights of either the parents or the child had been violated by the local authority? In the Court of Appeal, we decided that it could.[3] The House of Lords put us firmly in our place. We couldn't use the Human Rights Act to put something into the Children Act which deliberately wasn't there.[4]

Those were early days and we were still finding our way. Most of the big decisions were yet to come.[5] The routine day-to-day work of a Court of Appeal judge consists of deciding applications for permission to appeal and helping to decide full appeals. These days, anyone who wants to appeal against the trial court's decision in a civil or family case has to have permission (unless their liberty is at stake). Most applications are decided by a single judge on the papers. It takes up a lot of time. The test is whether an appeal would have a real prospect of success (or there is some other compelling reason for the court to hear it). This involves predicting how a bench of two or three other judges would look at the case: not always easy. Most applicants had a lawyer but a goodly proportion of applicants in family cases did not: they were acting for themselves. We would hear their applications in court, because it was felt that they would not take 'no' for an answer without a hearing. Feelings could run high and I was glad of the reassuring presence of my clerk, Ayo Onatade, if trouble was expected. There were a lot of angry and disappointed fathers who had been denied contact with their children. Some of these were helped by a 'McKenzie friend'[6] from one of the fathers' organisations. These are not allowed to speak for the applicant, but can sit beside a litigant in person, take notes and make quiet suggestions. Occasionally, it made more sense to let them speak. But there was always the risk that they would use the opportunity to run a political campaign rather than to help the client. There were other applicants who had fallen out with their lawyers and insisted on representing themselves, and others still who had run out of money because of the length of time and the number of hearings the case had taken. The Citizens' Advice Bureau in the Royal Courts of Justice would help them put together the 'bundle' of documents which the court needed but otherwise they were on their own. It was hard for them to understand what the court wanted to know. It was also hard for them to accept that the court would hardly ever interfere in the factual findings of the trial judge. But they were not always wrong. Some were very engaging. It was also easier to get a real sense of the family dynamics than when these were filtered through the careful submissions of a professional advocate. But it was hard to spot which of them did indeed have a good case and even harder to explain to those who did not have a good case why that was so and in a way which they could accept. It sometimes felt more like a social-work task than a judging task.

One unforgettable applicant was a delicate-looking woman who was aggrieved at the divorce settlement ordered by a district judge. She believed that her husband had been guilty of deception and wanted to sue the judge for being a party to that deception. I explained judicial immunity to her as best I could, but she was not convinced. Later that day, I was the junior judge hearing an interesting appeal about the water supply to a farm. I noticed the woman lurking at the back of the court. When we rose to leave, she came forward and declared that she was making a citizen's arrest of Lady Justice Hale for colluding in the fraud. As junior judge, I was supposed to wait until the seniors had left, so I stood still until the presider said 'Go on Brenda,' which I did. The woman was arrested by the tipstaff for contempt of court, but I don't think that anything came of that. She was perhaps a little mad but not bad.

Hearing the actual appeals was rarely so exciting. Everyone had a lawyer: the Bar Pro Bono unit would find barristers for any unrepresented applicant who had been given permission to appeal. We hardly ever heard evidence, only arguments about whether the trial judge had got the law or the process right. An exception was the appeal brought by the former MP Neil Hamilton in his unsuccessful libel action against Mohamed Al-Fayed, then the owner of Harrods. Al-Fayed had alleged that Hamilton had taken cash in return for asking questions in Parliament. The jury found that the allegation was true and Hamilton was ordered to pay the enormous costs. He then discovered evidence that 'Benji the Binman', a notorious Fleet Street operator, had been hunting in the rubbish bins outside his barristers' chambers and selling documents to Al-Fayed's people. He argued that this misconduct was enough to invalidate the claim or at least to deny Al-Fayed his costs. We had to try and find out what had happened. Al-Fayed had three stock answers to his cross-examination: 'No', 'I don't remember', or 'It's a possibility'. Eventually, the exasperated barrister asked him, 'Mr Al-Fayed, when you say "It's a possibility", do you mean "Yes"?' Predictably, the reply was 'It's a possibility.' Much laughter in court. We found that his people had indeed bought documents from Benji the Binman, but that there was no reason to think that the trial had been unfair. As I asked, 'What do people usually put in rubbish bins?'

While I was on the court, we would sit in the same panel of three judges for three weeks at a time. There was one reading day a week to prepare. The presiding Lord Justice would usually ring up over the weekend to say which of the cases listed for the following week he wanted me to take the lead in: this meant for a busy Sunday getting ready to give an oral judgment at the end of the hearing if necessary. This did not mean making up my mind in advance. It meant having a note with the chronology of the facts and the arguments clearly set out, so that it would be possible to tweak these and add a conclusion, in the light of the arguments during the hearing and the views of the other judges.

We would meet in the presider's room a quarter of an hour before the hearing to exchange preliminary views and in the corridor outside court at the end of the morning's sitting and just before the afternoon's sitting. It seemed to me that height was at least as important as gender in the dynamic of these corridor meetings: if the other two judges were tall, they would talk to one another; if one of them was short, he would talk to me; it was best if we were all short. But most of them were tall – my dear friend from National Family Mediation, Thelma Fisher, at a memorial service for Lord Havers (a former Lord Chancellor) in the Temple Church, remarked 'There's an awful lot of Normans here' (meaning tall, all-conquering men). At the end of the hearing we would reach our conclusions: not always the same as our preliminary views. If these were reasonably straightforward, the designated judge would give an oral judgment there and then. Some preferred this because it got the job done. Some even took a 'macho' pride in being able to do it.

But it was always possible to 'reserve' judgment to be given in writing at a later date. This was usual if the case was long or particularly complicated. It was also considered good manners to do this if we disagreed. To expect a dissenter to launch into a reasoned dissent having only just heard how the majority were explaining their decision was thought inconsiderate (although it had certainly been done in the past). And it was by no means unknown for people to change their minds when they saw the arguments written down. What had started two to one in one direction might become two to one or even unanimous in the other. The writer of the leading judgment might turn out to be a dissenter. The law is not always simple and straightforward. The advantage of writing, apart from clearer thought and greater accuracy, is proper grammar and punctuation. If an oral judgment has to be transcribed, what has sounded quite fluent and coherent when spoken out loud can look very different on the page.

Whether written or oral, a judgment has three audiences. First and foremost are the parties and their lawyers: they must understand why they have won or, more importantly, lost. Second is the court which will hear any appeal against the decision: they must know whether the result has been properly reasoned. Third is the wider legal and general public to whom we are accountable: they must be reassured that we are not reaching arbitrary and inexplicable decisions. A typical appeal court judgment will first explain what was decided in the lower court, and why; it will then give an account of the relevant law – some of it in legislation, some of it in the previous decisions of the courts; then it will explain the parties' arguments – about what the law is and how it applies to their case – in other words, why they should win; and finally it will reach a conclusion and explain why. It is not easy – or even possible – to do all this in a way which satisfies each of the audiences. But clarity about what has been decided and why is particularly important in our legal system: the decision of a higher court on a point of law is binding upon all the lower courts. Indeed, the decisions of the Court of Appeal are usually binding on that court too.

My two most notable cases in the Court of Appeal were definitely cases in which my gender played a part. What should be the measure of damages if a vasectomy or a sterilisation goes wrong and a woman becomes pregnant with a child she never meant to have? In particular, should she (and, if they are still together, the father) be entitled to the costs of bringing up the child? On general principles, there is little doubt that she should. She has suffered the personal injury of bearing and having a child whom she did not want to have. She should be entitled to damages for that injury and for the consequential financial loss, just as a man who is seriously injured at work is entitled to damages, not only for his 'pain, suffering and loss of amenity', but also for his loss of future earnings and the cost of looking after him if he is permanently disabled. But this made some judges uncomfortable: why should the health service, or the doctors' insurance company, pay to bring up a child in whatever standard of living the family enjoyed?

Matters came to a head in a Scottish case.[7] Catherine McFarlane was born in 1992. Her parents already had four children. In 1989 her father had a vasectomy and was later told that his sperm count was negative. Her parents therefore took no contraceptive precautions and Catherine was conceived. Assuming that they could prove negligence, either in the performance of the operation or in the advice they were given, could they claim damages for the cost of bringing her up, as well as for her mother's pain and suffering in carrying and giving birth to her? The Inner House of the Court of Session (the Scottish equivalent of the Court of Appeal) held that they could.[8] The court should abide by legal principle and leave the policy arguments against awarding damages to Parliament: on one side, every human life is valuable and a child is an incalculable blessing to her parents; on the other side, a child is not always a blessing, may bring real hardship, and parents are entitled to limit the size of their family. The hospital appealed to the House of Lords.

The House of Lords granted the mother's claim relating to the pregnancy and birth, but not the parents' claim for the costs of bringing Catherine up. Lord Steyn, one of the Law Lords hearing the case, was quite blunt. From the point of view of 'corrective' justice, somebody who has harmed another without justification was required to indemnify the other, so the parents' claim should succeed. But if one looked at it from the point of view of the 'just distribution of burdens and losses among members of society', he was firmly of the view that 'commuters on the underground' (his substitute for the 'man on the Clapham omnibus' – the archetypal 'reasonable man' in lawyer-speak) would say that the parents' claim for upbringing should not succeed. I do not know how he knew that. There had been no public opinion poll to inform him. And 'commuters on the underground' are a very small and unrepresentative section of society. In particular, they are less likely to include mothers who are struggling to bring up a large family on a limited income. I thought that they should have applied correct legal principles. If Parliament did not like it, it could always change the law.

Catherine was a healthy child. But what if the child was disabled? Scott Parkinson was born in May 1995. His mother already had four children. She was living with her husband in a cramped two-bedroomed house. She intended to go back to work and they planned to move to larger accommodation. In December 1993 she underwent a laparo-scopic sterilisation. Unfortunately, not only did the doctor performing the operation fail to apply a clip effectively to one of her fallopian tubes, two other clips dropped into her abdomen and were not removed. Negligence was admitted. She became pregnant about ten months later and was warned that the child might be disabled. The arrival of Scott was a catastrophe. She could not go back to work and the family could not move. The strain on the marriage was too much and Mr Parkinson left her before Scott was born. Scott had severe learning difficulties and behavioural problems. It was agreed that he could not be treated as a 'healthy child' as Catherine McFarlane had been. The judge held that the mother could claim the extra costs arising from his special needs but not the basic costs of maintaining him. In the Court of Appeal we unanimously agreed.[9]

In my judgment, I went to town on what it means to a woman to become pregnant and have a child that she never meant to have. I described the physical and psychological consequences of pregnancy. Along with these came a 'severe curtailment of personal autonomy. Literally, one's life is no longer one's own but also someone else's.' The process of giving birth is rightly termed 'labour': it is hard work, often painful and sometimes dangerous. The invasion of the mother's personal autonomy does not stop with giving birth. She inevitably has parental responsibility for the child. That responsibility is not

simply or even primarily a financial responsibility. The primary responsibility is to care for the child. Bringing up children is hard work. The
responsibility lasts twenty-four hours a day, seven days a week, all year
round until the child becomes old enough to look after him or herself.

To my mind, the damage suffered was not the financial cost of
bringing up a child but the responsibility of making or providing
proper arrangements for the care of the child. At the heart of the
House of Lords' decision in the *McFarlane* case was the feeling that
to compensate for the financial loss of bringing up a healthy child
was a step too far. A child brings benefits as well as costs. It is impossible to calculate the benefits, and invidious to distinguish between
different families in doing so. The only thing to do is to assume that
the benefits and burdens cancel one another out. (I called this a
'deemed equilibrium', a phrase which no one else liked, but it made
sense to me.) I commented that 'the notion of a child bringing benefit
to the parents is itself deeply suspect, smacking of the commodification
of the child, regarding the child as an asset to his parents'. The House
of Lords was a higher court, so the Court of Appeal was bound to
follow *McFarlane* whether we liked it or not. But it did not follow that
this limitation on ordinary principles should apply to the extra costs
of bringing up a disabled child. The defendant hospital did not appeal.

But what if the mother was disabled? Could she claim the extra
costs to her of bringing up a healthy child? Anthony Rees was born
in April 1997. His mother suffered from retinitis pigmentosa and was
severely visually handicapped. She was adamant that she did not want
children because she felt that her eyesight would mean that she could
not look after them. She was sterilised but it was admitted that the
operation was performed negligently and Anthony was conceived.
She was bringing him up herself with the help of her mother and
other relatives who lived nearby but it was a struggle for her. She
claimed damages for the full costs of bringing him up. In the Court
of Appeal, by a majority of two to one, we awarded her, not the full
costs, but the extra costs of bringing him up resulting from her disability. Once again, I focused on the legal and factual responsibility of
looking after the child. A seriously disabled mother needed help to
discharge this and deserved to be compensated. This time the
defendant hospital did appeal to the House of Lords.[10]

The mother tried to persuade Their Lordships to overturn the decision in *McFarlane* and give her the whole cost of bringing up Anthony. Because of this, the case was heard by seven Law Lords rather than by the usual five. She failed. But they agreed that Ms Rees should have something: but what? Three of the seven Law Lords would have given her the extra costs, as we had done. Four of them held that she could not get any of the costs of bringing up a healthy child. But they invented a wholly new remedy – giving her a conventional sum, put at £15,000, to recognise the wrongful invasion of the mother's right to live her life in the way that she had planned. I like to think that my explanation of just what this means to a woman had some effect. It was a victory of sorts, although not the one which I wanted.

That was a case in which we had quite intense discussions in the Court of Appeal. I had won one, but not both, of the others round to my point of view. We remained good friends. It is a feature of the collegiate atmosphere in an appeal court that we can disagree quite profoundly without falling out. Soon after I joined the court, Lord Justice Judge (later to become Lord Chief Justice) and I disagreed about whether a house buyer, Mr Farley, could claim damages for the distress and inconvenience caused when his surveyor negligently failed to discover that the house was affected by aircraft noise. Lord Justice Judge thought that he could. I thought that he couldn't because the evidence was that the value of the property was not affected by the noise: he had lost no money and damages are not normally paid for mere distress and inconvenience. We were a two-judge court and I stood my ground. So the case was argued again before a different three-judge court which decided two to one in the same way that I had done. It then went to the House of Lords which unanimously decided that damages were payable.[11] This was a pragmatic decision, which I thought unprincipled, but of course I was not unhappy that Mr Farley got his £10,000. I expect that I dug my heels in because, as a very new Court of Appeal judge, I did not want to be charmed by a more senior judge into what I saw as the wrong decision. He did not hold it against me.

The other judges had, of course, all been barristers. Barristers thrive on argument. They can fight hard in court and remain on good terms. That camaraderie was apparent in the court and I hope that I was part of it, despite not having been a barrister for long. It was a special pleasure sitting with Dame Elizabeth Butler-Sloss, when she came back from sitting in the Family Division. We were both of us capable of having a good giggle and 'getting over heavy ground as lightly as one can' (as Georgette Heyer would have put it). It was even more special in February 2001 to sit, for the very first time, on a Court of Appeal panel consisting of three women – Dame Elizabeth, Dame Mary Arden (who became the third woman in the Court of Appeal in October 2000) and I. This caused quite a stir at the time, although it would not do so now that roughly a quarter of the Court of Appeal judges are women. As Joshua Rozenberg reported in the *Daily Telegraph*:

'I think My Ladies agree with me,' said Dame Elizabeth Butler-Sloss yesterday, using the words for the first time as she criticised the Official Solicitor for not seeking to move a mentally ill prisoner to hospital. Though an all-woman Court of Appeal had never sat before, none of the three male counsel was sharp enough to earn himself a place in history by addressing Dame Elizabeth, Lady Justice Hale and Lady Justice Arden correctly as 'My Ladies'.

That mistake was not made when, many years later, counsel delighted in addressing the first Supreme Court panel to have a majority of women as 'My Ladies and My Lords'.

Two of the cases we heard that week were about the family. One was a shocking example of domestic abuse. A husband was in serious breach of an order not to molest his wife, which had a power of arrest attached. The worst breach was when he attacked his wife in the former matrimonial home with a Stanley knife and she had to have 'considerable' surgery to repair her cut hand. He also made repeated threats to kill her. He was arrested for breach of the order and had been in prison ever since. But he clearly had serious mental health problems. Soon after his remand to prison, two doctors had recommended that he be transferred to hospital under the Mental Health Act 1983. But this had not happened. We remanded him to prison under the Family Law Act so that the psychiatric reports, which ought to have been obtained earlier, could now be arranged. Knowing what to do with abusers who are seriously mentally ill is a very real problem: they are not amenable to the usual threats of imprisonment if they disobey an order. The only hope is psychiatric treatment but that is in short supply.

Next came round one of a most extraordinary story. It could not have happened before the advent of modern treatments for infertility. And it could not have happened had the Family Law Reform Act 1987 not introduced a rule that the husband of a woman who had a child by donor insemination would automatically become the legal father. The whole object of that Act was to remove the differences between children whose parents were or were not married to one another. So in 1990, this rule was extended to unmarried partners (provided that the woman was being treated in a licensed clinic in this country) and also to *in vitro* fertilisation (IVF) and other treatments involving donated sperm or eggs. To tell the story, I have to quote the exact rule which then applied to unmarried partners: 'If ... the embryo or the sperm and eggs were placed in the woman, or she was being artificially inseminated, in the course of treatment services provided for her and a man together ... then ... that man shall be treated as the father of the child.'[12]

Our case was about a little girl who was born in February 2000. Her mother had been in a relationship with a Mr B for some years and they were desperate to have a child. But Mr B became infertile after cancer treatment, so they went to a licensed clinic. They first tried treatment by donor insemination but this failed, and so in 1998 they moved on to IVF using donor sperm. The mother signed a form consenting to the treatment. Mr B signed an acknowledgment on the same form that they were being 'treated together' and that he would become the legal father of any resulting child. Her eggs were harvested and fertilised. Twelve embyros were produced. Two of these were implanted but neither resulted in a successful pregnancy. The rest were frozen.

The couple then separated and the mother began a relationship with another man. In 1999 she went back to the clinic. Her new partner came with her. The mother pretended that he was the same man who had signed the form the year before. This time the treatment was successful and the little girl was born. Mr B found out and applied for contact with the child and for an order granting him parental responsibility for her. A parental responsibility order can only be made in favour of the man who is the father of the child (or, now, a step-father). Surprisingly, the parties agreed that Mr B was indeed the legal father of the child. The trial judge allowed him to have indirect contact with her, but postponed any question of direct contact until she was three years old and adjourned the application for parental responsibility indefinitely. Mr B applied to us for permission to appeal.

We refused permission, because we thought that the judge had made the right decision in the child's best interests. But we expressed surprise it had been conceded that Mr B was the child's legal father. Neither the court nor the other people affected could be bound by such a concession. We directed that the case be brought to the attention of the Human Fertilisation and Embryology Authority.[13]

Two years later, the case was back before a different Court of Appeal panel. Mr B had reinstated his application for parental respon-sibility, so the question of whether he was legally the child's father became the first issue. The same trial judge decided that he was. In the Court of Appeal we decided that he was not. Mr B argued that the 'treatment services' in question were those listed in the original consent form, which had begun when the couple were together, and were still continuing when the second implantation took place. The mother argued that they had to be 'treated together' at the time when the embryo was placed in her and by that time they had separated and were no longer being treated together. We agreed with the mother: the wording of the section clearly focused on the time when the embryo was replaced in the mother rather than on the earlier time when it was created.[14]

Look at the wording: what would you have decided? The trial judge had every sympathy for Mr B, who had so much wanted a child and had regarded the embryos as his. But what if a man in Mr B's situation did not want the child once he and the mother were separated and resisted being made financially liable for her? Where would your sympathies have been then? Sympathy, as the trial judge observed, is an unreliable guide to the interpretation of Acts of Parliament. But, as I suggested, 'it is helpful to consider whether the conclusion reached in a case where one's sympathies lie in one direction would be equally attractive in a case where one's sympathies would lie the other way'. It has become quite common in family cases for the advocates to ask the judge to think about what the fair solution would be were the parties' roles or genders to be the other way round.

But is it a good idea to make legal parents of people who are not the child's birth parents? The pressure came from doctors treating married couples for male infertility by donor insemination. They and their patients wanted to treat the resulting child in the same way as any other child born to a married woman. The law presumes that any child born to a married woman during the marriage (and within a possible gestation period thereafter) is her husband's child, but genetic studies had shown that this was not true in a surprisingly high proportion of cases (as many as one-third was often mentioned in conferences, but the scientific source was hard to trace). Birth registrations are not always accurate but the child can grow up in happy ignorance of the truth. Why should births resulting from donor insemination be any different? The counter-argument was that it is one thing for a mother (and perhaps also her husband) to conceal the identity of her child's father; it is quite another for the law deliberately to pretend that something is true when it is known not to be. And these days, the child is quite likely to find out the truth eventually, but not in a good way. So at first I had a great deal of sympathy with the counter-argument.

In 2008, the rule was extended to the mother's female partner. The concept of being treated together was replaced by a much more workable rule. Both the intended mother and the intended father, or other mother, must give written consent that the intended father, or other mother, shall be treated in law as the child's other parent. This can be withdrawn at any time and the consents must be in force when the mother is inseminated or the embryo or eggs and sperm are placed in her. Unfortunately, it did not come into force until 2009, after both of my grandchildren were born to my daughter's partner, as a result of donor insemination arranged by a licensed clinic in England. Fortunately, the children were born in Ireland and Irish law has now allowed my daughter to be registered as their other parent, with the full support of the children, who have always seen her in that way (and Julian and me as their grandparents). Whatever my reservations about the idea when it was first introduced in 1987, I thoroughly approve of it now.

This is only a very small sample of the wide and varied subject matter of the appeals we heard. I have fond memories of writing judgments about bringing to an end a disastrous contract to run a local authority's parks and gardens; about whether Falmouth estuary was a 'watercourse' for pollution control purposes; about the responsibilities of local authorities towards destitute asylum seekers; about when an employee could claim damages for psychiatric problems caused by 'stress at work'; and many, many more. My aim was, of course, to get the answer right (and sometimes to persuade the House of Lords that we had got the answer right). I always tried to write in clear and accessible language and to use as few words as I could. Typing my own judgments helped. My long experience as a law teacher also helped. Perhaps that is why I was popular with law students – so much so that the website *Legal Cheek* dubbed me the Beyoncé of the legal world! The route to the right answer, to my mind, was always through the correct legal principles – but interpreting and applying these with an understanding of the social or economic context of the case. The perspective of women, of children, and of other disadvantaged groups in society had too often been overlooked – the decisions dotted throughout this book illustrate my attempts to correct that.

11 Life of the Lady Law Lord

As we judges solemnly processed into the quire of Westminster Abbey on 1 October each year, arrayed in all our finery, how many of us noticed the elderly gentlemen dressed in sober morning suits, seated to our left as we passed through the screen? They were the 'Law Lords' – present and past Lords of Appeal in Ordinary and past Lord Chancellors – the highest judges in the land. But if they were judges, why were they not also in the procession? They were indeed judges, but not in the ordinary courts of England and Wales. They were members of the House of Lords.

Until 2009, the top court for the whole United Kingdom was a committee of the House of Lords. The House of Lords had heard civil appeals from England and Wales for centuries and after the Acts of Union of 1707, appealing to the House of Lords became very popular with the Scots. The Lord Chancellor would preside and the judges might be called upon to come and give their advice. That was why we still got our writs of summons to each new parliament, although our services were no longer needed. Originally, non-lawyer peers could sit and vote on the result. But in 1844 it was firmly decided that their votes would not be counted. The trouble was that there were not enough peers who held or had held high judicial office to do the work. An attempt to create a life peerage for a distinguished judge failed. Long delays built up.

Things stumbled on until the 1870s. Then there was a wholesale reform of the chaotic legal system of England and Wales: the plethora of separate courts were brought together in a single High Court, with a single Court of Appeal, together known as the Supreme Court of Judicature. English and Welsh appeals to the House of Lords were to be abolished and the plan was for Scottish and Irish appeals to go to the new Court of Appeal. Not surprisingly, this stirred up a 'Celtic hornets' nest'. The Scots and the Irish were proud of their separate legal systems and did not want to go to an English court. A successful campaign was launched to preserve the judicial House of Lords, not only for Scotland and Ireland, but also for England and Wales. The Appellate Jurisdiction Act 1876 restored the House of Lords as the final Court of Appeal for the whole United Kingdom. It also created 'Lords of Appeal in Ordinary', colloquially known as Law Lords, to solve the numbers problem – 'in Ordinary' meant that they were paid (the handsome salary of £6,000 a year, which Disraeli thought 'mouth-watering to a Scotsman', although the first two Scotsmen approached turned it down).

The first Law Lords were appointed peers only for as long as they remained judges, but they soon proved so useful to parliamentary business that in 1887 they became peers for life. To begin with, there were only two, one from England and one from Scotland, but the numbers gradually increased until they reached twelve in 1996. It became the norm for there to be two Law Lords from Scotland and there was usually, but not invariably, one from Northern Ireland. This showed that they were the top court for the whole United Kingdom, not just England and Wales.

At first they only heard civil appeals. But when a Court of Criminal Appeal was set up for England and Wales in 1906, they could hear appeals from that court, provided that the Attorney General certified that the case involved a very important point of law. There has never been any equivalent for Scotland. In 1936, it was laid down that civil appeals could only go to the House of Lords with permission, either from the court whose decision was under appeal or from the lords themselves. Permission would only be given if the case involved 'an arguable point of law of general public importance'. As Lord Bingham, senior Law Lord from 2000 to 2008, put it, the House of Lords 'dines à la carte'. In practice, most cases involved a very serious point of law or a very serious amount of money.

Cases used to be heard in the House of Lords Chamber (and still could be) – very grand, lavishly decorated in gold, with red leather benches, but very inconvenient for everyone: the Law Lords had little card tables for their papers and the barristers had only a shelf behind the bar of the Chamber at which to perch. But in the late 1940s, the Law Lords became a committee and moved into a committee room overlooking the river Thames. They may have been driven out by the noise and dust of the rebuilding after the bomb damage of the Second World War; or it may have been impossible to fit in the judicial business as well as the huge volume of parliamentary business setting up the welfare state. The Lord Chancellor, previously top judge, had less and less time to spend on judicial business and left things more and more in the hands of the most senior Law Lord.

The Law Lords were (almost) all distinguished lawyers, but some of the early ones were also active politicians: one of them was Lord Carson, who had famously said that 'Ulster will fight and Ulster will be right'. But politics did not come into their appointment after the Second World War and as time went on, they took less and less part in ordinary parliamentary business. Some did still speak, usually on legal or constitutional matters, and some chaired committees on legal subjects. But some Law Lords played no part at all in parliamentary business. Even if they had previously been in politics, they all sat on the cross benches in the Chamber, where the peers who do not take a party whip sit. In June 2000, they declared that, although they were full members of the House and entitled to play a full part in parliamentary business if they chose, they would not 'engage in matters where there is a strong element of party political controversy' and would bear in mind that, if they expressed an opinion on something which was later relevant to an appeal, they might not be able to sit (which, after all, is what the public paid them to do). Two of my fellow Law Lords were unable to sit on the four fascinating cases we had about the Hunting Act 2004 and its Scottish equivalent (of which more later) because they had voted against the 2004 bill.

Not everyone wants to sit in the highest court in the land, hearing the most difficult and important cases, along with some of the greatest legal minds in the country, but I saw it as the pinnacle of a judicial career. So how did I become a Law Lord? There was one false start. In the summer of 2002, it was known that there would soon be a vacancy among the Law Lords. All of the Law Lords appointed since 1876 had been men. Improving the gender balance in the judiciary was in the air. There was excited press speculation that I would be appointed to fill the vacancy – indeed, the reports were so confident that some people wrote to congratulate me! But I knew that it was not to be. Someone would have told me if it was. And sure enough Lord Justice Robert Walker became Lord Walker of Gestingthorpe on 1 October 2002. He was, of course, eminently well qualified for the post – technically very skilled, but also forward-thinking and with a strong sense of justice and morality.[1]

Technically, the Law Lords were appointed by Her Majesty the Queen on the advice of the prime minister. In modern times, the prime minister has acted on the advice of the Lord Chancellor. The Lord Chancellor would consult the Law Lords, at a round-table meeting in his office in the House of Lords. He would also consult the most senior judges in all parts of the United Kingdom. At some point in 2002, someone in the Lord Chancellor's Department must have floated the idea of my appointment to the press – why else would such confident predictions have been made? But someone or something must have persuaded the Lord Chancellor, Lord Irvine of Lairg, otherwise. It was a dark moment. I thought that someone must have blackballed me and my chance of reaching the highest court in the land had gone for ever. But I should not have worried. I was, after all, only fifty-seven and had been a full-time judge for less than nine years. I received a charming letter from Lord Hobhouse, another Law Lord (who was due to retire in 2004): 'This is just a note to say that no doubt your day will come.' He went on to advise me, as one who had sat in both the House of Lords and the Court of Appeal, to 'enjoy the Court of Appeal as long as you can'. Curiously, when I did reach the House of Lords, I enjoyed it even more than the Court of Appeal, as will become apparent.

In October 2003, Julian and I were on holiday in New Zealand. It was 8 p.m. We had travelled by ferry from Wellington in the north island to Nelson in the south island and then by train down the coast to Christchurch. We had just checked into our hotel room when I had a phone call from my clerk, Ayo Onatade. It was 9 a.m. in London. She read to me a letter from the prime minister, Tony Blair, explaining that there was shortly to be a vacancy for a Law Lord and asking whether, if he recommended my appointment to the Queen, I would accept it. Of course I would. But apparently the drill was to deliver a handwritten acceptance to Downing Street and I was on the other side of the world. It was a dream come true but it still felt like a dream until I got back to London the following week and duly delivered my acceptance. There were two more vacancies in January 2004, filled by Lord Justice Simon Brown, a long-serving member of the Court of Appeal, and Sir Robert Carswell, Lord Chief Justice of Northern Ireland. Ironically, as I was sworn in the day before them, I was senior to them both, although in reality I was much their junior, both in age and experience, but they didn't seem to mind.

At least one of the Law Lords looked upon my arrival with some trepidation (see the entry in Lord Hope's diary for 31 December 1993 quoted on page 101 earlier). Quite what the reason for his anxiety was, I cannot know. Maybe only the two Scottish Law Lords felt that way. Maybe they all did. They were all men with very limited experience of women as equal colleagues. Perhaps it was because I had never had any qualms about calling myself a feminist. And it does appear from other entries in David Hope's diaries that he was uncomfortable with my advocacy of greater gender and other diversity in the judiciary, which he saw as Brenda's 'agenda', and indeed my interest in issues concerning women and children generally. It is strange that challenging the male-dominated status quo in the law and the legal profession is seen as an 'agenda' whereas preserving it is not. We have seen how efficiently the protectors of the status quo can mobilise when they feel it under threat – for example, by meeting calls for diversity with the mantra of 'merit'. But mostly they have no need to be so vocal – so that agenda remains hidden and, no doubt for many, quite unconscious.

Before I was sworn in came the momentous matter of choosing a title which could be approved by Garter Principal King of Arms. The rule is that every peerage has to have a unique title. This applies even if the previous holder was a life peer who has died. Charles Hale was an Oldham MP from 1945 until 1968, was raised to the peerage as Baron Hale in 1972, and died in 1985. This meant that I could not be plain Baroness Hale. Julian rather fancied the alliterative, if inaccurate, 'Lady Hale of Swalydale' (the Swale being the river which flows through my home town). But I played safe and chose 'Hale of

Richmond', meaning of course the first Richmond in North Yorkshire, not the second one on the Thames. There are now four peers of that same Richmond: Baroness Harris of Richmond is a senior Liberal Democrat and a Deputy Speaker; Baron Hague of Richmond was our MP as well as leader of the Conservative Party and Foreign Secretary; and Baron Houghton of Richmond was Chief of the General Staff and is now constable of the Tower of London. That is quite a tally of peers for a small town with around 8,500 inhabitants. It is a tribute to how much we all love the place.

Then there was the business of a coat of arms. This is not compulsory but the College of Arms is very keen that those entitled to bear arms should have one – it is how they make their money. 'In for a penny, in for a pound' thought I. Several decades earlier, the plot of the short story which won me the competition in the *New Elizabethan* magazine had turned on a knowledge of heraldry. So I am the proud possessor of a wonderful document, sealed by Garter King of Arms, recording that the duke of Norfolk, Earl Marshall, had authorised him to grant me a coat of arms: not a shield, but a lozenge, because I am a woman. This is the description: 'Gules two scrolls in saltire Argent banded crosswise Vert attached thereto four Seals in cross Or all between four towers crenellations outward Argent.'

The idea for the towers – representing Richmond Castle – and the sealed scrolls – representing the law – came from my step-granddaughter Madeleine, then aged eleven. As a peer I was also entitled to supporters: 'Two Frogs Vert crowned Or.'

Garter was delighted that I had gone for something so unusual. He may not have known that it was a not very subtle tribute to Julian, my frog prince. There was also a 'device or badge': 'A Frog sejant fronting Or holding between the forefeet a Ranunculus Gules seeded sable.' Finally, there was the motto: *omnia feminae aequissimae* (women are equal to everything).

I was sworn in on 12 January 2004 to hold the office of Lord of Appeal in Ordinary 'so long as she shall well behave herself therein'. This created much mirth in the Chamber and Their Lordships liked the grin with which I greeted it. Lord Triesman, who was sworn in as a life peer immediately after me, was under no such obligation.

One of my guests, Catherine Fraser, chief justice of Alberta, wondered whether it was because I was a woman and thus in some way on probation. But it was no such thing. Since the Act of Settlement of 1701, the senior judiciary have held office *quamdiu se bene gesserint*, that is during good behaviour, rather than at Her Majesty's Pleasure, which was previously the case. Far from being a threat, it is a guarantee of their independence from the government. The Appellate Jurisdiction Act 1876 merely adopted this for the newly created Law Lords.

But was I really a Law Lord? The 1876 Act said that suitably qualified 'persons' might be appointed Lords of Appeal in Ordinary. But in 1886, women were not seen as 'persons' in the eyes of the law. In 1909, the House of Lords held that the word 'persons', in a section of the Representation of the People (Scotland) Act 1868 which gave university graduates the right to vote, did not apply to five women graduates of the University of Edinburgh.[2] It was not until 1929 that the Judicial Committee of the Privy Council held that the word 'persons' in the British North America Act 1867 could now include women – the constitution of Canada was a 'living tree' which could grow and develop over time within its natural limits.[3] So could the meaning of 'persons' in the 1876 Act also move with the times, and now include women? I hope so.[4]

Unlike Lord Hope, I am not a great diary keeper, but I did keep a diary of my first week in the House of Lords. Here are some extracts to give the flavour of how it all felt:

MONDAY 12 JANUARY

Big day when I am 'introduced' into the House of Lords. Arrive at House early and find that Ayo (my much loved and lamented former clerk) has done magnificent job moving, sorting and placing all my stuff in my new room. A good deal smaller than my room at RCJ [Royal Courts of Justice], but has beautiful bay window overlooking Westminster Abbey, Pugin furniture including wonderful wall clock, and ubiquitous TV monitor announcing business of the day (which I rapidly discover can not only show action in Chamber but also real TV programmes – not that I propose to spend my time watching Sky but there it is). Open relations with my new (shared) secretary. Sort out books and belongings so that I know where everything is. Not home yet. Feel very new.

Twelve noon go down to peers' entrance to greet my guests. Traditional to have a large lunch beforehand in peers' dining room so follow suit. Panic about whether guests will find right place, arrive in time, behave themselves, etc. Much touched that Catherine Fraser, chief justice of Alberta, and her husband have flown all way from western Canada to be with us. Brings home how momentous women in common-law world think this is. Feel very small.

Pudding just served when participants in ceremony – my two supporters, Garter King of Arms, and me – whisked off to get robed, have endless photos and rehearse ceremony. Robes a doddle after judicial kit – red wool with ermine trimmings but no collar and tabs, court coat, special shoes, wig or even hat. Most Law Lords have other Law Lords as their supporters, but I have two academics – Lord Flowers, former VC of London University, and Baroness O'Neill, principal of Newnham College, Cambridge – representing main ways in which I am just a bit different from others. Garter King of Arms (a national treasure) is genial and resplendent in his tabard ...

TUESDAY 13 JANUARY

Further sorting, getting to know new secretary, dealing with vast mound of accumulated correspondence, meeting legal assistant (four between twelve of us), finishing off paper for upcoming visit of Israeli Supreme Court for an intensive three-day exchange of views: my subject is 'Homosexual Rights'. Papers for cases this week and next begin to arrive.

2.30 go down to Chamber to watch two other new Law Lords introduced. Peers now beginning to get the hang of it, so less hilarity when Lord Carswell is told he must behave himself and Lord Brown of Eaton-under-Heywood (Lord Justice Simon Brown as we used to know him) provokes hardly a titter ('rampant sexism' says senior Law Lord when I innocently ask him why).

WEDNESDAY 14 JANUARY

Time to collect my parliamentary laptop with obligatory training course. Oh bliss! Parliament has network so can be plugged in all the time. And get emails whenever we want. Very different from judicial system, where we need to dial up specially and everyone wants to do it at the same time. Less bliss! It's so modern that it doesn't have a floppy drive. More new things to learn on top of everything else . . .

But the doorkeepers and police seem to have learned my face already, which makes it feel bit more like home.

Prepare for next day's sitting in Privy Council: seventeenth-century standing order says that junior is always asked to speak first, so I am vastly over-prepared.

Visit from three pro-chancellors of Bristol University to discuss new role as chancellor, taken on before I changed jobs so hope I can cope.

THURSDAY 15 JANUARY

First day of actual sitting: four petitions to Privy Council, three asking for permission to appeal and one asking for fresh evidence to be admitted in his fight to stay registered as a vet. Two petitioners acting in person, so some things quite like Court of Appeal. But others not: Judicial Committee of Privy Council sits in Downing Street, a very short walk away, so we all proceed there by car. We go into the committee room first, and then counsel and others are brought in. Registrar wears morning dress while we are all in suits (I've carefully chosen to wear black skirt suit with white blouse and bright patterned scarf). Everyone else goes out if we want to confer. Then back to normal as all stand when we leave at end of proceedings. None of the petitions has been allowed . . .

FRIDAY 16 JANUARY

Hopefully last press interview for a long time: whole idea of giving press briefing last November was not to have to do any more. But of course they keep asking. And this one is for Bristol University's alumni magazine which wants profile of new chancellor so can't say 'no'. Say how nice it is to strengthen links with academic world once more (no disrespect to court world, of course, but there is more to life than litigation).

House and Privy Council virtually never sit on Friday, so there's time to prepare for next week. I've been lucky to have such a light load this week but will be sitting in Privy Council all next week on two cases: both look substantial and interesting (one's about whether police authority in British Virgin Islands is directly or vicariously liable for policeman who took police gun and used it to shoot at his girlfriend's new boyfriend but hit a bystander). And there's a pile of petitions for leave to appeal to House of Lords to plough through (though one has been taken away because they belatedly realised that I had sat on it in Court of Appeal – a problem for them at present with two new English Law Lords). So I'm not short of work.

Look round room as leave for weekend: two bulbs have now gone in ceiling light, deepening the gloom, but it's already beginning to feel like home.

A word about the Privy Council. It is a relic of empire. People from all over the British Empire could appeal to the monarch, who asked the lawyers on the Privy Council for their advice. In the nineteenth century, a Judicial Committee to do this was formalised. But most countries did away with such appeals once they gained their independence. The only countries that still use the Privy Council are Jersey, Guernsey and the Isle of Man (known as the Crown Dependencies); the few remaining British Overseas Territories (as former colonies are now known), such as Gibraltar, Bermuda and the Cayman Islands; and some small independent Commonwealth countries, of which the Bahamas, Trinidad and Tobago, Jamaica, and Mauritius are the largest.

The cases that come to the Privy Council are enormously varied. Some of these places have large offshore financial industries which can generate commercial disputes worth many millions. At the other extreme, there are some comparatively trivial civil disputes, because there is often a constitutional right of appeal if the case is worth more than what is now not a lot of money. They don't have to show that it raises an important point of law. Most of the criminal appeals arise because the independent Anglo-Caribbean countries still have the death penalty for murder which they inherited from England. All these countries, apart from the Crown Dependencies, have written constitutions modelled on those which were bequeathed to them by the United Kingdom when they gained their independence. The Privy Council has to interpret these: for example, was it

Cover of *Women and the Law*,
published 1984.

With stepson Tom, his wife Lieve, Julian and Julia,
at High Court swearing-in, 1994.

With stepdaughter Sarah, Julian and Julia,
at Court of Appeal swearing-in, 1999.

Introduced to the House of Lords,
2004.

The Law Lords with their clerk in Committee Room No. 1 in the Houses of Parliament, 2008.

With House of Lords' Judicial Assistant,
Rachel, 2005–6.

My Coat of Arms (for heraldic
description, see p. 178).

With Lord Neuberger, Lord Rodger
and Lord Hope, enjoying judgments
in the House of Lords, 2009.

In an even heavier robe, as Chancellor of the University of Bristol,
with Denis Burn, chair of Trustees, and Professor Eric Thomas, vice chancellor.

Cartoon by
Jessye Aggleton,
PhD student at the
University of Bristol.

Conferring a degree with delight,
University of Bristol, 2013.

The Supreme Court of the United Kingdom, formerly the Middlesex Guildhall.

The emblem and seal
of the Supreme Court
of the United Kingdom
(for explanation, see pp. 206-7).

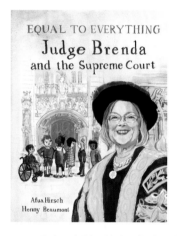

Cover of the children's book about
Judge Brenda, by Afua Hirsch and
Henny Beaumont, published by and
in aid of the Legal Action Group, 2019.

With Lady Black,
the second woman
in the Supreme
Court, processing
from York Minster
after the Legal
Service, 2019.

With artist David Cobley and the portrait now hanging in Gray's Inn hall
– the first woman since Queen Elizabeth I and the first to smile.

With Justice Ruth Bader Ginsburg,
after lecturing to the US Supreme Court
Historical Society on Magna Carta, 2015.

With Ayo, my clerk in the
Court of Appeal and PA in the
Supreme Court, and great friend.

Portrait photograph by Anita Corbin for her 'First Women' exhibition, in the Supreme Court library with the Gainsborough portrait of the Duke of Northumberland behind.

The Justices outside the Supreme Court before processing to the Legal Service in Westminster Abbey, 2 October 2017.

'Legacy, 2019' by Catherine Yass, in Courtroom No. 2 at the Supreme Court, featuring Cornelia Sorabji, Rose Heilbron, Brenda Hale and an unknown woman lawyer of the future, fundraising by Spark 21 and the First Hundred Years project.

The Supreme Court Justices and their Judicial Assistants, 2018–19. Penelope Gorman sitting in front of me.

A small selection of brooches, featuring *that* spider.

Jill and Brenda in The Heifer, Scorton, July 2021.

unconstitutional for Jamaica to replace appeals to the Privy Council with appeals to the Caribbean Court of Justice without using the special procedures necessary to amend the constitution? Somewhat to our surprise, we held that it was.[5] But that was not because we were anxious to hang on to these cases: we are happy to continue to offer the service if that is what the people of the independent nations want; but we are also happy to lose them if that is what they want. That some of us would miss the cases, the characters and the respite from an endless diet of 'points of law of general public importance' is beside the point.

I found the variety of the work, of the people and the places fascinating. We had to get to know the geography and the land-ownership system in the Cook Islands to resolve disputes which had been rumbling on for more than a century. We had to get to grips with the ethnic composition of the population of Mauritius in order to decide whether their voting system was fair. We had to brush up our French, because much of the law of Mauritius is derived from French law and the sources are in French. We had to understand the politics of Trinidad and Tobago, where the population is roughly evenly split between the African Caribbean and the Indian Caribbean communities. We even began to travel. Throughout its long history serving roughly a third of the world's population, the Privy Council had made the people come to them in London. But soon after I joined them, Lord Bingham accepted an invitation for us to spend a week sitting in the Bahamas. I was one of the five chosen to go. People found it hard to believe that I had mixed feelings. Who would not want to spend a week in the sunny Bahamas in December, staying in a hotel with its own private beach, being royally entertained and carefully looked after, each with our own car, driver and police protection officer – luxuries which we did not have in London? But what woman with a family Christmas to organise wants to be away at such a busy time? The visit went down well and there have been a few others to the Bahamas and Mauritius since.

Another enjoyable feature of the Privy Council was the variety of advocates who appeared there. There were London barristers who specialised in doing Privy Council work, but there were also local counsel who enjoyed the trip to London. There were some memorable characters among them: the great Sir Fenton Ramsahoye, a former Attorney General of British Guiana, who practised all over the Anglo-Caribbean, was said in 2006 to hold the record for the most appearances of a Caribbean lawyer before the Privy Council. We certainly saw a lot of him, usually leading Anand Ramlogan, who became Attorney General of Trinidad and Tobago. The custom was that local counsel would wear the same robes in London as they did at home: remarkably, in some very hot countries they were still wearing wigs.

I doubt whether any of us enjoyed the death-penalty cases. I was spared one of these soon after becoming a Law Lord. A nine-judge panel was assembled to resolve a conflict which had arisen between different decisions of the Privy Council: the issue was whether the compulsory death penalty for murder was unconstitutional. Everyone agreed that it was contrary to the constitutional prohibitions of 'cruel and unusual' or 'inhuman and degrading' punishment. The dispute was a highly technical one about the preservation of laws which pre-dated the constitution in question.

I would have been one of the nine, but it was decided that instead there should be an Anglo-Caribbean judge on the panel. Five of the judges (including the Caribbean judge) held that the compulsory death penalty was preserved and could not be modified to fit the constitution; four of them held otherwise.[6] Which way would I have decided? I cannot be sure. My personal views about the death penalty should not come into it: we are sworn to uphold the laws of the country in whose courts we are sitting. But if Lords Bingham, Nicholls, Steyn and Walker could reconcile it with their judicial consciences to hold as they did, it is unlikely that I would have disagreed with them. It is a mark of Lord Bingham's greatness that he decided to include a Caribbean judge on the panel, when he must have known that this would make it less likely that his own view would prevail.

The Privy Council used to sit in a particularly beautiful purpose-built committee room, originally designed by Sir John Soane, at 9 Downing Street. This was only a short walk from the Palace of Westminster. But the tradition was that the Law Lords would be solemnly driven between the two in an ancient Daimler limousine kept specially for the purpose. Downing Street was never happy that the parties, their lawyers and the public had to be allowed through the gates to take part, so they were delighted when the opportunity came to co-locate the Judicial Committee with the new Supreme Court of the United Kingdom.

I was not the first woman to sit on the Judicial Committee of the Privy Council. That honour goes to Dame Sian Elias, then the chief justice of New Zealand, who first sat in 2003. There was, of course, no lavatory for women judges. The registrar solemnly offered me the use of his until one was constructed, especially for me. Nevertheless, until I protested, the covering letter which came from his office with the case papers requested that 'His Lordship' bring the papers with him to the hearing. They seemed puzzled when I objected.

The doorkeepers in the House of Lords were much more understanding. Committee Room No. 1 on the committee corridor was dedicated to the Law Lords' use. We would emerge from the door at the end of the corridor in single file – of course in order of seniority – and bow to counsel standing further down the corridor before processing into the committee room. Traditionally, the doorkeeper leading us would shout 'Their Lordships' to announce our arrival. But I soon persuaded them to shout 'Their Lordships and Her Ladyship' and was rewarded with a quiet 'Well done, Brenda,' from Lord Hoffmann.

Some of the most entertaining cases to come before the House of Lords while I was there were the three attacking the Hunting Act 2004, which banned hunting certain wild animals with dogs, together with a fourth attacking the Protection of Wild Mammals (Scotland) Act 2002, which did much the same in Scotland. The Hunting Bill took up more parliamentary time than any other in the Labour government of 1997 to 2010. It was hugely controversial but not on wholly party political lines – there were Conservative opponents of hunting as well as Labour supporters. I well remember the dramatic atmosphere in the Palace of Westminster on 18 November 2004, when the bill received the royal assent without having been passed by the House of Lords.

Usually, of course, a bill needs the consent of the House of Commons, the House of Lords, and the royal assent before becoming law as an Act of Parliament. But since 1911 there has been a procedure for passing bills without the consent of the House of Lords if it passes the House of Commons a number of times over a minimum period of time. The House of Lords were persuaded to agree to this drastic reduction in their powers by the king's threat to create enough Liberal peers to vote the Parliament Act 1911 through. In 1949, the timetable was reduced, to make it easier for the Labour government to get through their legislation setting up the welfare state. This was done using the 1911 procedure.

The House of Lords usually backs down if its objections are rejected by the House of Commons and only a handful of Acts have been passed using the procedure as laid down in 1949. But one of them was the Hunting Act 2004. So the very first case about the Act to come before us in the House of Lords argued that it was not a valid Act of Parliament at all.[7] This was because, so the argument went, laws have to be passed by the Commons, Lords and Crown. In 1911 they had delegated their power, exceptionally, to the Commons and Crown. But a delegate cannot increase its own powers. That was what the Commons and Crown had done by changing the law in 1949. So the 1949 change was not valid and any Act passed using the 1949 procedure was not valid. A panel of nine Law Lords was assembled to hear the case. None of us had any difficulty in rejecting the argument. The Parliament Act 1911 was not delegating power to a new body but restricting the powers of the House of Lords. It expressly provides that a bill passed under its provisions 'shall become an Act of Parliament on the royal assent being signified thereto'. What could be clearer than that?

The case is exciting to law students because three of the Law Lords took the opportunity to discuss whether there were might be limits on what Parliament chose to do, whether or not it was using the new procedure. The traditional view, accepted since the Glorious Revolution of 1688, is that Parliament is sovereign. It can make or unmake any law it chooses. One parliament cannot prevent a later parliament changing the law. This puts the currently elected Members of Parliament in charge. That is democracy, UK-style. But was it right? Were certain things so sacrosanct that even Parliament could not change them? Lord Steyn suggested that it was not unthinkable that circumstances might arise in which the courts would have to rethink the principle – for example if there were an attempt to abolish judicial review of the legality of government action or the ordinary role of the courts in protecting the citizen from the state. Lord Hope pointed out that 'parliamentary sovereignty is no longer, if it ever was, absolute' and that 'the rule of law enforced by the courts is the ultimate controlling factor on which our constitution is based'. I suggested that 'the courts will treat with particular suspicion (and might even reject) any attempt to subvert the rule of law by removing governmental action affecting the rights of the individual from all judicial scrutiny'. Without the words in brackets, my view would have been unobjectionable. All three comments were roundly condemned as unhistorical and without authority by Lord Bingham himself.[8] I wonder whether they will surface in any future case which comes before the Supreme Court of the United Kingdom.

But how could it possibly be right for the case to be decided by a panel consisting entirely of members of the House of Lords? It is a fundamental principle of natural justice that no one shall be judge in their own cause – even an appearance of bias is enough to invalidate a judicial decision. Yet this was quintessentially a case about the respective powers of the House of Lords and the House of Commons. The fact that we unanimously decided it in favour of the House of Commons is neither here nor there. It greatly strengthened the case for setting up a Supreme Court, independent of Parliament.

That case had nothing to do with the pros and cons of banning the hunting of certain wild animals with dogs. The next two cases, which were heard together, claimed that the ban was an unjustified interference with human rights or with the fundamental freedoms protected by European Union law.[9] We also heard a similar attack on the Protection of Wild Mammals (Scotland) Act 2002, an Act of the Scottish Parliament which did much the same for Scotland as the 2004 Act did for England and Wales.[10]

The Scottish case was argued by Mr Brian Friend, a litigant in person. We all liked Mr Friend. He came to the House of Lords wearing a country gentleman's suit – he told us that he did have a city suit, but he was making a point about how important country pursuits were to him and to people like him. He felt that the ban had interfered with a core aspect of his personality and way of life. He came carrying a Conservative-supporting newspaper which had been strongly critical of the Human Rights Act to argue (contrary to the views of some of his friends) that the Human Rights Act was there to protect ordinary people who lead ordinary lives – not just the unpopular minorities whose cases hit the headlines. He was quite right about that.

The first argument was that the ban was an unjustified interference with the right to respect for private life, which is protected by Article 8 of the European Convention on Human Rights. Does the very public act of hunting wild animals with dogs feel like part of your 'private life'? We decided that it didn't. Private life is a very broad concept. It includes the personal and psychological space within which each individual develops his or her own sense of self and relationships with other people. But it does not cover everything that an individual might want to do in that private space; and it certainly does not protect things that can only be done by leaving it and engaging in a very public gathering and activity.

But was it an interference with freedom of association and assembly, protected by Article 11? This was more plausible. Article 11 is part of a trilogy of related rights – Article 9 which protects freedom of religion and belief, Article 10 which protects freedom of expression, and Article 11 which protects freedom of association. These are all about the freedom to share and express opinions and to try and persuade others to share them, essential political freedoms in any democracy. Hunt supporters could gather together to demonstrate against the ban. But did that mean that they had the right to gather together to chase and kill the fox or the stag or the mink or the hare? I thought not but Lord Bingham thought that it did. But if so, the interference was justified as part of a long line of measures to protect the welfare of animals, beginning with an Act to prevent the cruel and improper treatment of cattle in 1822. 'The familiar suggestion that the British mind more about their animals than their children does not lack a certain foundation in fact.' The Hunting Act had to be seen as 'the latest link in a long chain of statutes devoted to what was seen as social reform'. I agreed, although I hoped that the children had now caught up with the animals.

Lord Bingham felt very strongly that the protestors should not be able to win in the courts when they had so recently been defeated in

Parliament. If we had held that the ban was an unjustified interference with a Convention right, the result would have been different north and south of the border. The courts have no power to hold that an Act of the UK Parliament is invalid even if it does breach Convention rights – all they can do is make a declaration to that effect and leave it to the government and Parliament to decide what, if anything, to do about it. That is all part of the sovereignty of Parliament. But the Scotland Act 1998, which set up the Scottish Parliament, states that an Act of the Scottish Parliament which breaches Convention rights is 'not law'.[11] If Mr Friend had succeeded in his arguments, the Scottish Act would have been invalid, whereas the Hunting Act would not.

The alleged breaches of European Union law were more esoteric. Did the ban interfere with the free movement of goods within the European Union by inhibiting the sale of Irish hunting horses and greyhounds in England? Did it interfere with the freedom to provide services within the European Union by inhibiting hunting-based holidays here for people from other European countries? We weren't very sure of the answers. But we decided that the ban was justified on grounds of public policy. There is a famous case from Germany in which the European Court held that Germany was entitled to ban a game which involves the simulated shooting of people with laser guns, because this infringed the fundamental value of human dignity enshrined in the German constitution.[12] Here the real killing of certain wild animals for fun infringed a fundamental value enshrined in the UK's animal-welfare legislation.

Mr Friend and the Countryside Alliance complained to the European Court of Human Rights in Strasbourg that our decision meant that the United Kingdom had violated their rights under the Convention. The Strasbourg court agreed with us on all points and found their complaints 'manifestly ill-founded'.[13] This was, I think, a very good example of how effective the Human Rights Act 1998 has been. Because the rights protected by the European Convention are now also protected by UK law, we can consider whether they have been breached in the same way that the Strasbourg court would do. We are talking the same language. That is why the UK has lost far fewer cases in Strasbourg since the Act came into force than it did beforehand.

Entertaining though these cases were, there was nothing about them in which my gender might have made a difference to my thinking. But I can think of at least three cases where it certainly did so. In the first,[14] the male defendant was twenty-two years older than the female complainant. They lived in the same village and their families were friends. The complainant began working for him on Saturdays and during the school holidays. On many occasions when she was between the ages of thirteen and fifteen, the defendant had vaginal sexual intercourse with her: a classic case of abusing a position of trust. He also had oral sexual intercourse with her when she was thirteen. He was found guilty of indecent assault in relation to both types of intercourse. He appealed against his conviction for the vaginal sexual intercourse, though not for the oral, but he did not argue that he had not done it.

Since 1885, it had been an offence (colloquially known as 'statutory rape') to have intercourse with a girl aged thirteen to fifteen irrespective of her consent. This was a response to the widespread practice of selling young girls into prostitution against their will, to satisfy the insatiable demand of powerful men for sex with virgins, so vividly exposed by W. T. Stead in a famous series of articles entitled 'The Maiden Tribute of Modern Babylon', published in the *Pall Mall Gazette* in July 1885. It was vigorously opposed by people who feared that householders with young sons would no longer be able to employ female servants aged under fifteen – perhaps because of the fear that what were seen as the natural activities of those sons would now be criminal, or because of the fear of unfounded accusations, or both. The fear of unfounded accusations led to a rule that a prosecution could only be brought within three months of the alleged event – apparently the thinking was that if the girl became pregnant (and thus was undoubtedly a victim of the crime) she would be so likely to name the wrong man as the father that an accusation could only be made before any pregnancy became apparent (being obviously a girl of loose morals she would also be a liar – a classic case of blaming the victim). The time limit was progressively raised, reaching twelve months in 1928. But once the initial 'reasoning' had gone, it is not clear why the time limit was kept at all. The same conduct also constitutes the offence of indecent assault and in 1922 it was provided that the consent of a girl under sixteen was no defence to an indecent assault. There was no time limit for prosecuting that offence. That is how the law remained when it was all consolidated in the Sexual Offences Act 1956.[15]

In this case, the complainant did not disclose what had happened to her until she was seventeen. We do not know why, although we do know that there are many reasons why victims do not disclose until much later, especially if they have been groomed or threatened by their abusers. This meant that, because of a law originally conceived over a century earlier and in a different moral universe, the defendant could not be prosecuted for the offence of unlawful sexual intercourse but he could be prosecuted for indecent assault. There was no doubt about what he had done. The argument was that it was an 'abuse of process' to prosecute him for indecent assault when he could not be prosecuted for unlawful sexual intercourse. The other Law Lords held that it was an abuse. I disagreed. The delay had not meant that the defendant could not have a fair trial. There were no policy reasons against allowing him to be prosecuted for the offences which he had undoubtedly committed – teenage girls needed to be protected against just this sort of behaviour. How to explain to his victim or anyone else that he could be prosecuted for the oral but not for the vaginal intercourse? The only unfairness would be that done to her and the many others in her situation, if he were not. I think that Lord Judge, who was then Lord Chief Justice, would have agreed with me. The other Law Lords hearing the case did not.

The next case was about the scope of the defence of duress in criminal cases.[16] Advances in forensic science have made many crimes easier to detect and more difficult to defend, so the defence of duress – being forced by threats to commit the crime – is being raised much more frequently, and often by some very unattractive people. Judges do not like it, because it is so difficult to disprove. They are keen to maintain an objective approach to whether a reasonable person would have given way to the threats. The appellant claimed that he had been forced to commit a burglary by fear of extreme violence from the boyfriend of the woman for whom he worked, who ran an 'escort agency' and was involved in prostitution. But you cannot claim duress if you have voluntarily put yourself in a situation where you can foresee that you may be exposed to such threats. The question was whether this applied where he could foresee the risk of being compelled by threats of violence to do *something* or only where he could foresee the risk that he would be compelled to commit crimes. The other four Law Lords chose the former. I would have chosen the latter.

My main concern was for the wives and families of violent men: 'the battered wife knows very well that she may be compelled to cook the dinner, wash the dishes, iron the shirts and submit to sexual intercourse. That should not deprive her of the defence of duress if she is obliged by the same threats to herself or her children to commit perjury or shoplift for food.' It was one thing to deny the defence to someone who chose to become a member of a criminal gang; quite another thing to deny it to someone who had very different reasons for being associated with the criminal and then found it difficult to escape. During the hearing, I had thought that others agreed with me on the 'battered wife' question, but somehow it did not emerge in the majority judgment. It was in that judgment that I also confessed to being a 'reasonable but comparatively weak and fearful grandmother', who would have liked the defendant's personal characteristics to be relevant to whether she should have resisted the threats.

In those two cases, I was on my own: part of the long struggle to get the male judiciary to see things from the woman's point of view. But in the third no struggle was necessary. It brought together the cases of two women who admittedly had a well-founded fear that they would face persecution if returned to their home countries. A refugee is defined in the Geneva Convention relating to the Status of Refugees of 1951 as a person who, 'owing to a well-founded fear of being persecuted for reasons of race, religion, nationality, membership of a particular social group, or political opinion' is outside his country of origin and unable or unwilling to return because of that fear. Gender is not in the list of reasons for facing persecution, but during the 1990s the world woke up to the fact that women might be persecuted in ways which are different from the ways in which men are persecuted and that they may be persecuted because of the inferior status accorded to them in their home countries. So the question was whether they would be persecuted because of their 'membership of a particular social group'.[17] Mrs K was an Iranian woman whose husband had been arrested and detained without charge or trial. Soon afterwards the Revolutionary Guard came to her home and raped her. Later they went to her young son's school and made enquiries about her. Fearing for her own and her son's safety, she fled. Ms Fornah was a Sierra Leonean who came to this country at the age of fifteen and feared that she would be subjected to female genital mutilation (FGM) against her will if she returned. The lower courts had held that neither woman feared persecution 'for reasons of their ... membership of a particular social group'.

I am afraid that I started my judgment by saying that 'the answer in each case is so blindingly obvious that it must be a mystery to some why either of them had to reach this House'. Mrs K faced persecution because she was a member of her husband's family. The family is the original and quintessential social group: 'the cohesion and solidarity of a family means that any individual can be got at through the medium of the other individuals in the group'. Why then had she failed in the lower courts? Because it was not known whether her husband was being held because of his political opinions or for some other reason. The Court of Appeal had earlier held that if the 'primary member of a family' was not persecuted for a Convention reason then the 'secondary members' cannot be said to be persecuted for a Convention reason.[18] There was no warrant for this in the Convention or for the sexist assumption that her husband was the primary member of the family and she was secondary. Her claim had to be looked at in its own right: once the definition was applied to her, it was clear that she qualified.

Ms Fornah faced persecution because she was a member of a tribe in Sierra Leone which practised FGM, as did all the indigenous tribes in that country. Why then had she failed in the lower courts? Because a 'particular social group' cannot be defined solely by reference to the persecution it fears – there must be some other characteristic which binds it together. The Court of Appeal (by a majority – it is no coincidence that Lady Justice Arden had disagreed) had thought that this applied to her. They were misled by the fact that FGM is a once-and-for-all event – once done, it cannot be undone or repeated. So members of the group who have been cut are no longer at risk; and if the group is defined as those who have not been cut, it looks as if they are being defined solely by the persecution they fear. This is a good example of the convoluted reasoning which can sometimes blind us to the obvious. The Court of Appeal missed the blindingly obvious fact that Ms Fornah faced persecution because she was a female member of a tribe within Sierra Leone which practised FGM – they shared the immutable characteristics of being female, Sierra Leonean and members of their tribe. They would do so irrespective of whether the tribe practised FGM and irrespective of whether they had, or had not, been cut. I would have defined the group in that way. Lord Bingham would have gone further and defined it as all Sierra Leonean women. I think that Their Lordships would have decided these cases in the same way whether or not I had been a member of the panel: but some think that my presence did make a difference.[19]

But the judgment in the House of Lords of which I am most proud is a short concurrence in the case of *Ghaidan v Godin-Mendoza*.[20] Article 14 of the Convention bans discrimination on the ground of sexual orientation in the enjoyment of the right to respect for the home. The Rent Act 1977 provided that if a couple were 'living together as husband and wife' the survivor could succeed to the tenancy of their home. We had a duty, if possible, to 'read and give effect' to the Act so that it was compatible with the Convention rights.[21] Was it possible to read those words so as to include a same-sex couple? We held, by a majority of four to one, that it was. Once again, I went to town, this time on the importance of equal treatment:

> Such a guarantee of equal treatment is also essential to democracy. Democracy is founded on the principle that each individual has equal value. Treating some as automatically having less value than others not only causes pain and distress to that person but also violates his or her dignity as a human being ... Second, such treatment is damaging to society as a whole. Wrongly to assume that some people have talent and others do not is a huge waste of human resources. It also damages social cohesion, creating not only an underclass, but an underclass with a rational grievance. Third, it is the reverse of the rational behaviour we now expect of government and the state. Power must not be exercised arbitrarily. If distinctions are to be drawn, particularly on a group basis, it is an important discipline to look for a rational basis for these

distinctions. Finally, it is a purpose of all human rights instruments to secure the protection of the essential rights of members of minority groups, even when they are unpopular with the majority. Democracy values everyone equally even if the majority does not.

Unlike Lord Hobhouse, I enjoyed sitting in the House of Lords even more than in the Court of Appeal. We had more time to research and think about the cases than they did. We were not bound by previous Court of Appeal decisions as they were. We could try and find the right result in principle to some very difficult problems. We agreed about the right result far more often than we disagreed. The ethos was less 'macho' than in the hard-pressed Court of Appeal. During my time in the Lords, five of Their Lordships retired and were replaced by five more men. Sadly, I was to be the first and the only woman Lord of Appeal in Ordinary.

12 Creating the Supreme Court

16 October 2009 was a great day for the justice system in the UK. Her Majesty the Queen came to open the new Supreme Court in the old Middlesex Guildhall. The prime minister, Gordon Brown, and the leader of the opposition, David Cameron, and other leading politicians were there. There were distinguished visitors from overseas, including John Roberts, chief justice of the Supreme Court of the United States. This shows what a big deal the whole Anglo-American legal world thought it was. The Lord Chancellor, Jack Straw, made a speech; the Poet Laureate, Andrew Motion, read a poem composed for the court; and the Archbishop of Canterbury, Rowan Williams, said a prayer. Her Majesty toured the building, speaking to many groups of people, including the justices' spouses gathered in the lobby outside the principal courtroom. She so charmed my republican husband that he became a monarchist 'for this reign only'. She completed her tour by unveiling a fine bronze relief by Ian Rank-Broadley, who does her image on our coinage, showing her in garter robes with hand outstretched as if bestowing her jurisdiction upon us.

Was it really such a great day? Views were decidedly mixed. I was in favour, but I had joined the Law Lords knowing that their days were numbered, and was happy to be leaving the red benches, splendid though they were. Some very senior figures had gone public with their support. These included the senior Law Lord, Lord Bingham,[1] Lord Steyn, then the third most senior Law Lord,[2] and Lord Phillips, a former Law Lord who was then Master of the Rolls and was later to become Lord Chief Justice of England and Wales and the first president of the Supreme Court.[3] Some of the other Law Lords were strongly against it, but had not yet gone public with their views. So it is scarcely surprising that, when the government announced their package of constitutional reforms in June 2003, they thought that establishing a Supreme Court to take over from the Law Lords would be relatively uncontroversial. They were wrong about that. There was principle and pragmatism on each side.

In principle, there are three separate institutions of government – Parliament which makes the laws, the government which runs the country, and the judiciary who interpret and apply the laws. In the UK constitution, and in the many other 'Westminster-style' constitutions around the world, the government and Parliament are not separate – the government is chosen from those Members of Parliament whose party can command a majority in the House of Commons. But in all those other constitutions, the judiciary are completely separate from both Parliament and government. In practice, the judicial work of the House of Lords had become entirely separate from its legislative work and the Law Lords played less and less part in parliamentary business. So, argued Lord Bingham, we 'do not belong in a House to whose business we can make no more than a small contribution'. The Law Lords were a court and should be seen as such by the public and the outside world. Nor should they, as Members of Parliament, be called upon to decide disputes between the different Houses of Parliament[4] or between the government and Parliament.[5]

It also seemed to me that the character of the House of Lords had changed dramatically after 1999 when all but ninety-two of the hereditary peers had been removed (although a few were given life peerages instead). The House had become much more politically balanced. It felt more able to flex what remained of its muscles. The more politically effective the Lords became, the less appropriate it was for the Law Lords to be there. We got many lobbying letters, asking for our support for various political causes: I had a standard reply to the effect that, as a serving judge, I did not think it right to take part in parliamentary business. One persistent lobbyist responded by asking me to lend my support in my judicial capacity – showing just how confusing our position was.

Nor could the position of Lord Chancellor be defended. He was a senior member of the Cabinet responsible for a government department which spent a great deal of public money and ought really to be accountable to the House of Commons. He was Speaker of the House of Lords. But he was also head of the judiciary and could still sit as a judge if he wanted to: both Lord Hailsham and Lord Mackay occasionally did. Lord Irvine declared that he would not sit on cases in which the government was involved – of which there were many – or concerning legislation which he had promoted. But he remained in charge of the courts and responsible for the recruitment, appointment, deployment and discipline of the judiciary. Could this be reconciled with Article 6 of the European Convention on Human Rights, which guarantees the right, in both civil and criminal cases, to a 'fair and public hearing within a reasonable time by an independent and impartial tribunal established by law'? Ironically, the Human Rights Act 1998 had been piloted through the House of Lords by Lord Irvine himself.

So constitutional clarity and propriety were the main principled reasons for change. There were practical reasons as well. The Law Lords took up a great deal of space in the Palace of Westminster. I had a whole room to myself with a beautiful view of Westminster Abbey, room No. 1 on the Law Lords' corridor. Next to me was an almost identical room shared by four parliamentarians, two of them working peers who were there most days when the House was sitting. I felt very guilty. Our registry and other offices also took up space. Yet many working peers did not even have a desk. Even so, there was not enough room for all of us. There were ten rooms on the Law Lords' corridor. Lord Brown had to have a rather less grand room next to our secretaries – in fact, he thoroughly enjoyed being at the heart of things, in a room which we all had to pass to get to the coffee point in the secretaries' room, but that's beside the point. Lord Saville had only a broom cupboard, because he was fully occupied with the Bloody Sunday Inquiry in Northern Ireland. We had space for only four secretaries, at a time when few of the Law Lords typed their own judgments and correspondence. Even more important, we had space for only four judicial assistants. They inhabited a room at the very top of the tower above the peers' entrance to the House of Lords, so they had to be fit as well as friendly.

There were some principled objections. There were people who thought that, far from being a threat to the independence of the judiciary, it was our great protection to have a senior politician at the heart of government whose role it was to defend our independence and the rule of law. Lord Mackay certainly took that view. That is why the Constitutional Reform Act 2005 requires the Lord Chancellor to swear an oath 'that I will respect the rule of law, defend the independence of the judiciary and discharge my duty to ensure the provision of resources for the efficient and effective support of the courts for which I am responsible'.[6] The Act does not require that the Lord Chancellor be a lawyer. I have heard no less than eight Lord Chancellors take that oath, four of them lawyers (Jack Straw, Kenneth Clarke, David Gauke and Robert Buckland) and four of them not (Christopher Grayling, Michael Gove, Liz Truss and David Liddington). They all spoke to it with apparent conviction. History will no doubt judge how their efforts compared with one another and with the efforts of their predecessors. Some have undoubtedly found it harder than others to retain the confidence of the judiciary.

But many of their difficulties stemmed from the political reasons which lay behind the surprise announcements of June 2003.[7] The prime minister and others had for some time been frustrated by the resistance of the Lord Chancellor and his department to the modernisation of the criminal justice system. They wanted to bring together all parts of the system – or at least the courts, the judiciary and the prison and probation services – into a single Ministry of Justice. Politics required this plot to be hatched in secret, without the knowledge of Lord Chancellor Irvine or his senior advisers. But the effect of bringing together the apparently ever-open jaws of publicly funded legal services and the prison and probation services, was that the courts and the judiciary, whose jaws were not ever-open, were squeezed between them. This was made much worse in 2010 when austerity brought severe cuts to all parts of the justice system. It has been struggling to recover some of the lost ground ever since.

Funding was another objection to removing the Law Lords from Parliament. While we were there, our running costs came from Parliament, which can vote for itself the resources which it needs. Government departments, on the other hand, have to put in bids to the Treasury, which decides upon the spending plans to be put before Parliament. Would it really make us more independent if our funding had to come through the departmental budgeting process rather than directly from Parliament? Not only that: we were now going to have to pay for a great many services which we had previously enjoyed in the Palace of Westminster – our building and its maintenance, our library, our IT, our communications, our catering and a great deal more. The new court would inevitably cost much more than the Law Lords had done. Not surprisingly there were some, including Lord Neuberger, later to become the second president of the court, who questioned whether the benefits were worth the expenditure, at a time when the other courts were feeling the pinch. Fortunately, both these problems were later resolved. Even so, in the early days, we had to take trouble to emphasise that we were completely separate from the Ministry of Justice.

There was also a fear that, once we were no longer part of Parliament, both Parliament and the government would feel freer to criticise our decisions – we would no longer be seen as 'one of us' and given some protection or 'cover'. Allied to that was the fear that, once we moved out of Parliament and became known as the 'Supreme Court', we would get ideas above our station and somehow assume the powers of Supreme Courts in other parts of the world, in particular to strike down Acts of the UK Parliament. Ross Cranston MP,[8] for example, put it to Lord Bingham that both the United States Supreme Court and the High Court of Australia got bolder once they moved into their own prestigious accommodation. Lord Bingham was able to point out that the High Court of Australia could hardly be described as an activist court. Other scholars were more apocalyptic. Professor Diana Woodhouse, for example, suggested that 'in the long term, it is possible to see parliamentary sovereignty being replaced as the defining principle of the constitution by a more robust version of the separation of powers'.[9] The new justices had no such radical ambitions: for us, it was very much business as usual. I firmly believe that the Supreme Court has carried on the role which the Law Lords had carried on for decades, if not centuries, no more and no less.

Once the Constitutional Reform Act 2005 had set up the new court, a great deal of work had to be done to make it a reality. First was the search for a suitable building. The Law Lords solemnly examined no less than six possibilities, but only two of them were serious: the 'new' wing of Somerset House and the Middlesex Guildhall. The new wing of Somerset House is separated by a hidden roadway from the elegant eighteenth-century quadrangle of buildings fronting onto the Strand. It was formed in the mid-nineteenth century by making a row of houses into a single building and adding an elaborate entrance facade fronting onto the approach to Waterloo Bridge. Aesthetically, it was the more pleasing building. But there were objections: it had too much accommodation for us; but it had no large rooms which would be suitable for our hearings; the only possibilities were close to the road and ready targets for attack (as Lord Carswell, from Northern Ireland, pointed out); and the Scotsmen thought that it was too close to 'legal London' – the Royal Courts of Justice and the Inns of Court – for a court which was to serve the whole of the United Kingdom.

The Middlesex Guildhall was ideally situated: on the western side of Parliament Square, with the Houses of Parliament opposite on the east, the Treasury offices to the north, and the 'royal peculiar' of Westminster Abbey to the south. All four pillars of the constitution would be represented round the square: Parliament, the government, the judiciary, and the Crown (in my view, it should be renamed Constitution Square but that is not going to happen).

The Guildhall was opened in 1913 as the headquarters of Middlesex County Council: in fact once the London County Council was formed in 1889, the site was no longer actually in Middlesex, but the Middlesex magistrates had had a court building there since the early nineteenth century. The architect was James Gibson, but much of the design was the work of his partner, Frank Peyton Skipwith. Pevsner calls the style 'art nouveau Gothic' but in reality it is an eclectic mix of Gothic, Renaissance, and Arts and Crafts, described at the time as 'full of human fancy' and looking as if its creators had been having fun doing it. You only have to look at the elaborate stone carvings on the outside of the building to agree with this.

Like all such buildings, it had a council chamber, two courtrooms for the quarter sessions (for trials by jury) and the petty sessions (for trials by magistrates), cells in the basement, a library, meeting rooms and offices. The county of Middlesex was abolished by the Local Government Act of 1963, but the building continued to be used as a courthouse for jury trials. It was closed for some years in the 1980s and reopened as a Crown Court by Lord Mackay in 1987: there is still a stained-glass panel commemorating this in the lobby outside the main courtroom. There were no fewer than seven courtrooms, each with its associated jury room, lifts for bringing the defendants up from the cells in the basement, a jury muster area, probation offices, a mess for the barristers to lunch in, a dining room for the judges, and numerous other offices for the staff.

When the Law Lords inspected the building in 2006, it was a mess: dirty and dingy, its lavish ornamentation obscured by the clutter. The two original courtrooms had fine traditional furniture designed for criminal trials – a justices' bench 'halfway up the wall', a dock, a jury box, a witness box, benches for the barristers and solicitors, press and public galleries. None of these did we want or need. We wanted something much more like our House of Lords committee room. It was hard for some of the Law Lords to imagine what the Guildhall might be like if we got rid of it all. Some of them also had unhappy memories of appearing before a former chairman of the bench, Sir Ewen Montagu, who had a fine reputation as a soldier but not as a judge. A deep gloom descended on the party. But it was the obvious choice. Not only was the location ideal, it was exactly the right size, and it could not long continue to be used as a criminal court on such a security-sensitive spot. In March 2007 some of us attended the farewell sitting of the Middlesex Guildhall Crown Court. The sadness of the judges who had sat there and the staff who had worked there was palpable – that in itself sent us a message that, for all its clutter, this was a building that people loved to work in.

Over the next two years, it was transformed – remarkably, given the tight budget. The architects were Feilden + Mawson, who also brought in Foster + Partners to advise. Meetings were held with the Law Lords, first to discuss what they hoped for from the building, and then to secure their approval of the plans as they developed. The Law Lords formed a small subcommittee to liaise with the Ministry of Justice officials masterminding the move. Lord Hope was in the chair, and concentrated upon the administration, staffing and finances; Lord Mance was concerned with security issues; and I was concerned with the building and its refurbishment. People sometimes ask whether this was gender-stereotyping. But the truth is that I relished the task.

I like making my homes beautiful, warm and welcoming, but also practical. I had seen glimpses of what the building might become when we had first gone round it. Westminster City Council required us to have an art strategy and Elsie Owusu, one of the team at Feilden + Mawson, suggested that I should chair an 'art panel'. Our first job was to devise and implement an art strategy, but this soon developed into overseeing every aspect of the interior design.

The architects' plan was to strip out all the Crown Court trappings that we did not need, thus liberating the two large light wells inside the building. These were roofed over with glass and used as a café and part of the library. A major coup was to persuade Westminster City Council and English Heritage that we could take out the original courtroom and council chamber furniture and level the floors. Even so, we were not keen to use the old quarter-sessions courtroom for our hearings – it had a large balcony used as the public gallery which would have loomed over us. The architects were sure that the authorities would not let us take it down. This may well be because from it can be seen three little carvings of real people hidden amongst the elaborate stonework – as stonemasons used to do in medieval cathedrals. They represent David Lloyd George (Chancellor of the Exchequer in 1913), Henry Fehr (the sculptor who designed the stone carvings) and Carlo Magnani (the Italian anarchist refugee who did the carvings – delightfully apt in a court which hears many cases about refugees and terrorists).

Foster + Partners had the brainwave of turning this courtroom into our library, extending it down into the basement, with a book-lined gallery and reading shelf at ground floor level. The bookshelves, here and in the justices' rooms, were designed by Luke Hughes, who specialises in making furniture for sensitive historical locations (and who was told by his father, who sat in the Guildhall as a judge, that this was hopeless as a courtroom but would make a wonderful library). Aesthetically, it certainly has the 'wow' factor. It has an ornate fan-vaulted ceiling, which looks like stone but is made of plaster, with an exuberant royal coat of arms in the centre, and corbels supported by allegorical queen-like figures representing law, justice, government and the like. Symbolically, the law books it contains, going back to the very earliest law reports and Acts of

Parliament, represent the evolution of the law over the centuries and show that everything we do has its roots in that history – we are not making it up as we go along.

Surrounding the library at the heart of the building are our three courtrooms. The large council chamber in the centre of the building, above the library, became our principal courtroom – designed to hold up to nine justices but as it turned out able to accommodate eleven. Now we could sit in larger panels whenever we wanted to. In the House of Lords, the senior Law Lord had to ask for a larger committee room if he wanted a larger panel and compete with the parliamentarians for it. Larger panels became much more frequent in our early days, although they calmed down later. The room has a spectacular hammer-beamed roof, the original bronze light fittings, wooden panelling and stained-glass windows. The aldermen's benches, and the bench-ends carved with old kings, queens and heraldic beasts, the finials and armrests carved with animals, from the councillors' benches, have been reused for the benches on which the public sit. The old petty-sessions courtroom on the north side of the ground floor has kept its wooden panelling, stone carving and stained-glass coats of arms in the windows. A brand-new double-height courtroom has been created on the first and second floors to the south side of the building, overlooking Westminster Abbey.

All three courtrooms have new furniture specially designed for us by Tomoko Azumi, skilfully incorporating our IT needs, all clean lines and no clutter, but unfortunately all too frequently covered in the papers and computer screens with which we work. The lawyers had to be discouraged from barricading themselves in behind massive boxes of files. Lord Hope and I decided that we could do away with the central podium from which counsel used to harangue us in the House of Lords: instead, we would sit round a notional elliptical table, with a curved bench for the justices facing a curved bench for the lawyers. The leading barristers can have their juniors sitting beside them. We can see exactly what is going on. The atmosphere is a little more like a learned seminar than a battle between courtroom gladiators – but only a little. I would much have preferred the barristers to address us sitting down (as used to happen in family cases in the county courts). Lord Hope says that is because I wasn't an advocate for long and don't understand how important it is to stand up to the judges. But one very experienced advocate did ask if he could address us sitting down, so perhaps not everyone feels that way.

Once all the clutter was cleared away, the wealth of original decoration was revealed – the exuberant carvings in stone and wood, the stained-glass medallions showing the coats of arms of successive High Sheriffs, the bronze light fittings, the elaborate leaded lights in the internal screens and windows and the door furniture which matched them. We wanted to combine these with some modern features. We made a virtue out of necessity by using our small budget for artwork to add value to what there had to be in any event. We had to have glass screens and doors – to separate the security-screened from the unscreened in the entrance hall, to create an entrance into the library from the entrance hall, to give structure to the new modern courtroom. So we decided to decorate these screens with words and pictures, designed by Bettina Furnée. The judicial oath, adorned with our four plants, is etched on the screen across the entrance hall, telling everyone who enters that our mission is to 'do right to all manner of people after the laws and usages of this realm, without fear or favour, affection or ill will'. A facsimile of the Magna Carta decorates the entrance to the library, with the vital words 'to no one will we sell, to no one will we deny or delay, right or justice' picked out. The screen in the new courtroom proclaims on each side the words of Eleanor Roosevelt: 'Justice cannot be for one side alone but must be for both.' Richard Kindersley has carved many other appropriate quotations into the woodwork and glass in the library. My personal favorite is from Francis Bacon: 'Judges ought to be more learned than witty, more reverent than plausible, and more advised than confident.'

Of course, not everyone liked what we had done. One commentator, who had brought an unsuccessful legal challenge to the decision to allow us to refurbish the building, accused us of robbing it of its 'robust masculinity'. Just so. The law should also be in touch with its feminine side. It was reassuring that Prince Charles, who had been sympathetic to the challenge, was obviously impressed with what he saw when he visited the court for our tenth anniversary in 2019.

We also had to have our own seal. It had at first been thought that we would use the royal coat of arms which is on display in most courts. But there were problems. It is controversial in Northern Ireland. It is also controversial in Scotland, where the quarterings are different from those used in England. So we recruited Yvonne Holton, herald painter to the court of Lord Lyon King of Arms (the Scottish herald), to design something specially for us. This was not an easy task. But eventually she came up with just the thing, a design featuring a different plant for each part of the United Kingdom: a Tudor rose for England, a thistle for Scotland, a flax flower for Northern Ireland, and a leek for Wales. All are enclosed within the symbol which is both the sign for Libra – the scales – and the Greek letter omega – the last letter in the alphabet, signifying the final fount of justice.

And we had to have carpets. Elsie had a brainwave: to recruit Sir Peter Blake, the leading British pop artist, famous for his record sleeves for the Beatles, The Who and Band Aid. He swiftly came up with a design which featured stylised versions of the four plants, enclosed in dynamic twisting rope circles. It comes in three basic colourways: the green is used in the two traditional courtrooms and in the corridors; the blue is used in the modern courtroom, the justices' and some meeting rooms; and the red is used in the library and in the rooms allocated to the president and deputy president. It is light and bright and vibrant. It complements the original grass-green tiling on the walls of the corridors and staircases, providing colour and interest in spaces which would otherwise lack it. It was disappointing that, contrary to what we were originally led to believe, the rooms to be occupied by our secretaries, our judicial assistants, the registry and some of the staff had to make do with dull carpet tiling: no doubt there were bureaucratic reasons but it seemed a petty and mean-minded economy.

Another regret was that we were only allowed to convert the building if we kept alive the memory of Middlesex by continuing to house the collection of portraits which had belonged to Middlesex County Council. Some of these are first-rate. There are two portraits of Hugh Percy, for whom the earldom and later the dukedom of Northumberland were revived in the eighteenth century. The portrait of him as an earl, by Sir Joshua Reynolds, in an elaborate Chippendale frame, hangs in Courtroom 3. The portrait of him as a duke, by Thomas Gainsborough, hangs in the library. As Lord Lieutenant of

Middlesex, he had donated the land on which the building's predecessors had stood. There are many other portraits of Lords Lieutenants
of the County, of chairmen of the Middlesex magistrates or the county
council, and other Middlesex notables. My personal favourite is the
portrait by Nathaniel Hone the Elder of Sir John Fielding. He was
brother to Henry Fielding, the eighteenth-century novelist who wrote
Tom Jones, and succeeded him as chairman of the Middlesex magistrates. They were both notable penal reformers and responsible for
setting up the Bow Street Runners, ancestors of the Metropolitan
Police Force. Sir John was known as the 'blind beak' – a blind man
who was said to be able to identify 2,000 regular villains by their
voices. I used to find looking at his portrait very inspiring when things
got difficult in Courtroom 1 – if he could do it, so perhaps could I.

Fine though some of these portraits are, it is a shame that we have
to fill our walls with so many images of 'dead white men'. There is
one darker-skinned man – an Indian judge who sat in the Privy Council
in the 1930s – but there are no women. This is not a good message
for a twenty-first-century court, which ought to be visibly committed
to equality and diversity, to send to all the young women and members
of minority ethnic groups who are or want to be lawyers, to all the
litigants whose cases are heard in the court, and to all the members
of the public who visit us. Thanks to Spark 21 and the First Hundred
Years project, we have made a start towards redressing the balance:
there is now an exciting new artwork in the modern Courtroom 2,
by Catherine Yass, celebrating one hundred years of women in the
law. It features four photographic images, made to look like stained
glass, of Cornelia Sorabji, the first woman to study law at Oxford
University; Dame Rose Heilbron, one of the very first successful
women barristers; myself as the first woman to sit on the Supreme
Court; and an unknown young woman lawyer of the future.

Now that we had more space we could also have more staff. It
turned out that the justices didn't need any more secretaries. Most
now do their own typing and emails have replaced much correspondence. But we were able to go up to eight judicial assistants (JAs)
at first and have since gone up to twelve, so that each justice can have
one of his or her own. This is still far fewer than the three or four
'law clerks' which each justice of the US Supreme Court can have.

Another difference from them is that I hope and believe that our JAs are never asked to write our judgments for us: we all 'roll our own'. We use the JAs for writing 'bench memos' to summarise applications for permission to appeal and for doing research, either for the cases we are hearing or for the many lectures which we give. Mine were invaluable in helping with two new editions of my book *Mental Health Law*. I am grateful to everyone who worked for me, but especially to Ayo Onatade, my clerk in the Court of Appeal and my PA in the Supreme Court, and Penelope Gorman, my JA for some years before I retired. I was deeply touched when Penelope and a group of former JAs clubbed together to give me a magnificent painting of Courtroom 1 by Alison Pullen as a retirement gift.

The light, bright and welcoming building was also meant to represent the openness and transparency of the business done within it. No more would intrepid visitors have to brave the intimidating entrance to the Houses of Parliament, the policemen armed with sub-machine guns, the labyrinthine route to Committee Room 1 on the committee corridor, where the seats for the public were uncomfortable and few. They could walk in from Parliament Square, be greeted by our friendly security guards, directed through security to a reception desk, take a self-guided tour of the building, visit our café and exhibition space with its interactive displays, read summaries of the cases being heard that day, and pop into the courtrooms to see what was going on. Many people do so, although many others still do not yet realise that they can.

But there is no need to come to the building to watch our proceedings. From the first, we had insisted that the general prohibition of filming and photography in courtrooms should not apply to us.[10] Our courtrooms were equipped with unobtrusive cameras and our proceedings were filmed. It was not long before they were also live-streamed so that anyone could tune in, and now they are also available on catch-up. The cameras are operated by the court's own contractors in accordance with the court's own rules. This is very different from letting the media in with their own cameras to film how and what they want. It also means that the media can watch from the media room at the court or in their own offices rather than coming into the courtrooms.

There was a fear that filming might tempt the barristers to 'grandstand' or play to the gallery, but that has not really happened. In high-profile cases in the House of Lords, they always used to have some opening words which were designed for press consumption, and that has not changed. But mostly they concentrate on persuading us rather than on impressing an audience. I can think of only one example where the barrister's speech was clearly aimed at an audience rather than at us. I don't think that the justices are tempted to play to the gallery either – it is more important to keep up with what is going on. Broadcasting our proceedings was particularly valuable in the two cases brought by Mrs Gina Miller, both of which generated enormous public interest. Viewers could see that we were not having a political debate about whether or not the UK should leave the European Union. We were having a serious debate about important constitutional issues concerning the allocation of powers between government and Parliament.

One issue which came up very soon after we had left the Lords was titles. At first, we were all members of the House of Lords, but when Lord Saville retired from the Supreme Court in 2010, Lord Justice Dyson was appointed to replace him. He was referred to as Sir John Dyson, while the rest of us were 'Lord' or 'Lady'. This made him uncomfortable, although he would not have been alone for long. One solution would have been to do as the Act says: 'The judges other than the president and deputy president are to be styled "Justices of the Supreme Court".'[11] Their Lordships were not too keen on this. Another was to ask Her Majesty to bestow courtesy titles on the justices, as is done for the senior Scottish judges. The Labour government declined to do this, but the Coalition government which took office after the 2010 election did do it. All the Supreme Court justices now have the courtesy title of Lord or Lady. But I am kicking myself for not protesting about the sexism involved. The wives of courtesy lords become courtesy ladies, but the husbands of courtesy ladies do not become courtesy lords (a man can bestow his rank upon his wife but a woman cannot bestow her rank upon her husband). A twenty-first-century court should not be lending itself to such practices.

Freed from the constraints of the House of Lords, we could develop our own ways of giving judgment. In the House of Lords, we held a mock debate in the Chamber on the motion that 'the report of the appellate committee be agreed to'. Our judgments were technically speeches in that debate. But we all voted for the motion whether or not we agreed with the result. In the Supreme Court we produce three explanations for our decisions. The only authoritative one is the judgment itself – a long written account of the problem, the background, existing legal materials, the arguments, and the reasoning which leads to the solution. We developed a firm practice of having one leading judgment giving the majority view – usually with a single author but sometimes jointly written. Justices who agree with the majority view can write their own 'concurrences' but we try not to have several 'stand-alone' judgments, each reaching the same conclusion for slightly different reasons (as was not uncommon in the House of Lords). Justices who disagree are of course free to do so and explain their reasons. Given that all our cases are by definition arguable, it is surprising that dissent is comparatively rare: over the first ten years of the court's operation, the unanimity rate was almost 80%.

To arrive at our decisions, we carried on the practice in the House of Lords. Immediately after the hearing, we would have a meeting where each justice, beginning with the most junior, would give a provisional view of the answer, with brief reasons. From this it would usually emerge what the majority decision was likely to be. The presider would identify someone to write the leading judgment. That person would circulate drafts to which the others would respond with comments and suggestions. Dissenters were asked to wait until they had seen the draft before circulating one of their own, but occasionally a dissenter would jump the gun, hoping to persuade others to agree with him. The majority did sometimes change hands, but not often. More often, a justice who had originally taken a different view would come round to the majority. A few justices engaged in active lobbying for their point of view, but most did not. Generally, dissent was reserved for matters of real principle on which the dissenter felt strongly.

I was not the most frequent dissenter in those first ten years. That honour goes to Lord Rodger. I came fifth (out of the nineteen surveyed) for dissents and sixth for solo dissents. Two of my solo dissents were particularly memorable. In *Radmacher v Granatino*,[12] a nine-judge panel was convened to decide what weight should be given to pre-nuptial agreements if the couple came to divorce. The facts were unusual because it was the wife who was extremely wealthy, heiress to a German industrial fortune, and the husband, an investment banker turned research scientist, who was making the claim. They had entered into an agreement in Germany before they married, in which the husband had agreed to make no claims at all upon his wife. He had not had any independent legal advice but he was an intelligent man who knew what he was doing. They married in London and lived in London for most of their married life, except for a spell in New York for the husband's work. Their two children were born here. They divorced here. It had been a long-standing rule of English law that it was contrary to public policy for a married couple to agree, whether before or during the marriage, what the financial consequences of any future separation would be. The original reason for this rule was that such an agreement might encourage them to separate: hence it did not apply to an agreement made when or after they did separate. Nor was any agreement binding on the court if they came to divorce. This was to protect the economically weaker party – almost always the wife – and, perhaps more importantly, the public interest in not leaving her destitute and dependent on public funds. In *Radmacher*, the majority held that the old rule that prenuptial agreements were not binding on the parties was obsolete; that although they were not binding on the divorce court, the court should give effect to an agreement which was freely entered into by the parties, unless in the circumstances at the time of the divorce it would not be fair to hold them to it; in this case, the husband should be kept to the agreement, except for having a capital sum to provide a home and an appropriate standard of living for the children when they were with him.

I disagreed with the unnecessary and illogical ruling that the agreement was binding on the parties, without insisting on any of the procedural safeguards which are required in countries where such agreements are binding. The object of premarital and pre-separation agreements, unlike separation agreements, was to deny the econom-ically weaker party the financial provision to which she or he would otherwise be entitled. There was a gender dimension to the issue 'which some may think ill-suited to a court consisting of eight men and one woman'. (I might have added, eight men who mostly had backgrounds in commercial or property law, rather than in the subtleties of personal relationships.) The court should not impose any sort of presumption or starting point on the statutory factors governing financial remedies on divorce, but should give full weight to the agreement if it was fair to do so. The majority's decision treated the parents as if they had never married. This so-called enemy of marriage declared that 'Marriage still counts for something in the law of this country and long may it continue to do so.' The modest provision made for the husband should last for his life, not just until the children grew up. This was a complicated subject upon which there was a large literature. Knowledgeable and thoughtful people might legitimately hold different views. It was much more suitable for examination by the Law Commission, which had a current project on marital agreements.

I have often wondered what would have happened had the husband been fabulously wealthy and the wife an investment banker turned research scientist. One of my fellow justices did voice the view that the husband was a 'cad' for even trying to save something from the wreckage of his marriage.

I don't think that my fellow justices were offended by my dissent in that case, but they were undoubtedly offended by my dissent in the case of Elaine McDonald.[13] This featured in my imaginary conversations with the schoolchildren who visited the Supreme Court in the charming children's book by Afua Hirsch and Henny Beaumont, *Equal to Everything: Judge Brenda and the Supreme Court*:

'Is all your work about children?' Anoushka's shyness slipped away.
'No,' said Lady Hale. 'In one case, a lady, famous for ballet,
Now old, needed help at night to get up and go to the loo.
But the council said she should wear nappies when she needed to do
a poo!
I thought that wasn't fair at all. You wouldn't like that, would you?'
'On no,' said the children, giggling, 'what a horrible thing to do.'

The council had a legal duty to assess what her needs were as a disabled person and then a duty to provide what was necessary to meet those needs. I agreed with Age Concern (who intervened in the case) that it was irrational to meet the need of a person, who was not incontinent, for help to go to the lavatory at night with incontinence pads, designed to meet the quite different need of an incontinent person. I was troubled by the contrary view, which logically meant that the council could supply incontinence pads, whether she needed to urinate or defecate during the night or indeed during the day. I didn't mean to upset my fellow justices, but I am afraid that my references to defecation touched a raw nerve. Another senior woman judge later remarked upon the gender dimension: it is so much easier for men to urinate into a bottle than it is for women to do so, so perhaps the men could not envisage being in the ballerina's situation. But they could envisage the defecation problem. Despite their upset, we managed to stay friends.

Dissents are not always in vain. They can sometimes point the direction in which the law is travelling or even produce the desired outcome. Lord Kerr and I dissented in a case challenging the refusal of the Secretary of State to provide free abortions in England for women and girls from Northern Ireland who were unable to get them there.[14] There was such an outcry that the Scottish government announced that it would provide them, and the Secretary of State soon changed his mind.

There were many more cases in which my fellow justices shared my views. There are two of which I am particularly proud, because they established the importance of looking at things from the point of view of the women and children involved.

The first is *Yemshaw v Hounslow London Borough Council*[15] which turned on the question of what is meant by the word 'violence'. Is it limited to hitting or threatening to hit (as the Court of Appeal had twice held), or can it include a much wider variety of abusive behaviour? A mother who had left the family home with her children would be entitled to rehousing unless she was intentionally homeless. She would not be regarded as intentionally homeless if it was probable that staying in the home would lead to 'domestic violence or other violence' against her. Her husband had never actually hit her but she was afraid that he would do so and she complained of other abusive and oppressive behaviour – behaviour which we would now call coercive control. We decided that although 'physical violence' was one natural meaning of the word violence, it was not the only natural meaning, and in this context it applied to 'physical violence, threatening or intimidating behaviour and any other form of abuse, which directly or indirectly may give rise to the risk of harm'. Much of the material to support this conclusion was supplied by the Secretary of State for Communities and Local Government, who intervened in the case. But I was later grateful to the editors of *The Archers* for their powerful story showing how a person could be completely dominated by being deprived, first of a job, then of contact with her family and friends, then of finance and a mobile phone, and finally of all confidence in her own abilities and even sanity. The listeners could hear all this happening to Helen Archer, but her family and friends could not.

The second is *ZH (Tanzania) v Secretary of State for the Home Department*,[16] where the issue was the weight to be given to the interests of children when deciding whether to remove their parents from the country. The mother had an 'appalling' history of making false claims to stay in the UK and obviously deserved to be sent back to her home country. But while here she had had two children, both of them British citizens, who had lived here all their lives. If their mother had to leave, they would have to leave too, as there was no one else to look after them. They would lose their home, their friends, their school and all the other benefits of their British citizenship. The United Nations Convention on the Rights of the Child requires that, in any official action concerning children, 'the best interests of the child shall be a primary consideration'.[17] We held that this applied when considering whether this interference with the children's private and family lives could be justified: their interests had to come first, although they could be outweighed by other considerations. The children were not to be blamed for their mother's behaviour. This same principle applies to many other types of official action which interfere with a child's rights under the European Convention, not just to immigration decisions.

When the written judgment (or judgments) has been prepared, agreed and edited, it is not read out in court. It is published, in print and online, together with a two-page 'press summary'. This is not a press notice designed to catch the eye, but a deadpan account of the decision: the hope is that if the media – and anyone else – is interested, they will read the summary and report the decision accurately. As well as this, the author of the leading judgment goes into court on the day the judgment is published and delivers an even shorter explanation, aimed at the general public, hopefully in a way which anyone can understand. In some of the more technical cases, this is no easy task, but it is a challenge which some of the justices relish. It is live-streamed and also appears on the court's own YouTube channel.

As part of our 'mission to inform' everyone about the court and the justice system generally, there is a programme of outreach to schools, colleges and universities. We have many visits from school and student parties – they can be shown round the building, hear a talk about our work, sit in for a while on a hearing, and sometimes meet one of the justices too. My fondest memories are of visits from primary-school children. Like almost everyone else, their view of the justice system is taken from television courtroom dramas. But when they are shown that the law is about issues of justice, fairness and equality in all areas of life, they quickly get the point. We also have an 'Ask a Justice' programme for schools which are too far away to visit. They send in questions and a justice spends half an hour answering them over Skype or FaceTime. All the justices go out and about talking to schools, universities and many other organisations and groups – the only problem is that certain institutions rarely ask, whereas others take it for granted that they can secure a justice when they want one. I tried my best to go to as many of the former sort as I possibly could. My last visit before lockdown was to the brand-new law school at the delightful University of Chichester – which scores highly for their personal concern for each one of their very diverse group of students.

Universities like having law schools. They are comparatively cheap to run and attract well-qualified candidates. This means that many young (and not so young) people who would never have dreamt of trying to become lawyers in the past can now do so. The quality I have seen is fantastic. The profession needs people from many different backgrounds if it is to become truly reflective of the people and businesses that it is there to serve. But it is a worry that so many people are hoping to go into the law at a time when the number of traditional law jobs available is shrinking. I always tried to encourage students to think flexibly, to remember that there are many different uses to which a good legal brain can be put, outside the traditional fields of private practice as a barrister or solicitor, and to leap at whatever opportunities come their way – just as I have tried to do.

One of those opportunities came my way in 2012 when Lord Phillips retired as president of the court. I was then the longest serving and most experienced member of the court (apart from Lord Hope, who was soon to retire as deputy president). I thought that my varied career had given me the skills necessary for the job. I had experience of management in the university and at National Family Mediation. I had experience of leading teams at the Law Commission and elsewhere. I had long experience of chairing meetings, often very difficult meetings. I was a good communicator with a worldwide reputation. But others thought that Lord Neuberger, then Master of the Rolls, was the obvious candidate.[18] And so he turned out to be. I was soon very glad that he had got the job. I could learn from him and focus on becoming his deputy when Lord Hope retired in 2013. Lord Hope has been indiscreet enough to reveal that, although I had strong support from outside the court and interviewed well, the other candidate for deputy president had more support from inside the court. Perhaps in my four years as deputy president I managed to win them over.

Much of the outreach work of the court could in theory have been done in the House of Lords. But setting up the Supreme Court gave it an added impetus. We had our own small team dedicated to communications and interaction with the public, who kept coming up with good ideas and putting them into operation. We were no longer an obscure and anomalous part of the much larger institution. We were one of the three essential pillars of the constitution, and visibly so.

13 What is the Supreme Court For?

It is easy to see why the top court in the country should not be part of the House of Lords. But why do we have a top court at all? Were they so wrong in the 1870s to think of abolishing the Law Lords altogether? There are at least three reasons why they were wrong.

The first is the most mundane. In theory at least, the decisions of the Supreme Court ought to be better than those of the lower courts. The Supreme Court only hears appeals which raise an arguable point of law of general public importance. This means three things. First, it has to be a point of *law* – not a question of fact and only a question of procedure or the exercise of discretion if it raises an important point of principle.[1] Second, the point has to be *arguable* – if the law is clear, we don't interfere just because the Court of Appeal may have got its application wrong. Third, the point has to be 'of general public importance' – it has to matter to many more people than the parties to the particular case. The interpretation of a one-off contract may matter millions of pounds to the parties, but it doesn't matter at all to anyone else. The interpretation of the contracts of doctors working in the NHS, on the other hand, matters to a great many people, the doctors directly and their patients indirectly.

There is another consideration: this may not be the right case for the Supreme Court. The point may be difficult and important, but the appeal panel may feel that the Court of Appeal so obviously got the answer right that there is no point in putting the parties to the delay, the expense and the uncertainty of a further appeal: that was why, for example, we didn't take the cases which had successfully challenged the new pension schemes for firefighters and for judges on the ground of age discrimination.[2] Or the point may be difficult and important, but the case has become moot – the individual's problem has been resolved in another way. But if we do nothing, the Court of Appeal's decision will be binding on all the other courts even though we think it may be wrong. So we may have to take the case anyway.[3]

This ability to 'dine à la carte' means that we hear far fewer cases than the lower courts do. In the year April 2019 to April 2020, for example, the Supreme Court heard eighty-one appeals: in only ten of these had the lower court given permission to appeal. The Court of Appeal of England and Wales deals with thousands of cases every year. We have far more time to devote to the cases we do hear. We also have a great deal of help. The advocates who appear in the Supreme Court are, generally speaking, of the highest quality. They also know that we shall be interested in the bigger picture: the social or economic context in which the problem arises, the historical development of the law, and the way the problem has been solved in other countries. So they present us with a good deal of material which may well not have been put before the Court of Appeal. And we can ask our judicial assistants to research things which they have not put before us.

The Supreme Court, unlike the Court of Appeal, is not bound by the previous decisions of the Court of Appeal. It can even depart from the previous decisions of the House of Lords or the Supreme Court if justice requires this, although this is rare. It can stand back and look at the problem as a matter of principle. It is also far less likely to come to decisions which are difficult to reconcile with one another. A rare example happened when the court adopted different approaches to the 'illegality defence' – that is, whether some unlawful conduct on the part of the claimant might invalidate the claim.[4] We had to assemble a nine-judge court to decide between them.[5]

Perhaps the final advantage of the Supreme Court is safety in numbers – the five or more heads in the Supreme Court are thought better than the two or three in the Court of Appeal (although, as I have remarked earlier, this is not such an advantage if they all look and think alike).

Of course, the lower courts will not always agree that the Supreme Court's decisions are better. That is human nature. I can think of a few decisions of mine in the Court of Appeal which I thought that the House of Lords was wrong to overturn: the most obvious example was the blind mother whose sterilisation failed.[6] But their decision is the law and has to be loyally followed. The same is true, of course, of the House of Lords and Supreme Court decisions from which I dissented.

The second reason for having an apex court covering the whole of the United Kingdom is that there is a great deal of law which applies throughout the UK and ought to be interpreted in the same way in England, Scotland, Wales and Northern Ireland. A Scottish journalist once asked me (apropos a lecture I was about to give), 'Is there such a thing as UK law? Doesn't it just mean applying English law to the whole UK?' No it does not. Great swathes of the modern law are contained in Acts of the UK Parliament, and regulations made under them, which apply throughout the UK or at least Great Britain. Obvious examples are nationality, immigration and asylum law, extradition, employment and equality law, and much of social security law and tax law, as well as the laws implementing the international treaties to which the UK is a party. The Supreme Court can resolve differences in their interpretation which have arisen between different parts of the UK. Even if there have been no differences, the Supreme Court can provide an authoritative interpretation which is binding on all parts of the UK. The lower courts in England and Wales, Scotland and Northern Ireland would regard each other's decisions as persuasive but not binding.

There are also some areas of judge-made law which everyone agrees should be the same throughout the UK. The law of negligence, much of which has been developed in cases from Scotland, is the most obvious example.[7] A lesser-known but equally important example is ordering the disclosure of government documents which are relevant in court proceedings but which the government wants to keep secret. In an English case about disclosing the documents revealing why a submarine had been lost on a trial voyage during the Second World War, the Law Lords held that they were bound to accept a minister's certificate that it was not in the public interest to disclose them.[8] But then they held that in Scotland the court did have power to overrule a minister's objections.[9] In 1966, the Law Lords announced that they would, in future, decline to follow their own previous decisions if justice required this. Their first use of this new-found power was to decide that the Scottish approach should be adopted throughout the UK.[10] This is but one example of a noticeable trend towards a greater willingness to challenge the government which developed in the 1960s.

This brings us to the third and most important role of the Supreme Court – and the Law Lords before it – as a guardian of the constitution of the United Kingdom. Famously, the United Kingdom is one of only four countries in the developed world which do not have a written constitution (the others are New Zealand, Israel and the Isle of Man). But that does not mean that we do not have a constitution. We obviously do. We have the same set of institutions that they all do – a parliament, a government, a judiciary and a head of state. Their powers and the relations between them are set out in a mixture of laws and practices (known as conventions). But they are not all set out in a binding written document which is usually harder to change than other laws.

Our constitution is more complicated than it used to be, now that both lawmaking and governmental powers have been devolved to the Scottish Parliament, the Welsh Senedd, the Northern Ireland Assembly and their respective ministers. This means that the Supreme Court has to rule on whether what they have done is within the powers which the UK Parliament has given them – just as the Supreme Court of the United States has to rule on whether the states which make up the Union have acted within their powers. This is not a new role for us – the top court has had it since a parliament was set up in Northern Ireland following the island's partition in 1921. But it has become a great deal more prominent – and more politically sensitive – since 1998, when devolution was extended to Scotland and Wales.

Most of the examples of how it works have come from Scotland, usually on appeal from the Scottish courts in a real dispute between real parties. For example, the Scottish government is not allowed to act incompatibly with the Convention rights. Defendants in criminal cases have successfully challenged long-established features of the Scottish criminal justice system on this ground. This has brought the

Supreme Court into territory which had previously been off limits, because there is no right of appeal in Scottish criminal cases,[11] and provoked the wrath of some prominent people in Scotland.[12]

Acts of the Scottish Parliament, for example, can be challenged because the subject matter is reserved to the UK Parliament, or because they 'modify' one of the laws listed in the Scotland Act 1998, or because they are incompatible with human rights law or (until Brexit) with European Union law. A motorist complained that the powers to sentence for motoring offences had been increased because road traffic is reserved to the UK Parliament;[13] the insurance industry complained that making employers pay damages for asymptomatic pleural plaques caused by exposure to asbestos violated their human rights (yes, insurance companies do have human rights);[14] the tobacco industry complained that a ban on cigarette vending machines and other restrictions on the sale of tobacco products related to reserved matters;[15] and the alcohol industry complained that the introduction of a power to fix a minimum price for each unit of alcohol sold in off-licences was contrary to EU law.[16] These complaints all failed, but one or two have succeeded.[17] The Supreme Court tries to respect the democratic will of the Scottish people if it can: the Scottish Parliament is not just another public authority.

Such issues can also be referred direct to the Supreme Court as an abstract question by one of the law officers – the Attorney General for England and Wales, the Attorney General for Northern Ireland, the Counsel General for Wales, the Lord Advocate (the equivalent of the Attorney General in Scotland), and the Advocate General for Scotland (the UK government's law officer for Scotland) – if they want to know whether what the Scots, the Welsh or the Irish have done is within their powers. This does not often happen but when it does the context can be highly political. Brexit generated some heated arguments between the UK government and the Scots, the Welsh and the Irish. Early in 2018, the Scottish Parliament tried to legislate to provide for the continuity of EU law in Scotland after Brexit. The UK government did not want them to do this, because it planned to do the same for the whole United Kingdom. So the Attorney General and the Lord Advocate referred the Scottish Act to the Supreme Court before it received the royal assent. We held that most of the Act was within the powers of the Scottish Parliament when it was passed. But we had to judge whether it would be valid when it received the royal assent and became law. And by then the UK Parliament had passed the UK Act. This meant that much more of the Scottish Act was outside the powers of the Scottish Parliament. So both sides were to some extent vindicated. This was essentially a political battle between the UK and Scotland. But deciding the case did not involve deciding the political questions. It involved a great deal of detailed and mind-numbing comparison between the provisions of the Scotland Act 1998, the UK Withdrawal from the European Union (Legal Continuity) (Scotland) Act and the European Union (Withdrawal) Act 2018.[18] Hotly contested political battles don't necessarily generate exciting legal disputes.

Sometimes, however, we are grateful for a reference, as we were in what has been called the 'gay cake' case.[19] Gareth Lee is a gay man who supported the introduction of gay marriage in Northern Ireland. He wanted to take a cake bearing the legend 'Support Gay Marriage' (with cartoon characters of a same-sex couple) to a party in support of the campaign. He ordered one from the Ashers Baking Company. This is run by a family of devout Christians who believe that the only form of marriage consistent with biblical teaching and therefore acceptable to God is between a man and a woman. They decided that they could not fulfil the order. Mr Lee, backed by the Equality and Human Rights Commission, complained that he had been discriminated against on the ground of sexual orientation and on the ground of religious belief or political opinion. The bakers denied discrimination and also argued that to read the relevant legislation in such a way as to make them liable would conflict with their right to freedom of expression under Article 12 of the European Convention on Human Rights: just as you must be free to say what you like (within certain limits) so you must be free *not* to say things with which you profoundly disagree. Mr Lee won on both grounds before the district judge and on the ground of sexual orientation before the Northern Ireland Court of Appeal. The bakers wanted to appeal to the Supreme Court and we thought that the case did indeed raise arguable points of law of general public importance. But they had no right of appeal, so we were grateful to the Attorney General for referring the case to us.

We held that the bakers had not discriminated against Mr Lee, or anyone with whom he was associated, on the ground of sexual orientation: their objection was to the message, not to the man. The same applied to his political opinions: their objection was not to the man, but to the opinion he held. However, as the connection between the man and his opinion was so close, we also held that it would be incompatible with the bakers' Convention rights to make them liable for refusing to publish a message with which they profoundly disagreed, so the legislation should not be read in that way.[20]

Not everyone will agree with our analysis. It remains to be seen what the European Court of Human Rights will make of the case. But I was much comforted by its reception later that same day. My daughter Julia and I were 'in conversation' at a dinner organised by 'Out Leadership' (an offshoot of 'Out on the [Wall] Street', an association of LGBT+ people who work in the finance industry). Everyone there appeared to understand why we had decided the case as we had – the mere fact that the case had something to do with sexual orientation did not mean that a particular individual had been treated less favourably because of his own or his associates' sexual orientation. The gay men there were much more concerned about the approach of UK law to surrogacy arrangements – which are not legally enforceable in this country.

But what about the court's role in relation to central government and the UK Parliament? Judicial review of the legal validity of administrative action has been with us for centuries: government ministers, officials and public authorities of all kinds have to act within the limits of the powers they have been given by Parliament or the common law. The rule of law applies just as much to them as it does to the rest of us. If Parliament does not like what the judges have decided, it can always change the law. It was established in the Glorious Revolution of 1688 that the UK Parliament is sovereign: it can make *or unmake* any law. Unlike Supreme Courts in other parts of the world, such as Canada and the United States, the UK courts cannot strike down a provision in an Act of the UK Parliament – unless that Parliament has given them the power to do so.

The Human Rights Act 1998 does not give them that power.[21] The European Communities Act 1972 was another matter. That did sometimes require the courts to give precedence to European Union law even over a provision in an Act of the UK Parliament which was incompatible with it. In the so-called 'metric martyrs' case, the court recognised that the European Communities Act was of such constitutional significance that the powers it gave to the UK government to give effect to EU law, which required the use of metric measures and labelling, were not impliedly repealed by the Weights and Measures Act 1985, which allowed the use of the old imperial measures.[22] But that did not prevent the UK Parliament from expressly repealing the 1972 Act and taking away that power: Parliament can make or unmake any law.

Each of the first three presidents of the Supreme Court has had to preside over a case of the highest constitutional importance concerning the relationship between Parliament and the other branches of government. Lord Phillips presided in the case of *R v Chaytor*.[23] In May 2009 the *Daily Telegraph* had the 'scoop of the year'. It bought the unexpurgated records of the expenses claims made by Members of Parliament and began publishing a series of articles revealing these. Members could claim for expenses incurred 'wholly, exclusively and necessarily to enable [them] to stay overnight away from [their] only or main home for the purpose of performing [their] duties as a Member of Parliament'. The claims were shocking because they revealed three things: first, that most members who could do so claimed sums very close to the maximum allowed and the outlandish things for which some of them claimed; second, that some members had claimed for things which were not within the rules; and third, that a few members had made false claims for expenses that they had not in fact incurred, which is a criminal offence.

In 2010, the Director of Public Prosecutions, Keir Starmer, decided that three MPs and one member of the House of Lords should be prosecuted for false accounting. Each was committed for trial in the Crown Court. Each claimed that he could not be prosecuted because what he had done was covered by parliamentary privilege: it was protected either by Article 9 of the Bill of Rights of 1689 or by the wider concept of matters which are within the 'exclusive cognisance' of Parliament. The trial judge and the Court of Appeal rejected that claim and they appealed to the Supreme Court. A nine-justice panel was convened to hear it.

Article 9 of the Bill of Rights of 1689 says this: 'That the Freedome of Speech and Debates or Proceedings in Parlyament ought not to be impeached or questioned in any court or place out of Parlyament.' The object then was to allow members to say what they pleased in the course of parliamentary debates. But could it be said that submitting a claim for expenses, provided for in rules laid down by resolutions of the House of Commons, to the Fees Office in the Palace of Westminster, part of the administration of the House, was a 'proceeding in Parliament'? The answer was 'no': proceedings in Parliament related to the process by which the House took action or reached a decision, in which members took part by speaking, voting, giving notice of a motion, presenting a petition or report or the like: in other words, taking part in the 'core or essential business' of Parliament.

Nor could it be said that the claims were within the exclusive cognisance – or jurisdiction – of Parliament. Parliament did not claim jurisdiction, let alone exclusive jurisdiction, over 'ordinary crimes' committed within the Palace of Westminster or by its members. The House only has power to punish for conduct which is a contempt of Parliament; not all ordinary crimes will be such a contempt; and the House's powers and procedures are inadequate to deal with the more serious crimes (after all, Prime Minister Spencer Perceval was murdered in the Lobby of the House of Commons in 1812). Indeed, far from claiming exclusive jurisdiction, the House authorities had asked the police to investigate. Obviously, if the House itself had intervened in support of the defendants, we would have given very careful consideration to its claim. But, as Lord Phillips explained, it was established long ago that the courts are the judge of the extent of Parliamentary privilege.[24] Acts of Parliament may, of course, determine it, but mere assertion cannot.

We were unanimous in rejecting the appeal and I do not recall that any of us found it difficult. The prosecutions went ahead and all four defendants either pleaded or were found guilty and sentenced to terms of imprisonment. There were a few later prosecutions for similar offences. However, the decision proved very important when we came to decide the cases brought by Mrs Gina Miller and Ms Joanna Cherry MP challenging the advice given by Prime Minister Boris Johnson to

Her Majesty that Parliament should be prorogued. But before we come to that, there was the important constitutional case decided under the presidency of Lord Neuberger.

The referendum in June 2016 had produced a majority of nearly 52% in favour of leaving the European Union. The referendum was not legally binding on the government or Parliament but the government had declared that it would respect the result. In practice it was binding. Prime Minister Theresa May announced that on 29 March 2017 she would give notice to the European Union that the United Kingdom intended to leave. This time feelings were running high. Little did I think that a long-arranged trip to Malaysia would get me into hot water with the press.

Supreme Court justices are asked to take part in many interesting conferences and events, but there is none more luxurious than the annual lecture in memory of Sultan Azlan Shah in Kuala Lumpur. Sultan Azlan Shah was a distinguished jurist who rose to the highest judicial office in Malaysia before unexpectedly becoming sultan of the State of Perak and later king of Malaysia. The lecturer is (literally) royally entertained by the sultan's son in Kuala Lumpur and on the island of Langkawi; there are opportunities to meet the Malaysian judiciary and legal profession; and, most memorable of all, there is a dinner after the lecture which is followed by a karaoke session. The lecturer is among those commanded to sing. The idea is to find something where everyone can join in, so I contributed my usual party piece: 'On Ilkley Moor Bar t'Hat'. The chorus is easy to pick up, but the Yorkshire dialect words and accent are not. They all thought that I was singing in another language. But a Japanese judge who was there told me that it is a well-known hymn tune in Japan.

The title of my lecture had been agreed months before it was delivered in November 2016: 'The Supreme Court: Guardian of the Constitution?'. Little did I realise at the time how topical it was about to become. Just before I left for Malaysia, a Divisional Court of the High Court of England and Wales had decided the case of *R (Miller and others) v Secretary of State for Exiting the European Union*.[25] The question was whether the government could give notice of withdrawal from the European Union without the authority of Parliament. I thought that it would be discourteous to my hosts, given the title of my lecture, not to explain what the issues were. This is what I said:

> Article 50 of the Treaty of the European Union provides that 'any Member State may decide to withdraw from the Union in accordance with its own constitutional arrangements' (Article 50(1)). A Member State which decides to withdraw shall notify the European Council of its intention. The Council is then expected to negotiate and agree upon the arrangements for withdrawal with the Member State. These have to be agreed by the Council, acting by a qualified majority, and by the European Parliament (Article 50(2)). However, the treaties shall cease to apply to the State in question from the date of the entry into force of that agreement or, failing that, two years after the notification, unless the Council unanimously agrees to extend the period (Article 50(3)). The issue is whether giving that notification falls within the prerogative powers of the Crown in the conduct of foreign relations or whether it falls foul of the rule that the prerogative cannot be used in such a way as to frustrate or substantially undermine an Act of the United Kingdom Parliament. The argument is that the European Communities Act 1972 grants rights to individuals and others which will automatically be lost if the Treaties cease to apply. Such a result, it is said, can only be achieved by an Act of Parliament. Another question is whether it would be enough for a simple Act of Parliament to authorise the government to give notice, or whether it would have to be a comprehensive replacement for the 1972 Act.
>
> The contrary argument is that the conduct of foreign affairs, including the making and unmaking of treaties with foreign powers, lies within the prerogative powers of the Crown (what you would call the executive power of the Federation). The EU Referendum Act 2015 neither expressly nor by implication required that further parliamentary authority be given to begin the process of withdrawal. The basis on which the referendum was undertaken was that the government would give effect to the result. Beginning the process would not change the law.
>
> Just before I left to come here, a unanimous Divisional Court held that the Secretary of State does not have power under the royal prerogative to give notice to withdraw from the European Union.

The court held that, just as making a treaty does not change the law of the land, unmaking it cannot do so, but triggering Article 50 will automatically have that effect. What has to be done instead is perhaps not so clear. But the case is destined for our court, so I must say no more.

When I got back to London, the lecture was put on our website, as is the usual practice. Our wise young director of communications checked it over and did not see anything to frighten the horses. But such was the febrile atmosphere of the time, with feelings running extraordinarily high on each side of the argument, that my query about 'what has to be done instead' was seized upon as indicating anti-Brexit bias. This was as nothing compared with the vitriol heaped upon the Divisional Court, consisting of the Lord Chief Justice, the Master of the Rolls (his second in command), and Lord Justice Sales, a distinguished Court of Appeal judge who was soon to become a Supreme Court justice: their photographs appeared in the *Daily Mail* under the banner headline 'Enemies of the People'. Nothing could, of course, have been further from the truth. By asserting the fundamental principles of the constitution which governs us all, they were standing up for the people and for Parliament. Unfortunately, the Lord Chancellor, Liz Truss, who had sworn an oath to protect the rule of law and the independence of the judiciary, did not instantly leap to their defence. It would have been so easy. The script would have gone something like this:

> We have a free press in this country and you are free to write and publish what you like. But it is my duty, as the member of the government sworn to defend the rule of law and the independence of the judiciary, to tell you that you are wrong. These are not enemies of the people but senior members of the judiciary deciding the case in accordance with the law. If they have got the answer wrong, the Supreme Court will put them right.

She might have gone on to warn them to 'beware what you wish for. If you bring senior members of the judiciary into disrepute for doing their job, you may risk bringing the whole justice system into disrepute, and thus imperil the orderly administration of justice on which we all depend for our safety and security'. But she did neither. The Lord Chief Justice could not defend himself and his colleagues (although he was later able to let his views be known), nor could the president of the Supreme Court react, as we were due to hear the case in December.

Hearing the case involved more elaborate arrangements than we had ever had to make before. It was decided that all eleven of the then serving justices would sit:[26] we did not want it said that the result would have been different had a different panel sat. This meant squeezing eleven chairs and ten bookcases behind a bench designed for nine: fortunately, Lord Kerr did everything on his computer and did not need a bookcase. There were two applicants, Mrs Gina Miller and Mr Deir Dos Santos, and numerous other interested parties and interveners, including the Lord Advocate, the Attorney General for Northern Ireland, and the Counsel General for Wales. Everyone had a huge legal team: the government had seven barristers; Mrs Miller had five; Mr Dos Santos had three; the other parties had thirty-two between them. Among this huge array, it was a great disappointment that only five were women, and only one, Helen Mountfield QC, actually addressed the court (very effectively). As well as the barristers, there were of course their instructing solicitors, the media and the general public. The professionals were allocated seats which changed each day as the people speaking changed. There was a ticketing system for the main courtroom and the other two courtrooms, to which the hearing was relayed. All this put huge demands upon the court staff, who rose magnificently to the challenge (and were later rewarded by the justices with a ping-pong table which has proved very popular). The hearing was broadcast both on television and on our own website.

Amazing numbers of people, who had previously had little contact with the law, not only tuned in but watched all four days of the hearing. This despite the remark of one radio commentator that 'to say that the proceedings went at a snail's pace was unfair to snails'. But that is the way of legal argument and viewers can have been in no doubt that we were listening to complicated and learned legal argument: we were not debating the pros and cons of Brexit. I was relieved that Lord Sumption's ties got more attention than the dresses and brooches I wore each day.

By the time the case came to us, the legal debate had changed somewhat. Although the government did still argue that parliamentary approval for triggering the Article 50 process was not needed, the serious argument was about whether the European Communities Act 1972 contained that approval within its own terms. That turned it into a question of statutory interpretation rather than the constitutional separation of powers. Lord Hughes put it very neatly.[27] There are two well-understood rules: rule one that the government cannot change the law made by an Act of Parliament or the common law; rule two that the making and unmaking of treaties is a matter of foreign relations within the competence of government. Mrs Miller's case was that because there was an Act of Parliament to give effect to our joining the (then) EEC and making European rules part of UK law, there has to be another Act of Parliament to authorise service of notice to leave. The government's case was that the 1972 Act would simply cease to operate if the UK leaves. It was only designed to have effect while we were members. Left to himself, Lord Hughes would have agreed with the government, as did (at greater length) Lord Reed and (for rather different reasons) Lord Carnwath. The rest of us co-operated in a joint judgment agreeing with Mrs Miller. The 1972 Act was designed to make the ever-changing law of the European Union automatically into the law of the United Kingdom. It did not follow that it authorised the government to cut off that entire source of law completely and make such a fundamental change in the UK's constitutional arrangements, as well as changing the legal rights and duties of individuals and enterprises.

There was another argument, raised by Scotland, Wales and Northern Ireland, that withdrawal from the EU would fundamentally change the devolution settlements with each of those countries. It would mean that the UK Parliament would be able to legislate for matters which had previously been governed by EU law, even if the subject matter would otherwise have been devolved to them. It would also be in breach of the 'Sewel Convention': under this, although the UK Parliament retained the right to legislate for matters which were devolved to those countries' legislatures, it was recognised that it would not 'normally' do so without their consent. The convention had been expressly incorporated into the Scotland Act 1998.[28]

Speed was of the essence if we were to decide the case in time. After the hearing, Lord Neuberger asked us all to circulate a short paper giving our conclusions on the main issues. This speeded up our deliberations and soon made the majority view on the main issue clear. Lord Neuberger worked very hard on the judgment over the Christmas vacation, actively seeking the help of other justices, and incorporating our views so that we could present a united front. Lord Hodge from Scotland and Lord Kerr from Northern Ireland worked on the devolution issues, where we were unanimous in rejecting the argument.

The reaction to our judgment, when it was delivered on 12 January 2017, was much more restrained than the reaction to the High Court judgment had been. Perhaps televising the snail's pace debate had had an impact. Perhaps everyone had realised that it was no big deal: the agreed answer to my innocent question was that a one-clause bill authorising the government to act would be enough. Perhaps the reaction to the *Daily Mail* headline had had a sobering effect. But the *Daily Mail* did a clever thing: it published photographs of Lord Reed, Lord Carnwath and Lord Hughes under the banner headline 'Champions of the People'. You have to admire the ingenuity and sense of humour.

Parliament duly passed the European Union (Notification of Withdrawal) Act on 16 March 2017 and the prime minister, Theresa May, gave the notification on 29 March as planned. The two years would expire on 29 March 2019. In between those dates, I became president of the Supreme Court. By a quirk of fate, Lord Neuberger and I had different retirement ages. He had to retire at the age of seventy, whereas I could go on until I was seventy-five.[29] In fact, he generously decided to retire in September 2017, before he had to and before the start of the new legal year. He wanted his successor to have a good run at the job and he wanted his successor to be me. The post was advertised, as was now standard practice, but I was the only applicant. Whatever their views when I applied to be deputy president, my fellow justices must have decided that they could bear the thought of me as president. By then, I really did think that I could do the job. I had learned a lot from watching how well Lord Neuberger did it. We had made a good team. Indeed, we had sat together more often than is usual while I was deputy president: was that because he enjoyed it or because he did not quite trust me to preside in court? There were still some qualms, imposter syndrome never quite defeated, but I was told in no uncertain terms by Lord Kerr, wise friend and mentor to us all, not only that I had to apply but that I would get the job. Even so, the interview was rigorous. The appointing commission had to be satisfied that I was properly qualified. The most memorable moment came when I was asked whether I thought about how my male colleagues felt when I was so vociferous about there needing to be more women! I said something anodyne but inwardly I was seething. Are men such delicate flowers that their feelings will be hurt if women push for more equal opportunities? Are we to be blamed for doing so? Or are we to feel sorry if they are afraid that they will lose their privileged position? Surely not. I wonder what would have happened if I had said what I really thought. As it was, in September 2017, a seventy-two-year-old woman succeeded a sixty-nine-year-old man as president of the Supreme Court of the United Kingdom. For a brief period, the top judges in Canada, Australia, New Zealand and the United Kingdom were all women.

But it is time to return to the Brexit saga. Mrs May had lost her majority in the House of Commons in the surprise election held on 8 June 2017. She was only able to form a government because of a 'confidence and supply' agreement with the Democratic Unionist Party of Northern Ireland. Parliament passed the European Union (Withdrawal) Act 2018. This would repeal the European Communities Act 1972 on 'exit day' but also required parliamentary approval for any withdrawal agreement negotiated by the government. Mrs May concluded a withdrawal agreement on 25 November 2018, but it was rejected three times by the House of Commons. She was effectively compelled to ask the European Council to extend the notification period from 29 March to 31 October 2019, which it did. Mrs May resigned as leader of the Conservative Party on 7 June 2019 and stood down as prime minister once the party had selected Boris Johnson as her successor. Parliament went into its usual summer recess and was due to return on 3 September 2019.

During August, the prime minister decided to advise Her Majesty that Parliament should be prorogued from a date between 9 and 14 September until 14 October: that is, for roughly five weeks out of the eight between 3 September and exit day on 31 October. Proroguing Parliament is quite different from going into recess. It brings the parliamentary session to an end. While Parliament is prorogued, neither House can meet, debate and pass legislation, debate government policy, ask written and oral questions of ministers, meet and take evidence in committees, in short engage in all the normal activities of Parliament. The bills currently being considered lapse automatically (unless deliberately carried over into the next session). During a recess, on the other hand, the Houses do not sit, but all the other parliamentary activities can continue as normal. Each House decides when to go into recess and can decide to return early if it wishes. Prorogation, by contrast, is a prerogative power of the Crown acting on the advice of the Privy Council, in effect the prime minister of the day. Parliament has no choice in the matter.

There had been suggestions in academic writings that something like this might happen. On 30 July, Ms Joanna Cherry MP, together with a cross-party group of seventy-five MPs and members of the House of Lords, brought proceedings in the Court of Session in Scotland claiming that it would be unlawful and seeking an interdict to prevent it. This was met by denials that the government had any intention of advising Her Majesty to prorogue Parliament 'with the intention of denying before Exit Day any further parliamentary consideration of withdrawal from the Union'. Weasel words, you may think. On 4 September, the Lord Ordinary (the first instance judge) refused the case, on the ground that it was not justiciable in a court of law.[30] Certain issues are 'inherently unsuitable for judicial determination' because of their subject matter:[31] the usual example given is the dealings of foreign states with one another. If the court had been asked to decide between two entirely political reasons for doing, or not doing, something which was clearly within the government's powers, that would almost certainly not have been justiciable. But when the court is asked to decide whether the government has acted within the limits of its legal powers, that is certainly justiciable. The Inner House (the appeal court) heard Ms Cherry's appeal later that week, delivered their decision with a summary of their reasons on 11 September and their full judgment on Friday 13 September.[32] They decided that the advice given to Her Majesty was justiciable, that it was unlawful because it was motivated by the improper purpose of stymying parliamentary scrutiny, and that the prorogation itself was unlawful and thus null and void. They gave permission to appeal to the Supreme Court.

Meanwhile, as soon as the prorogation was announced, Mrs Gina Miller began proceedings in the High Court of England and Wales, seeking only a declaration that the advice was unlawful. This was heard by a Divisional Court, consisting of the Lord Chief Justice, the Master of the Rolls and the president of the Queen's Bench Division, on 5 September and judgment was given 11 September.[33] They decided that the issue was not justiciable. But they granted a certificate so that the case could 'leapfrog' the Court of Appeal and come straight to the Supreme Court.

I was at Yale Law School in the United States during that week, attending the annual Global Constitutionalism seminar. This remarkable event brings together apex court judges from all over the world with leading academic constitutionalists to discuss contemporary constitutional issues. The idea is that the thoughtfulness of the academics and the decisiveness of the judges will generate stimulating debate and fresh ideas, all in the cause of promoting constitutional government and human rights. I have been attending the seminar as the UK member since 2004 and made many friends there, as well as learning a lot. There was great excitement at the conflicting decisions reached by the courts in Scotland and England. Not surprisingly, as almost everyone there came from a country with a written constitution, which the courts had a duty to interpret and apply, the general view was that the issue was justiciable, although not what the answer should be. I, of course, could only explain the story so far: I could not form any conclusions until we had heard the arguments.

One thing was absolutely clear: we had to hear and decide the case. There is only one UK Parliament. Either it had, or it had not, been validly prorogued. The Scots and the English could not both be right. Once again, we convened a panel of eleven justices. We are required to sit an uneven number,[34] so this was the maximum number of serving justices who could sit. One of the justices was difficult to reach in Africa but all the others were able to change their plans and make themselves available at short notice. We heard Mrs Miller's appeal against the English decision and the government's appeal against the Scottish decision, from Tuesday 17 to Thursday 19 September, together with interventions from the Lord Advocate, the Counsel General for Wales, a litigant from Northern Ireland, and the former prime minister Sir John Major KG, CH. We heard from Sir John because he could give (unchallenged) evidence from actual experience of the normal process of proroguing Parliament. There were also written interventions from Baroness Chakrabarti, CBE, PC, and the Public Law Project.

As with the first *Miller* case, there was intense public interest. The legal teams were not so many or so enormous but the courtroom was still packed, as were the two overflow courtrooms. The atmosphere might have been electric but the slow formality of legal proceedings has a very calming, even soporific, effect. Even so, the proceedings attracted a huge audience on television. The rest of the English-speaking legal world was also riveted: whether the government could indeed shut down Parliament for weeks without its consent was a matter of importance to many other countries with constitutions based on the 'Westminster model'.

Early on, we decided that the focus should be on the *effect* of the prorogation, rather than the motivation for it. If the matter was justiciable at all, and the effect was to frustrate the normal operation of Parliament at a crucial time in the nation's history, then it might be unlawful whatever the political motivation for it. Counsel for Mrs Miller, Lord Pannick QC, who spoke first to present her appeal from the English decision, picked this up straightaway and adjusted his argument accordingly. He was followed by Lord Keen QC, the Advocate General for Scotland, who presented the government's appeal against the Scottish decision. Next came Sir James Eadie QC, who responded to Mrs Miller's appeal in his usual avuncular fashion. Finally came Aidan O'Neill QC, counsel for Ms Cherry, who made a theatrical defence of the Scottish decision. This was probably the only time in the hearing when sparks flew.

By the Wednesday evening, we had heard all four of the main parties. So I decided to follow the same practice which Lord Neuberger had adopted in the first *Miller* case: I asked each member of the court to circulate a short paper, preferably on one side of A4, giving their answers to four questions: was the matter justiciable; if so, by what standards was the lawfulness of the advice to be judged; how did those standards apply to this advice; and if unlawful, what was the remedy? I asked that everyone circulate their memo at 9 a.m. on the Thursday morning, so that they were not reacting to one another.

On Thursday morning it was quite clear that we would hold that the advice was justiciable. The issue was not its political wisdom but whether it was within the bounds of the government's lawful powers. The precise criteria for judging its lawfulness required fine-tuning, but these evolved gradually by discussion during the day. The main question on which we had not heard full argument was what the remedy should be if the advice was unlawful. During the day, after we had heard from the interveners, we asked counsel for Mrs Miller and for the government to help us with this in their replies. Counsel for Ms Cherry, as respondent to the government's appeal, technically did not have a right of reply, but he did put in a very helpful written paper, to which the government replied in writing.

Our deliberations that afternoon took much less time than they might have done. It was clear that we were going to allow Mrs Miller's appeal and dismiss the government's appeal. Given the way the criteria were to be framed, the decision was likely to be unanimous. It had to be announced as soon as possible, otherwise there would be no point. Lord Reed and I were sent away to draft the judgment of the court over the weekend. We divided the judgment into five sections and decided who would do the first draft of each. I retired to the peace and quiet of North Yorkshire to do mine: I could take the most essential papers with me and all the voluminous documentation was available electronically. He and I exchanged drafts over the next two days and by Sunday morning we had a draft which we could share with the other justices. Everyone else had undertaken to be available to consider it by email. One of our number went on holiday to Sicily and sent us tantalising photos of him working on the draft with the bright blue sea behind him and the sun flooding into his apartment.

Everyone responded with helpful comments and suggestions. It was a truly collective endeavour. I was delighted by the constructive way in which everyone was pulling together. By Monday morning we had an agreed draft which we could send to the court to be processed in the usual way. I worked during the day on the summary to be read out in court and on Monday evening I travelled back to London to deliver it the next day.

Getting up that morning, I did think carefully about which dress I should wear. I have always been happier wearing dresses than suits. But suits were what was expected when I was in the Family Division of the High Court. So my husband Julian started giving me brooches to liven them up. The very first was an antique silver spider but there have been many more since then. I have never used my brooches to convey a specific message, as Madeleine Albright, the United States Secretary of State, used to do.[35] They were there to cheer me up and maybe others too. Most of my brooches are creatures of some sort – frogs, spiders, dragonflies, bees, etc. Each of my favourites has found its way onto a specific garment – a suit or a dress – where it stays. I chose to wear a demure black crêpe dress by Goat for the hand-down. It had always had a spider brooch, a dramatic jet and diamanté piece. But when I took the dress out of the wardrobe that morning, the usual spider brooch was missing (it still is). So I found another sparkly one: £12 from Cards Galore, Julian told me. I was completely unaware that The Who had recorded a song about 'Boris the Spider' who comes to a sticky end. If I had realised the speculation about hidden messages that it would provoke, I would probably have chosen something else – but what would people have made of a frog or a dragonfly or a bee?

What I was wearing that day is not important. I was more concerned with explaining to the world, in a way which I hoped that everyone would understand, a decision of the highest constitutional importance.[36] My summary was along these lines.

The first question was whether the lawfulness of the prime minister's advice to Her Majesty was justiciable. We held that it was. As long ago as 1611, the court held that 'the King [who was then the government] hath no prerogative but that which the law of the land allows him'.[37] However, there are two different questions. The first is whether a prerogative power exists and if so its extent. The second is whether the exercise of that power, within its limits, is open to legal challenge. This may depend upon what the power is all about: the exercise of some powers is inherently unsuitable for judicial review while others are not. However, all the parties to the case accepted that the courts have jurisdiction to decide upon the existence and limits of a prerogative power. We concluded that the case was about the limits of the power to advise Her Majesty to prorogue Parliament rather than its exercise.

The second question, therefore, was what were the limits of that power? Two fundamental principles of our constitution were relevant: parliamentary sovereignty and the government's accountability to Parliament. Parliamentary sovereignty would be undermined if the government could, through the use of the prerogative, prevent Parliament from exercising its power to make laws for as long as the government pleased. Not only that, in the words of Lord Bingham, 'the conduct of government by a prime minister and Cabinet collectively responsible and accountable to Parliament lies at the heart of Westminster democracy'. The power to prorogue is limited by the constitutional principles with which it would otherwise conflict.

Hence a decision to prorogue (strictly, to advise the monarch to prorogue) is unlawful if the prorogation has the effect of frustrating or preventing, without reasonable justification, the ability of Parliament to carry out its constitutional functions as a legislature and as the body responsible for the supervision of the executive. In judging any justification which might be put forward, the court must of course be sensitive to the responsibilities and experience of the prime minister and proceed with appropriate caution. But if the prorogation does have that effect, without reasonable justification, there is no need to consider whether the prime minister's motive or purpose was unlawful.

The third question, therefore, was whether this prorogation did have the effect of frustrating or preventing the ability of Parliament to carry out its constitutional functions without reasonable justification. This was not a normal prorogation in the run-up to a Queen's Speech. It prevented Parliament from carrying out its constitutional functions for five out of the possible eight weeks between the end of the summer recess and exit day on 31 October. This prolonged suspension of parliamentary democracy took place in quite exceptional circumstances: the fundamental change which was due to take place in the constitution of the United Kingdom on exit day. The House of Commons as the elected representatives of the people had a right to a voice in how that change was brought about. The effect upon the fundamentals of our democracy was extreme.

No justification for taking action with such an extreme effect had been put before the court. The only evidence of why the decision was taken was a memorandum from Nikki da Costa, Downing Street's director of legislative affairs, of 15 August. This explained why it would be desirable to hold the Queen's Speech to open a new session of Parliament on 14 October. It did not explain why it was necessary to bring parliamentary business to a halt for five weeks before that, when the normal period necessary to prepare for the Queen's Speech is four to six days. It did not discuss the difference between prorogation and recess. It did not discuss the impact of prorogation on the procedures for scrutinising the delegated legislation which would be necessary to achieve an orderly withdrawal from the European Union, with or without a withdrawal agreement, on 31 October. It did not discuss what parliamentary time would be needed to secure parliamentary approval for any new withdrawal agreement.[38]

We were bound to conclude, therefore, that the decision to advise Her Majesty to prorogue Parliament was unlawful because it had the effect of frustrating or preventing the ability of Parliament to carry out its constitutional functions without reasonable justification.

The final question, therefore, was what the legal effect of that finding was and what remedies the court should grant. The government argued that the Inner House could not declare that the prorogation was 'null and of no effect' because it was a 'proceeding in Parliament' which, under the Bill of Rights of 1689 cannot be 'impeached or questioned' in any court. But prorogation is not a proceeding in Parliament. It takes place in the House of Lords Chamber in the presence of members of both Houses, but it is not their decision. It is something which has been imposed upon them from outside. It is not something on which members can speak or vote. It is not the core or essential business of Parliament which the Bill of Rights protects. Quite the reverse: it brings that core or essential business to an end.

The prime minister's advice to Her Majesty was unlawful, void and of no effect. The Order in Council to which it led was also unlawful, void and of no effect and should be quashed. When the Royal Commissioners walked into the House of Lords to deliver it, it was as if they had walked in with a blank sheet of paper. Parliament had not been prorogued.

It was a big moment when I walked into the crowded courtroom. My default facial expression is a smile – often an unconscious one – but that would not have been appropriate, so I had to school my face. Our security staff were on high alert and more visible than they normally are. Julian watched from the balcony – someone was afraid for his safety if feelings got out of hand. But of course everyone was well behaved – there was not a sound apart from the audible gasp when I announced that 'this is the unanimous judgment of us all'. But people who had been following the hearing closely cannot have been surprised at the result – why else would we have been so interested in remedies on the final day? Clive Coleman, the BBC's legal correspondent, had been virtually spot on in Radio 4's *Today* programme that very morning.

We expected the intense interest from the UK. We probably did not expect the intense interest from all over the English-speaking world. People saw the broadcast in the strangest places – Dubai airport, for example. We also did not expect that an enterprising company would produce a tee-shirt that very evening sporting a sparkly spider decoration, which raised thousands of pounds for Shelter, the homelessness charity. Equally unexpected was the use of spiders by people who wanted to show their support – including the pikemen who escorted the procession to and from the annual legal service in York Minster that October, each of them wearing a little spider pin. No doubt there will have been plenty to show their disapproval, but on social media which we didn't see.

It seems that, among the general public, opposition to, or support for, our decision is strongly correlated with support for, or opposition to, Brexit. But, as I have tried to explain, our decision had nothing to do with the arguments for and against Brexit. It would have been the same, whatever the personal views of any of the justices about Brexit (which I do not know). Our personal views and experience of life influence our decisions only if they are relevant to the legal issues, which in this case they were not.

It was undoubtedly the most important case in my judicial life and the whole court can be justly proud of what was achieved. Once again, the two fundamental principles of our constitution, the sovereignty of Parliament and the rule of law, had been vindicated. But legal life and political life are two quite different things. Parliament returned the following day and reasserted its will amidst noisy scenes. Exit day was postponed once more. Parliament was prorogued again, but this time for only a few days before the Queen's Speech which had been arranged for 14 October. We went along in our finery to hear it, knowing full well that there was likely to be a general election and another Queen's Speech before the year was out. And so it turned out to be. I felt very sorry for Her Majesty. She could so easily have been spared it all if that had been the plan from the outset.

But does that mean that our decision was ultimately futile? No, it does not. We are not concerned with the pros and cons of what the politicians decide to do: to leave the European Union; to agree the terms on which to leave, including special arrangements for the island of Ireland; to agree a fresh trading relationship with the European Union. I do not know the political views of my fellow justices (although I could make a good guess in one or two cases). Such political questions are not discussed in court and rarely round the lunch table. Our job is to decide the cases which come before us according to law. We cannot refuse to decide them, however much we might prefer not to be dragged into some which are essentially political disputes. From time to time, it is our job to decide that those in political power have acted unlawfully. Political power and legal power are not always the same thing. The rights and freedoms of every individual and enterprise within the country depend upon those in political power acting within the powers which the law has given them. Otherwise is tyranny.

Afterthoughts

I retired on 10 January 2020, three weeks short of my seventy-fifth birthday, looking forward to a very full year ahead. There were fourteen cases over which I had presided awaiting judgment, including four where I was to write the lead. There were several foreign trips planned: to the Four Jurisdictions Family Law Conference (always a favourite), celebrating its twentieth anniversary by going to Malaga rather than to Liverpool (the four jurisdictions are Scotland, Ireland, Northern Ireland and the north of England), in January; a month sitting in the Court of Final Appeal in Hong Kong from February to March; a 'conversation' with Justice Stephen Breyer of the US Supreme Court at the University of California, Berkeley, in April; a family holiday in France to celebrate daughter Rachel's fiftieth birthday; the trip of a lifetime to New Zealand for the International Association of Women Judges conference, followed by a visit to the Cook Islands (still sending cases to the Judicial Committee of the Privy Council), in May; another 'conversation' at the Aspen Institute in Colorado in July; followed by the World Conference of the International Society on Family Law in Barbados; and the usual Global Constitutionalism seminar in Yale in September. There were many other visits, conferences and lectures planned (and four honorary degrees to add to the thirty-two my rarity value had already attracted). I had accepted several honorary academic appointments, including a professorship at University College London. There was the prospect of playing an active part in Chambers at 1 KBW (see p. 123) and of returning to the House of Lords as an active parliamentarian.

We made it to Malaga, but Hong Kong was postponed because of the developing Covid-19 pandemic there (which gave me time to work on the judgments). Julian made it to the World Senior Teams Chess

Championship in Prague at the beginning of March. I did a round of events, typical of my extra-judicial activities, which in retrospect were very risky: a panel discussion at Canada House to celebrate International Women's Day, at which Sophie Trudeau made a surprise appearance, shortly before testing positive for Covid-19; a lunch at the Bristol Merchant Venturers' Hall, also to celebrate International Women's Day; a performance of the wonderful musical *Come from Away*, about how the Newfoundlanders welcomed the passengers and crew of an airliner diverted from JFK on 9/11; a large and lavish reception for the LexisNexis awards, at which I was given a lifetime achievement award; a dinner to welcome me as the Sultan Azlan Shah Fellow at the Oxford Centre for Islamic Studies; and a reception in Gray's Inn to launch Women in Family Law: the sorts of activities which made my life so full and happy.

Then Julian's chess tournament was ended two days early by order of the Czech government. He made it home safely but on Sunday 15 March he had a mysterious fall in our London flat. Unbeknownst to us, because he had such a high pain threshold, he suffered two serious injuries. We made it up to Yorkshire by train on 18 March. His daughters took one look at his arm and took him off to A&E in Northallerton, where they quickly diagnosed a dislocated shoulder and sent him straight away to James Cook University Hospital in Middlesbrough to have it fixed. Even he found that hard to bear. But that was not all. Over the next few days, he became more and more disabled, unable to use his legs as he wanted to. On 25 March he fell out of bed in the middle of the night. An ambulance took him off to Darlington hospital. There they diagnosed bleeding between the skull and the brain and sent him to James Cook to have it washed out. This was done successfully on 27 March, agony for us because we could not be there. But first thing on the morning of 28 March I had a text from him: it must have taken him ages to do it, but what a relief to know that his mind was working again! He came home on 31 March and made a steady recovery, working on the next issue of *Emmet and Farrand on Title*, the conveyancers' bible, and playing chess online, while I looked after him and the house and worked on this book. It was lockdown but we had his two daughters, Sarah and Rachel, on-site, friends who could help with the shopping, a beautiful garden and walks from the house, and wonderful spring weather. It was, in his word, an 'idyllic' time.

Then on 17 July, setting up a DVD for us to watch after dinner, he suddenly found himself unable to breathe. Two ambulance crews kept up CPR all the way to the hospital but could not save him. He died of a pulmonary embolism – probably nothing to do with his earlier injuries. Up until then he had been so healthy that we all thought that he would live forever. We were able to give him a wonderful send-off: as a lifelong atheist, he had to have a wholly secular funeral service, but our kind friend, the former rector of Richmond, devised something which worked for them both; we could have only twenty mourners at the crematorium, but we could have thirty at an appropriate distance in a marquee in the garden – quite like old times – with food and drink and tributes in words and music from all the children and grand-children. He would have loved it (and who knows, perhaps he did?).

My life is now nothing like I expected it to be at the start of 2020. But I know full well how very fortunate I am, compared with so many whose lives have been turned upside down by Covid-19. And I can look back on a life which has been nothing like the life I expected it to be when I started out at Richmond High School for Girls all those years ago or at any of my other imposter moments. I hope that I have made a difference. I hope that I have encouraged many other young people to believe that they too can make it in the law. And I am not planning to give that up any time soon ...

Acknowledgements

I first thought of this book as a conventional lawyer's memoir, written mainly for people who were already lawyers and people who might be thinking of becoming lawyers. But my editor, Stuart Williams, and all the team at The Bodley Head have helped me transform it into something which I hope has been written for a much broader readership than that – anyone who is interested in the momentous changes which have taken place in our society during my lifetime. The words are still all my own, but some of them are rather different from the words I might first have chosen. I am enormously grateful to Stuart and the team for what we have achieved together.

I am also grateful to those who have allowed me to reproduce their work to illustrate the story:

Richmond in early autumn: Mark Denton

St. Mary's Church, Bolton on Swale: Mark Whyman

Girton College, Alfred Waterhouse: The Mistress and Fellows, Girton College, Cambridge

Cartoon of Brenda Hale as Chancellor of Bristol University: Jessye Aggleton

United Kingdom Supreme Court emblem: This logo has been reproduced with the permission of the Supreme Court of the United Kingdom

Panoramic photograph of the UK Supreme Court: Natasha Bennett

Equal to Everything: Legal Action Group, illustrated by Henny Beaumont

Lady Brenda Hale from the series 'First Women UK' by Anita Corbin

The Justices outside the Supreme Court, 2017: UK Supreme Court

The Supreme Court Justices and their Judicial Assistants, 2018–19: Kevin Leighton

'Legacy, 2019': Catherine Yass; Legacy 2019 by Catherine Yass, artwork reproduced with the permission of the artist and Spark21/ First 100 Years.

Notes

1 Village Life

1 *Oxfordshire County Council v Oxford City Council* [2006] UKHL 25, [2006] 2 AC 674, para 129; the case held that the Trap Grounds, a stretch of waste land in north Oxford, could be registered as a town or village green despite looking nothing like the traditional picture I painted.

2 A Family Life

1 Renamed St Edmund's School in 1897 and now an independent school for boys and girls.
2 *R v Birmingham City Council, ex parte Equal Opportunities Commission* [1989] AC 1155.

3 Why Law?

1 F. W. Maitland, *The Constitutional History of England*, Cambridge University Press, 1908, p. 281.
2 (1607) 12 Co Rep 63, 77 ER 1342.
3 (1610) 12 Co Rep 74, 77 ER 1352.
4 *R v Hampden* (1637–8) 3 State Trials 825.
5 (1670) 124 ER 1006.

4 University Life

1 Neither Dame Elizabeth Lane, the first woman High Court judge, nor Dame Elizabeth Butler-Sloss, the first woman Court of Appeal judge, had university degrees.
2 I am grateful to her relative, whom I met at a High Sheriff's dinner, for allowing me to copy the letter.

3   *In re B (A Child) (Residence: Second Appeal)* [2009] UKSC 5, [2009] 1 WLR 2496.

4   *In re G (Children) (Residence: Same Sex Parent)* [2006] UKHL 43, [2006] 1 WLR 2305.

5   www.supremecourt.uk/news/permission-to-appeal-hearing-in-the-matter-of-charlie-gard.html; www.supremecourt.uk/news/permission-to-appeal-determination-in-the-matter-of-alfie-evans.html.

6   *Girton: Thirty years in the life of a Cambridge College*, compiled by Marilyn Strathern, Third Millennium Publishing, 2005, p. 79.

5 Manchester – A Double Life

1   Sweet & Maxwell, 1975; 6th edition, 2017.

2   Sweet & Maxwell, 1976; 4th edition, 1993.

3   Butterworths, 1983; 6th edition, 2009.

4   Basil Blackwell, 1984; republished on open access by the Institute of Advanced Legal Studies, 2018.

6 A Feminist, Frank and Fearless

1   *Turley v Allders Department Store* [1980] ICR 66.

2   *Webb v EMO Cargo (UK) Ltd* [1992] 1 WLR 49.

3   *Webb v EMO Cargo (UK) Ltd* [1994] QB 718.

4   *Webb v EMO Cargo (UK) Ltd (No 2)* [1995] 1 WLR 1454.

5   *Skyrail Oceanic Ltd v Coleman* [1981] ICR 777.

6   *Gill v El Vino* [1983] QB 425.

7   *R v Wandsworth London Borough Council, ex parte Nimako-Boateng* (1984) 11 HLR 95.

8   *Davies v Johnson* [1979] AC 264.

9   *Richards v Richards* [1984] AC 174.

10 410 US 113 (1973).

11 *R (Carson) v Secretary of State for Work and Pensions* [2005] UKHL 57, [2006] 1 AC 173, Lord Hoffmann at para 15.

12 *Amoena (UK) Limited v Revenue and Customs Commissioners* [2016] UKSC 41, [2016] 1 WLR 2904.

13 Constitutional Reform Act 2005, s 64(1) and s 63(2).

14 [2001] *Public Law* 489.

15 *Eve was Framed: Women and British Justice*, Vintage, 1993, pp. 48–9.

16 *Judges*, Oxford University Press, 1987, p. 51.

17 'Declining the Brief' in *Ashes and Sparks*, Cambridge University Press, 2011.

18 [2010] UKSC 42, [2011] 1 AC 534, see p. 211.

7 Public Life

1 Law Commissions Act 1965, s 3(1).
2 *Reform of the Grounds for Divorce: The Field of Choice*, Law Com. No. 6, 1966.
3 *Financial Provision in Matrimonial Proceedings*, Law Com. No. 25, 1969.
4 Law Com. No. 33, 1970.
5 Law Com. Nos. 26 and 23, 1969.
6 Divorce Reform Act 1969; Matrimonial Proceedings and Property Act 1970; Nullity of Marriage Act 1970; Law Reform (Miscellaneous Provisions) Act 1970.
7 *Second Report on Family Property: Family Provision on Death*, Law Com. No. 61, 1974.
8 *Matrimonial Proceedings in Magistrates Courts*, Law Com. No. 77, 1976.
9 Inheritance (Provision for Family and Dependants) Act 1975; Domestic Proceedings and Magistrates' Courts Act 1978.
10 *Solemnisation of Marriage in England and Wales*, Law Com. No. 53, 1973.
11 *First Report on Family Property: A New Approach*, Law Com. No. 52, 1973.
12 *Third Report on Family Property: The Matrimonial Home (Co-ownership and Occupation Rights) and Household Goods*, Law Com. No. 86, 1978.
13 *Whitehouse v Lemon* [1979] AC 617.
14 *Offences against Religion and Public Worship*, Working Paper No. 79, 1981.
15 *Offences against Religion and Public Worship*, Law Com. No. 145, 1985.
16 Criminal Justice and Immigration Act 2008, s 79.
17 Session 1983–4, HC 360.
18 *Review of Child Care Law: Report to Ministers of an Inter-Departmental Working Party*, HMSO, 1985.
19 *The Law relating to Child Care and Family Services*, Cmnd 62, 1987.
20 *Family Law. Illegitimacy*, Law Com. No. 118, 1982.
21 *Report of the Inquiry into Child Abuse in Cleveland*, Cmnd 412, 1988.
22 An incomplete draft was attached to the Law Commission's report, *Guardianship and Custody*, Law Com. No. 172, 1988, and the gaps were filled in as it went through Parliament.
23 *Facing the Future: A Discussion Paper on the Ground for Divorce*, Law Com. No. 170, 1988; *The Ground for Divorce*, Law Com. No. 192, 1990.
24 *Domestic Violence and Occupation of the Family Home*, Working Paper No. 113, 1989; Report, Law Com. No. 207, 1992.
25 See John Eekelaar and Sandford Katz (eds), *Marriage and Cohabitation in Contemporary Societies*, Butterworths, 1980, ch. 10.
26 Soon to become a long-serving and much respected member of the Scottish Law Commission.
27 *Rape within Marriage*, Working Paper No. 116, 1990.
28 *R v R* [1992] AC 599.

29   *Rape within Marriage*, Law Com. No. 205, 1992.

30   *In re F (Mental Patient: Sterilisation)* [1990] 2 AC 1.

31   *Mentally Incapacitated Adults and Decision-Making: An Overview*, Consultation Paper No. 119; *A New Jurisdiction*, Consultation Paper No. 128; *Medical Treatment and Research*, Consultation Paper No. 129; and *Public Law Protection*, Consultation Paper No. 130.

32   *Mental Incapacity*, Law Com. No. 231, 1995.

33   *Who Decides? Making Decisions on behalf of Mentally Incapacitated Adults*, Cm 3808, 1997; *Making Decisions: The Government's proposals for making decisions on behalf of mentally incapacitated adults*, Cm 4465, 1999.

34   See, for example, *Family Matters: Work in Child Protection and Family Law at the Nuffield Foundation, 1995–2001*.

35   Professor Liz Trinder et al., *Finding Fault? Divorce Law in Practice in England and Wales*, Nuffield Foundation, 2018.

8 Onto the Bench

1   After the case of *Anton Piller KG v Manufacturing Processes Ltd* [1976] ch. 55, in which the Court of Appeal held that such orders were possible in exceptional circumstances.

9 Family Life in the Family Division

1   'The view from Court 45' (1999) 11 *Child and Family Law Quarterly* 377.

2   *TB v JB (Abduction: Grave Risk of Harm)* [2001] 2 FLR 515.

3   *Re B (Children)* [2001] EWCA Civ 625.

4   Articles 16(3) and 23(1) respectively.

5   *Christian Institute v Lord Advocate* [2016] UKSC 51, 2017 SC (UKSC) 29, para 73.

6   Children Act 1989, s 31(2).

7   Ibid., s 1(1).

8   Guaranteed by Article 8 of the European Convention on Human Rights and now part of our law by virtue of the Human Rights Act 1998.

9   Contact and residence orders have since been replaced with comprehensive 'child arrangements' orders but they do the same thing.

10   Now enshrined in the Children Act 1989, s 1(2A), (2B).

11   My judgment in *Re D (Contact: Reasons for Refusal)* [1997] 2 FLR 48; taken up by the president of the Family Division in *Re L (A Child)(Contact: Domestic Violence)* [2001] Fam 260, with the benefit of expert psychiatric advice [2000] *Family Law* 615; an excellent example of interdisciplinary co-operation.

12 Children Act 1989, ss 11A to 11P, following a report of that name from the Children Act Advisory Subcommittee of the Family Justice Council.

13 [2001] 1 AC 596.

14 Implementing the Law Commission's proposals of 1995.

15 *Re S (Hospital Patient: Court's Jurisdiction)* [1995] 1 All ER 449.

16 *Re S (Hospital Patient: Court's Jurisdiction)* [1996] Fam 1.

17 *Re S (Hospital Patient: Foreign Curator)* [1996] Fam 23.

18 The general rule is that an English power of attorney ceases to have effect if the donor loses capacity, but in 1985 it became possible to make one which would survive incapacity, provided that certain formalities were complied with.

19 *Buchanan v Milton* [1999] 2 FLR 844.

20 Superior Courts Act 1981, s 116.

10 My Lady, Lord Justice

1 The Family Division were offered three-week slots in the Court of Appeal each term and I chose one whenever I was high enough in the picking order (which did not depend on how high one was in the pecking order).

2 For examples, see pp. 187 and 215.

3 *In re W and B (Children: Care Plan)* [2001] EWCA Civ 757, [2001] HRLR 50.

4 *In re S (Children) (Care Order: Implementation of Care Plan)* [2002] UKHL 10, [2002] 2 AC 291.

5 There is a good example of what the duty to 'read and give effect' can achieve on p. 194.

6 So called after *McKenzie v McKenzie* [1971] P 33, where the Court of Appeal ruled that a litigant in person was entitled to have such assistance.

7 *McFarlane v Tayside Health Board* [1999] 2 AC 59.

8 1998 SLT 307.

9 *Parkinson v St James and Seacroft University Hospital NHS Trust* [2001] EWCA Civ 530, [2002] QB 266.

10 *Rees v Darlington Memorial Hospital NHS Trust* [2003] UKHL 52, [2004] 1 AC 309.

11 *Farley v Skinner* [2001] UKHL 49, [2002] 2 AC 732.

12 Human Fertilisation and Embryology Act 1990, s 28(3).

13 *In re D (Parental Responsibility: IVF Baby)* [2001] EWCA Civ 230, [2001] 1 FLR 972.

14 *In re R (A Child) (IVF: Paternity of Child)* [2003] EWCA Civ 182, [2003] Fam 129.

256   *Spider Woman*

11 Life of the Lady Law Lord

1 It is worth reading his dissenting judgment in the Court of Appeal in *Porter v Magill* [2001] UKHL 67, [2002] 2 AC 357.
2 *Nairn v University of St Andrews* [1909] AC 147.
3 *Edwards v Attorney General of Canada* [1930] AC 124.
4 'The House of Lords and Women's Rights: Am I really a Law Lord?', (2005) 25(1) *Legal Studies* 72–84.
5 *Independent Jamaica Council for Human Rights (1998) Ltd v Marshall-Burnett* [2005] UKPC 3, [2005] 2 AC.
6 *Matthew v State of Trinidad and Tobago* [2004] UKPC 33, [2005] 1 AC 433.
7 *R (Jackson) v Attorney General* [2005] UKHL 56, [2006] 1 AC 262.
8 Tom Bingham, *The Rule of Law*, Penguin, 2011, p. 167.
9 *R (Countryside Alliance) v Attorney General, R (Derwin) v Attorney General* [2007] UKHL 52, [2008] 1 AC 719.
10 *Whaley v Lord Advocate* [2007] UKHL 53, 2008 SC (HL) 107.
11 Section 29(1) and (2)(d).
12 *Omega Spielhallen- und Automatenaufstellungs-GmbH v Oberbürgermeisterin der Bundesstadt Bonn*, Case C-36/02 [2004] ECR I-9609.
13 *Friend v United Kingdom* (2010) 50 EHRR SE6.
14 *R v J* [2004] UKHL 42, [2005] 1 AC 562.
15 It has since been replaced by the Sexual Offences Act 2003, which takes an entirely different approach.
16 *R v Hasan (Aytach)* [2005] UKHL 22, [2005] 2 AC 467.
17 *K v Secretary of State for the Home Department, Fornah v Secretary of State for the Home Department* [2006] UKHL 46, [2007] 1 AC 412.
18 *Quijano v Secretary of State for the Home Department* [1997] Imm AR 117.
19 E. Rackley, 'What a difference difference makes: gendered harms and judicial diversity', (2008) 15 (1–2) *International Journal of the Legal Profession* 37–56.
20 [2004] UKHL 30, [2004] 2 AC 557.
21 See p. 158.

12 Creating the Supreme Court

1 Lectures for JUSTICE, the British branch of the International Society of Jurists, 2001, and the Constitution Unit at University College London, 2002.
2 'The case for a Supreme Court', (2002) 118 *Law Quarterly Review* 382.
3 *The Times*, 22 May 2001, and the *Independent*, 18 June 2001.
4 See p. 186.

5 See pp. 228 and 235.

6 Promissory Oaths Act 1868, s 6A, inserted by Constitutional Reform Act 2005, s 17.

7 Vividly explained by Frederic Reynold QC, in *High Principle, Low Politics, and the Emergence of the Supreme Court*, Wildy, Simonds and Hill, 2019.

8 Later to become a highly respected High Court judge, having made his name, like me, as an academic and public servant rather than a practising barrister.

9 (2004) 24(1 and 2) *Legal Studies* 153.

10 Constitutional Reform Act 2005, s 47.

11 Ibid., s 23(6).

12 [2010] UKSC 42, [2011] 1 AC 534.

13 *R (McDonald) v Kensington and Chelsea Royal London Borough Council* [2011] UKSC 33, [2011] 4 All ER 881, curiously not reported in the official Law Reports.

14 *R (A and B) v Secretary of State for Health* [2017] UKSC 41, [2017] 1 WLR 2492.

15 [2011] UKSC 3, [2011] 1 WLR 433.

16 [2011] UKSC 4, [2011] 2 AC 166.

17 Article 3(1).

18 Whether there was a 'stop Brenda' campaign, as some have suggested, I am not qualified to say.

13 What is the Supreme Court For?

1 E.g. *Radmacher v Granatino* [2010] UKSC 40, [2011] 1 AC 534, p. 211; *In re B (A Child) (Residence: Biological Parent)* [2009] UKSC 5, [2009] 1 WLR 2305, p. 57.

2 *Lord Chancellor v McCloud and others; Sargeant and others v London Fire and Emergency Planning Authority and others* [2018] EWCA Civ 2844, [2019] ICR 1489.

3 E.g. *MS (Pakistan) v Secretary of State for the Home Department* [2020] UKSC 9, [2020] 1 WLR 1373, about whether an immigration tribunal is bound by the National Referral Agency's decision that a person is not the victim of trafficking.

4 *Hounga v Allen* [2014] UKSC 47, [2014] 1 WLR 2889; *Les Laboratoires Servier v Apotex Inc* [2014] UKSC 55, [2015] AC 430; *Bilta (UK) Ltd v Nazir (No 2)* [2015] UKSC 23, [2016] AC 1.

5 *Patel v Mirza* [2016] UKSC 42, [2017] AC 467.

6 *Rees v Darlington Memorial Hospital NHS Trust* [2003] UKHL 52, [2004] 1 AC 309; see p. 165.

7   Starting with the famous case of *Donoghue v Stevenson* [1932] AC 562.

8   *Duncan v Cammell Laird* [1942] AC 624.

9   *Glasgow Corporation v Central Land Board* 1956 SC (HL) 1.

10 *Conway v Rimmer* [1968] AC 910.

11 See p. 174.

12 E.g. *Cadder v HM Advocate* [2010] UKSC 43, [2010] 1 WLR 2601, 2011 SC (UKSC) 13.

13 *Martin v Most* [2010] UKSC 10; 2010 SC (UKSC) 40.

14 *AXA General Insurance Ltd v HM Advocate* [2011] UKSC 46, [2012] 1 AC 868, 2012 SC (UKSC) 122.

15 *Imperial Tobacco v Lord Advocate* [2012] UKSC 61, 2013 SC (UKSC) 153.

16 *Scotch Whisky Association v Lord Advocate* [2017] UKSC 76, 2018 SC (UKSC) 94.

17 E.g. *Salveson v Riddell* [2013] UKSC 32, 2013 SC (UKSC) 236; *Christian Institute v Lord Advocate* [2016] UKSC 51, [2016] SC (UKSC) 79.

18 *In re UK Withdrawal from the European Union (Legal Continuity) (Scotland) Bill* [2018] UKSC 64, [2019] AC 1022.

19 *Lee v Ashers Baking Co Ltd* [2018] UKSC 49, [2020] AC 413.

20 Another example of Section 3 of the Human Rights Act 1998, see pp. 158 and 194.

21 See p. 158.

22 *Thoburn v Sunderland City Council* [2002] EWHC 195 (Admin), [2003] QB 151.

23 *R v Chaytor* [2010] UKSC 52, [2011] 1 AC 684.

24 In the famous case of *Stockdale v Hansard* (1839) 9 Ad & E 1, 112 ER 1112.

25 [2016] EWHC 2768; [2017] 1 All ER 158.

26 The vacancy caused by the retirement of Lord Toulson had not yet been filled.

27 *R (Miller and another) v Secretary of State for Exiting the European Union* [2017] UKSC 5, [2018] AC 61, para 277.

28 See Scotland Act 1998, s 28(8).

29 This was because I was appointed a High Court judge before the magic date in 1995 when the Judicial Pensions and Retirement Act 1993 came into force, whereas he had been appointed afterwards.

30 [2019] CSOH 70, 2020 SC 13.

31 See *Shergar v Khan* [2014] UKSC 33, [2015] AC 359.

32 [2019] CSIH 49, 2020 SC 37.

33 [2019] EWHC 2381 (QB).

34 Constitutional Reform Act 2005, s 42(1)(a).

35 See Madeleine Albright, *Read my Pins: Stories from a Diplomat's Jewel Box*, Harper, 2009.

36 *R (Miller) v Prime Minister; Cherry and others v Advocate General for Scotland* [2019] UKSC 41, [2020] AC 373.

37 See p. 39.

38 As required by the European Union (Withdrawal) Act 2018, s 13.

Index